Reenvisioning Christian Ethics

Reenvisioning Christian Ethics

Special Issue Editor
Darryl W. Stephens

MDPI • Basel • Beijing • Wuhan • Barcelona • Belgrade • Manchester • Tokyo • Cluj • Tianjin

Special Issue Editor
Darryl W. Stephens
Lancaster Theological Seminary
USA

Editorial Office
MDPI
St. Alban-Anlage 66
4052 Basel, Switzerland

This is a reprint of articles from the Special Issue published online in the open access journal *Religions* (ISSN 2077-1444) (available at: https://www.mdpi.com/journal/religions/special_issues/Christian_Ethics).

For citation purposes, cite each article independently as indicated on the article page online and as indicated below:

LastName, A.A.; LastName, B.B.; LastName, C.C. Article Title. *Journal Name* **Year**, *Article Number*, Page Range.

ISBN 978-3-03928-394-1 (Hbk)
ISBN 978-3-03928-395-8 (PDF)

© 2020 by the authors. Articles in this book are Open Access and distributed under the Creative Commons Attribution (CC BY) license, which allows users to download, copy and build upon published articles, as long as the author and publisher are properly credited, which ensures maximum dissemination and a wider impact of our publications.

The book as a whole is distributed by MDPI under the terms and conditions of the Creative Commons license CC BY-NC-ND.

Contents

About the Special Issue Editor vii

Darryl W. Stephens
Reenvisioning Christian Ethics: An Introduction and Invitation
Reprinted from: *Religions* **2020**, *11*, 74, doi:10.3390/rel11020074 1

Antje Schnoor
Transformational Ethics: The Concept of Obedience in Post-Conciliar Jesuit Thinking
Reprinted from: *Religions* **2019**, *10*, 342, doi:10.3390/rel10050342 11

Kevin J. O'Brien
The Scales Integral to Ecology: Hierarchies in *Laudato Si'* and Christian Ecological Ethics
Reprinted from: *Religions* **2019**, *10*, 511, doi:10.3390/rel10090511 27

Kate Ott
Taking Children's Moral Lives Seriously: Creativity as Ethical Response Offline and Online
Reprinted from: *Religions* **2019**, *10*, 525, doi:10.3390/rel10090525 41

Ilsup Ahn
Reconstructing an Ethics of Credit in an Age of Neoliberalism
Reprinted from: *Religions* **2019**, *10*, 484, doi:10.3390/rel10080484 53

Tyler B. Davis
Liberating Discernment: Language, Concreteness, and Naming Divine Activity in History
Reprinted from: *Religions* **2019**, *10*, 562, doi:10.3390/rel10100562 69

Shaji George Kochuthara
Challenge of Doing Catholic Ethics in a Pluralistic Context
Reprinted from: *Religions* **2020**, *11*, 17, doi:10.3390/rel11010017 83

James Francis Keenan
Pursuing Ethics by Building Bridges beyond the Northern Paradigm
Reprinted from: *Religions* **2019**, *10*, 490, doi:10.3390/rel10080490 99

Luke Beck Kreider
Christian Ethics and Ecologies of Violence
Reprinted from: *Religions* **2019**, *10*, 509, doi:10.3390/rel10090509 113

About the Special Issue Editor

Darryl W. Stephens (Director of United Methodist Studies) teaches at Lancaster Theological Seminary, Pennsylvania, USA, and holds a Ph.D. in Christian Ethics from Emory University, Georgia, USA. Stephens has authored over 60 articles, chapters, and books for scholarly and church audiences and is a sought-after speaker, workshop leader, and editor. His scholarship on ethics at the juncture of church and society focuses particularly on sexual ethics, church polity, and ecclesial social teaching. His writings have been published in a variety of peer-reviewed journals, including *Journal of Religious Ethics*, *International Journal of Practical Theology*, *Methodist History*, *Methodist Review*, *Ecumenical Review*, *Religions*, *Theological Education*, and *Religious Education*. He is the author of *Methodist Morals: Social Principles in the Public Church's Witness* (University of Tennessee Press, 2016), *Out of Exodus: A Journey of Open and Affirming Ministry* (Cascade, 2018), and *Bearing Witness in the Kin-dom: Living into the Church's Moral Witness through Radical Discipleship* (United Methodist Women, forthcoming 2021). He is also co-editor of *Professional Sexual Ethics: A Holistic Ministry Approach* (Fortress Press, 2013), *Liberating the Politics of Jesus: Renewing Peace Theology through the Wisdom of Women* (T&T Clark, forthcoming 2020), and *Teaching Sexuality and Religion in Higher Education: Embodied Learning, Trauma Sensitive Pedagogy, and Perspective Transformation* (Routledge, forthcoming 2020).

Editorial

Reenvisioning Christian Ethics: An Introduction and Invitation

Darryl W. Stephens

Lancaster Theological Seminary, 555 West James Street, Lancaster, PA 17603, USA; dstephens@lancasterseminary.edu or dwstephens@alumni.rice.edu; Tel.: +1-717-875-4751

Received: 20 January 2020; Accepted: 4 February 2020; Published: 6 February 2020

Abstract: This article by the guest editor introduces the theme of this special issue of *Religions*, reveals some of his underlying convictions and assumptions regarding the task of reenvisioning Christian ethics, and introduces each of the eight articles in this collection. Rather than a discipline, Christian ethics might more accurately be described as a field of scholarly endeavor engaging a range of partner disciplines. Each contributor was invited to offer a distinct perspective on this task, contributing to a collective reenvisioning of the field. The guest editor describes his underlying convictions, that the task of reenvisioning Christian ethics is real, perspectival, dialogical, collaborative, and purposeful. Correspondingly, he sees the task as awe-filled, discerning, responsive, participatory, and hopeful. Envisioned is a confluence of intersectional, interdisciplinary, and intercultural approaches expanding beyond the academy and even beyond the Christian in order to partner with all members of global society for the common good, shared justice, and full flourishing of all of creation.

Keywords: Christian ethics; theological ethics; social ethics; ethical methodology; H. Richard Niebuhr; ecumenical ethics; Society of Christian Ethics

---

1. Introduction[1]

Christian ethics is a wide, varied field. So diverse are the methods and approaches, theological perspectives and starting points, and scopes of inquiry and purposes—dare we even call it a "discipline"?—that the field is rarely considered as a whole. Christian ethics includes historical, descriptive, critical, constructive, and applied projects on countless topics. Lending creative energy to this field of scholarly endeavor are a range of partner disciplines, including, most prominently, theology, philosophy, and sociology—each containing multiple schools themselves. The 2014 report on "The Future of Christian Ethics" by the 2020 Committee of the Society of Christian Ethics (SCE) identified twenty different academic fields partnered with Christian ethics.[2] To envision the entire field of Christian ethics is a difficult task; to reenvision the entire field, perhaps impossible for one person. Thus, to explore the theme "Reenvisioning Christian Ethics," I invited papers offering a distinct perspective from their primary partner discipline, each contributing to a composite reenvisioning of the field. The purpose of this special issue of *Religions* is to reenvision Christian ethics by refracting

---

[1] A word of thanks is due to Patricia Beattie Jung for her collegial encouragement and support leading to my taking on the role as guest editor; to Kevin O'Brien for his insightful, often challenging, and always encouraging conversation and feedback on the initial call for papers and this introductory essay; and to the entire staff of MDPI, all of whom exhibited the highest level of professionalism and competency, including assistant editors Bingjin He, Mamie Lu, Carrie Liang, Joy Ji, Kate Yang, Macy Zong, Angelia Wang, and Michelle Cai.

[2] The SCE identified 20 different academic fields listed with ethics in the job title or as co-primary in the job description, based on data collected from the *Chronicle of Higher Education* for the years 1998–1999 and 1999–2000 and from the American Academy of Religion (AAR) Annual Meeting Jobs Listings for the years 2001–2012 (SCE 2014).

our collective vision through the prisms of diverse academic and methodological perspectives in this vast field of inquiry, study, and practice. This introduction identifies my underlying convictions and assumptions, presents the articles comprising this volume, and challenges scholars of Christian ethics to reenvision the field of Christian ethics today.

2. Underlying Convictions and Assumptions

The shared endeavor to reenvision the field necessarily embraces a wide range of understandings of Christian ethics. I do not impose any normative definition of the field or its purposes, which I believe are multiple. Nevertheless, one can infer several of my underlying convictions from the way in which I have framed this task, convictions that I presently make explicit. My understanding of reenvisioning Christian ethics can be described as real, perspectival, dialogical, collaborative, and purposeful. Correspondingly, I see the task as awe-filled, discerning, responsive, participatory, and hopeful.

2.1. Real and Awe-filled

Reenvisioning necessarily presumes that there is something to see. Christianity is a religion based on the belief in one God in three persons, embodying truth and love. My understanding of Christian ethics is premised on a reality shaped by this unity—what Howard Thurman (1980) described as "the sound of the genuine" and what H. Richard Niebuhr understood as "that transcendent absolute for whom ... whatever is, is good" (Niebuhr 1970, p. 112). Thus, not only do I imply some commonality, no matter how distant, between various approaches to Christian ethics, I also expect some coherency—not in the sense of coming to the same answers from different angles but in the sense of contributing to our thinking about a shared reality, despite differences in how we may experience it. "The world is an intelligible whole in which all things are related to one another and to God" (Lovin et al. 2017, p. xxiv). My ontological realism should not be confused with a strategic compromise to be "realistic" or an identification with a particular school of thought, such as Christian Realism. It is a more basic conviction, an awe-filled sense of creaturely relation to our Creator, who shapes the arc of the universe—that orienting "center of value" at the heart of H. Richard Niebuhr's "radical monotheism" (Niebuhr 1970). Christian ethics shares this with theology: it "allows human beings to advance particular descriptions and normative claims about what is most essentially real or true" (Scharen and Vigen 2011, p. 3). Thus, I prioritize with Niebuhr the question "What is going on?" and expect a glimpse of something real in response (Niebuhr 1978, p. 60). My approach to reenvisioning the field of Christian ethics presumes an underlying reality in God, no matter our perspective.

2.2. Perspectival and Discerning

An assumption of shared reality does not necessarily imply a clear understanding or identical experience of that reality. Philosophy is filled with stories illustrating the difficulty of truth and perception, from Plato's cave to the folktale from India about six blind men describing an elephant. Humanity's unrelenting desire for knowledge continually chafes against the limitations of our perspectives, which are the only windows we have available to see the real, "For now we see through a glass, darkly ... " (1 Corinthians 13:12, KJV). Our glimpses of the real and true are necessarily partial and incomplete. Just as all theology is contextual, all Christian ethics is perspectival.

Acknowledging the perspectival nature of moral vision does not commit me to recognizing every perspective or interpretation therefrom as equally valid or ethically binding, though. A perspectival approach does not mean that "anything goes."[3] Recognizing the validity of differing perspectives no more leads to extreme relativism than recognizing an underlying reality leads to absolutism.

---

[3] Scharen and Vigen (2011, p. 61) make a similar point addressing the fear of relativism in relation to prioritizing human experience, particularly embodied knowing, as a source for Christian theology and ethics.

It does, though, raise the possibility of error. My own perspective could be wrong, misinformed, or myopic—particularly so when warped by the forces of social privilege and refracted through hegemonic power (see, for example, Block 2019). There is need for discernment. Perspective, though limiting, provides vantage for critical discernment; in fact, it is the only vantage for critique I have. There is no "view from nowhere." To exercise critical discernment is to stand somewhere, despite the limitations of perspective.

Reenvisioning presumes that what is seen can be seen anew, in a different and perhaps more helpful way, and for this, we need assistance from others. James Gustafson describes "the fault of rationality" as misconstruals of reality based on my limited perspective, compounded by my refusal to "submit them to criticism and correction by others" (Gustafson 1981, pp. 300–1). I would add, we particularly need criticism and correction from persons with perspectives that differ from our own. For example, as a white, cisgender male of comfortable economic status in the U.S., I must be open to the corrective insights of black womanist ethics, which draws on moral struggles and oppressions that are not part of my own experience (Cannon 1988, pp. 5, 6). For this reason, a perspectival and discerning approach to reenvisioning Christian ethics must also be dialogical and responsive.

2.3. Dialogical and Responsive

Christian ethics is an ongoing task subject to continual revision, requiring critical dialogue and appropriate responsiveness. The nature of scholarly collaboration should lead to constructive dialogue across difference, offering mutual critique and deeper insight. Whether through communicative ethics (Benhabib 1992; Habermas 1990), cross-disciplinary intersections (Gustafson 1996), or interdisciplinary conversation (Jung et al. 2010; Lovin and Maudlin 2017), a dialogical approach open to mutual critique enables continued learning. David Hollenbach's "dialogic universalism" is a good example of this kind of learning (Hollenbach 2003, pp. 10–16). Scholars of Christian ethics engage in dialogue and mutual critique not only with each other but also with the magisterium (Curran 2018), the lived contexts of churches and denominations (Stephens 2016, p. 195), "communities of shared practice" (Jenkins 2013, p. 99), marginalized communities (De La Torre 2014; West 2006), new realities (Lovin 2008), the earth itself (Moe-Lobeda 2013; Rasmussen 1996), or a combination thereof (Harris 2017). At their best, perspectival insights can lead, for example, to awareness of intersectionality and other social realities laden with power (Kim and Shaw 2018, p. 107) and to valuing the particularity and countermemory of marginalized groups (Townes 2006, p. 23). The task of reenvisioning Christian ethics demands that we be appropriately responsive to this mutually critical dialogue.

Responsiveness implies vitality and relationship. Unresponsiveness is an indication of death. To respond, then, is to be alive in some way. Responsiveness shows an awareness of others, a capacity to be open to their influence, and to change through that interaction.[4] Responsiveness is necessary for relationship. Not all relationships are healthy, though. Appropriate responsiveness implies recognition of the other and sensitivity to context, needs, and power dynamics. Appropriate responsiveness demands different things of different persons. Recognizing my own social location, appropriate responsiveness demands of me humility (cf. Lovin et al. 2017, p. xxix; Scharen and Vigen 2011, pp. 17, 18). For others, from different social locations, the task of Christian ethics may demand boldness, courage, fortitude, and audacity. Constructive dialogue and appropriate responsiveness, especially across difference, are means by which our vision can be improved, adjusted, or otherwise clarified—even as we acknowledge the limitations inherent in our individual perspectives. To do this task well, reenvisioning Christian ethics should also be collaborative and participatory.

---

[4] These are fundamental insights of process theology and ethics.

2.4. Collaborative and Participatory

Collaboration is at the heart of Christian ethics. I agree with Paul Marten's assessment of the SCE's futuring report, that, due to the complexity of ethical issues, "what is increasingly needed ... is a recognition that Christian ethics necessarily is a field where collaboration is ubiquitous, both in the classroom and in research" (Martens 2014). Collaboration is not optional. This shared work, or co-laboring (*colaboración*), involves individuals as well as entire communities in the task of Christian ethics. Emilie Townes, for example, emphasizes that "dismantling the cultural production of evil ... must be a group project" (Townes 2006, p. 160; see also Soto Albrecht and Stephens 2020). It is in our struggles for wisdom and survival, "en la lucha," as Ada María Isasi-Díaz (2004) described it, that we encounter the real. Reenvisioning Christian ethics can be an emancipatory praxis. When Christian ethics is done in participatory community, when we partner with each other to gain perspectives unavailable to any one person, we build networks capable of transcending our limited perspectives. For this task, we need each other.

Reenvisioning Christian ethics is not just for students in the classroom or members of the scholarly guild. Our collective task requires bringing faith communities and the wider public into our discursive and scholarly spaces, not merely as subjects of research but as interlocutors defining and shaping what it means to do Christian ethics (Scharen and Vigen 2011, p. xxii). Scholars of Christian ethics need to engage churches and practitioners (clergy, social workers, community organizers, journalists, bus drivers, and many others) as essential conversation partners. Furthermore, our task also requires that, as scholars, we move out into the community, roll up our sleeves, and view everyone around us as potential collaborators in this most practical endeavor, learning to hear and live in harmony with the sound of the genuine. We might even be audacious enough to attempt "pragmatic solidarity with those who suffer" (Scharen and Vigen 2011, p. 24) as we join in the struggle. However, participatory collaboration is a means, not a guarantee, of widening perspectives and gaining greater insight into what is really real or, as Townes puts it, "the true-true" (Townes 2006, p. 161). Crowd sourcing can quickly degenerate into group think, reifying one's own perspective through echo chambers of like-minded individuals. Both outcomes are possible. Reinhold Niebuhr's depiction of "immoral society" (Niebuhr 1960) may be just as appropriate as Paul's depiction of the church as a body with many members (1 Corinthians 12:12). Collaboration is a shared task that demands dialogue and critique.

2.5. Purposeful and Hopeful

Finally, the act of reenvisioning—and, indeed, Christian ethics itself—has a normative dimension. The task is purposeful. Though our individual motivations may differ widely, we do not enter this dialogue or participate in mutual critique without some aim. Whether seeking eudaimonia, rest in God, or full human flourishing, I presume that we each participate in the collaborative effort of Christian ethics for a reason. These reasons are diverse and multiple, motivating some to witness to an eschatological community of peace (Hauerwas 1983) and others to disruption (West 2006). As Traci West (2006) describes it, the task of Christian ethics is necessary "when racism and women's lives matter". Whether grounded in a present reality of hopelessness (De La Torre 2017) or a conviction that what we do as scholars might make some positive difference in this world (Lovin et al. 2017, p. xxxi), the ongoing work of Christian ethics entails some kind of hope for the future. Thus, reenvisioning Christian ethics is, in the end, I believe, a hopeful task.

3. Contributions to the Task of Reenvisioning the Field of Christian Ethics

This special issue of *Religions* represents merely one moment of collaboration and dialogue within the ongoing task of reenvisioning Christian ethics. This effort makes no attempt at comprehensiveness or systematic overview, in contrast to a recent treatment of theological ethics (Junker-Kenny 2019). There are many perspectives and voices that I tried to include in this issue, many scholars whose competing commitments prevented them from contributing an article in this particular collaboration.

As a corrective to the limitations of this scholarly effort, I encourage readers to draw connections between these essays and other forums, such as Syndicate Theology (https://syndicate.network/about/); to further these conversations through professional guilds such as the American Academy of Religion (AAR), the Society of Christian Ethics (SCE), and the Society for the Study of Christian Ethics (SSCE); and to participate in those uncertain, "incompetent communities" (Jenkins 2013, p. 20) that have so much to teach us about living morally in an ambiguous world.

The scope of this special issue is necessarily broad, though each individual contribution is well-focused, indicating how advances and insights from one location might effectively contribute to or prompt new developments in other locations in this field. Each author was invited to provide a vision of the field of Christian ethics from a distinct perspective, as follows: identify the primary partner discipline, method and approach, theological perspective and starting point, and scope of inquiry and purpose; name key insights developed from that perspective; describe ways in which this perspective has impacted other perspectives and approaches in the field; and suggest ways to reenvision Christian ethics through these perspectival insights. Individual authors may or may not share my underlying convictions, as described above. Readers engaging this sampling of perspectives on the task of reenvisioning the field of Christian ethics are encouraged to participate through agreement, disagreement, argument, and continued, critical dialogue.

In "Transformational Ethics: The Concept of Obedience in Post-Conciliar Jesuit Thinking," Antje Schnoor employs conceptual history, specifically *Begriffsgeschichte* according to Reinhart Koselleck, to illustrate how the pursuit of social justice became a form of religious obedience within the Society of Jesus. Her analysis reveals a bidirectional flow of social and theological influences, resulting in an emphasis on responsibility and conscience within Jesuit practices of leadership and ethics more generally. The article raises awareness of historical context for shaping ethical values, thereby suggesting that the task of reenvisioning Christian ethics is itself situated within and influenced by a social history of ideas.

In "The Scales Integral to Ecology: Hierarchies in *Laudato Si'* and Christian Ecological Ethics," Kevin J. O'Brien draws upon ecological theory and environmental ethics to assess the use of scale and hierarchy in Pope Francis's encyclical *Laudato Si'*. Drawing on Bryan Norton's attention to spatial and temporal scales in moral argument, O'Brien observes, "Pope Francis's integral ecology is a powerful example of global environmental ethics." However, O'Brien questions the hierarchical assumptions of the encyclical, arguing that all hierarchies are social constructions and must be interrogated and acknowledged as such. Citing Francis's unreflective use of hierarchies ordering relationships by gender, species, and the divine, O'Brien calls for a more inquisitive integral ecology. Acknowledging the limitations of all hierarchical assumptions, O'Brien reenvisions Christian ethics as a self-critical endeavor operating at multiple scales simultaneously.

In "Taking Children's Moral Lives Seriously: Creativity as Ethical Response Offline and Online," Kate Ott reenvisions Christian ethics through sustained attention to child moral agency. Drawing on John Wall's concept of childism as a methodology for social change, she engages in conversation with psychologists, child development theorists, educators, theologians, and philosophers as well as her own experience leading children's programs to consider children as full moral agents. Childist ethics emphasizes particularity, decenters rational individualism, and upends linear moral developmental models. Children's responses to the impact of digital technologies illustrate a reenvisioning of Christian ethics through creativity, play, and improvisation.

In "Reconstructing an Ethics of Credit in an Age of Neoliberalism," Ilsup Ahn engages economic and social theory to expose the social and environmental costs of financialization, a global, economic process based on credit contributing to the erosion of social capital and increased inequality. Drawing on David Harvey's scholarship on neoliberalism, Ahn observes a disturbing result: "the increasing economic inequality paradoxically destroys its own basis—social capital." In order to reconnect social and financial capital in a just way, he lays the groundwork for a theological reconstruction of moral credit, recovering a sense of credit as "a form of gift [that] should be all-inclusive and thus available to all." Ahn thereby reenvisions Christian ethics as a call to churches to promote financial justice by engaging in political activism to rebuild social capital.

In "Liberating Discernment: Language, Concreteness, and Naming Divine Activity in History," Tyler B. Davis examines the criterion of objectivity for discerning God's activity in the world, illustrated by narratives about meteorological events in history. Drawing on Alice Crary's expansion of objectivity in ethical theory, Davis rejects any conception of objectivity that would demand abstraction over concretization. He argues, instead, for a "concrete objectivity" as the basis of discernment within liberation theology, as expressed by Beatriz Melano Couch and James Cone. Such liberating discernment claims a Christological criterion in the lives of crucified peoples and can only be articulated in language emerging from the material struggles of the oppressed. Davis, then, "re-envision[s] Christian ethics as language accountable to the God of the oppressed" discerned through the concrete praxis of liberation.

In "Challenge of Doing Catholic Ethics in a Pluralistic Context," Shaji George Kochuthara shows the need for and possibility of constructing a pluralistic approach in Catholic ethics. The Indian context provides a richly pluralistic environment of cultures and religions for this discussion. To establish a theological grounding within the Catholic tradition, he engages documents of the Second Vatican Council and subsequent developments within Church teachings, including the International Theological Commission's document, "In Search of a Universal Ethic: A New Look at the Natural Law." Two issues, ecological ethics and sexual ethics, serve to illustrate potential rapprochement within both Catholic and Hindu traditions. He concludes by offering a number of basic considerations necessary for constructing a pluralistic approach to ethics, including: appreciative, non-judgmental listening; collaboration along the way; mutual study of texts and traditions; critical evaluation; humility; and solidarity. In this way, Kochuthara reenvisions Christian ethics through ongoing dialogue amidst difference in pluralistic contexts.

In "Pursuing Ethics by Building Bridges beyond the Northern Paradigm," James Francis Keenan reenvisions Christian ethics through new and emerging forms of scholarly praxis. Specifically, he promotes collegiality among Christian ethicists across the globe, illustrated by the work of Catholic Theological Ethics in the World Church (CTEWC). He describes the development of this network as an attempt at bridge-building between scholars of the Global North and Global South, "respond[ing] to the challenge of pluralism by answering the call to dialogue from and beyond local culture." CTEWC was created to address the problem of insularity among ethicists in the Global North, dominated by a "northern paradigm." He narrates in detail the creation, growth, and challenges to CTEWC as this network achieved international and regional conferences, published a monthly newsletter, sponsored visiting scholars, provided PhD scholarships, and launched an international book series. Citing the long-term benefits of these cross-cultural, interdisciplinary conversations while naming the institutional realities that prioritize individual scholarship over collaboration and co-authorship in the academic job market, Keenan issues an invitation to reenvision Christian ethics as a collective endeavor requiring connection and collaboration among global scholars.

In "Christian Ethics and Ecologies of Violence", Luke Beck Kreider seeks to combine environmental ethics with peace and conflict studies to address what he terms "ecologies of violence". Recognizing "the deep entanglement of ecological and sociopolitical systems", the author facilitates a more integrated moral analysis by identifying four illustrative types of ecologies of violence: ecological drivers of conflict and peace; environmental consequences of war; land conflict; and structural violence conveyed through environmental systems. He then interrogates recent works in Christian ethics addressing these topics and challenges the authors to further collaboration and deeper engagement. Recognizing both cosmological and pragmatic challenges, he calls not only for improving moral imagination and practical strategies but also for a new approach to ecologies of violence: "a dialogical method" characterized by "integration, critique, collaboration, and exchange" across boundaries of culture, politics, theology, and community. Inspired by Traci West, Krieder reenvisions Christian ethics "as dialogical negotiation over intersectional problems with the goal of 'building more ethical communal relations.'"

4. Implications for Christian Ethicists and Our Guilds

The responsibility of Christian ethicists to join with members of global society for more rigorous ethical thought, reflection, and action is more important now than ever. We live in an age of "wicked problems," anthropogenic climate change foremost among them (Jenkins 2013, p. 171). We also live in an age of alternative facts. As a colleague recently observed, "Who would've thought that in the Potter Box, the dimension labelled 'facts' would become the most difficult and contested part of ethical methodology?"[5] When the "real" recedes from view, morality has precarious standing. We must be intentional about engaging with many disciplines and with persons inside and outside the academy (Edwards 2014). Reenvisioning Christian ethics as real, perspectival, dialogical, collaborative, and purposeful is timely and urgent work.

This special issue of *Religions* is one, small part of this ongoing effort. Contributors have offered a fascinating array of perspectives, engaging conceptual history, multiple spatial and temporal scales self-critical of assumed hierarchies, play and improvisation inspired by children's moral agency, political activism to rebuild social capital, the concrete praxis of liberation as a criterion of discernment, bridge-building among global scholars, ongoing dialogue within a pluralistic context, and dialogical negotiation about intersectional problems. Each of these perspectives has enriched my own understanding of Christian ethics. These authors challenge us to consider more deeply the value of intersectional, interdisciplinary, and intercultural approaches. Yet, I believe the task of reenvisioning Christian ethics requires even more of Christian ethicists and the guilds that support us as scholars. We must look beyond academia.

Reenvisioning this field requires seeing as valid Christian ethicists who work outside the academy. The SCE's "2020 Committee," tasked in 2012 with investigating the current status of and future prospects for Christian ethics, raised a question about the "academic captivity" of the field: Has the field of Christian ethics become too "professionally distinct" and "disciplinarily reflexive"? (SCE 2014). This question, however, was offered as "provocation" and was not explored by the Committee. The report itself reflected the academic insularity in question. When a major report on "The Future of Christian Ethics" concerns itself mainly with the production and placement of PhD-trained scholars in U.S. academic institutions—and whether the academic job market will sustain them—our vision is indeed too narrow. Would a law school strive to train only as many graduates as are needed for future faculty needs? PhD graduates who apply their studies to work outside of the academy should be considered valid and successful placements by a PhD program. Furthermore, while labor relations with contingent faculty are an important ethical issue within higher education (James Keenan 2020), the designation "non-tenure track" is an inadequate description of the many Christian ethicists who interact (or who might potentially interact) with the SCE without academic tenure. The SCE, for example, could do more to engage with and include professional Christian ethicists who work primarily in hospitals, churches, NGOs, and other social institutions. What would it look like to view these Christian ethicists not in terms of their standing (or lack thereof) within the academy but rather in terms of their standing in a larger field of Christian ethics, of which the academy is only one part? Again, provocatively but with no exploration, the SCE futuring report asked, "How ought we to understand Christian Ethics' multiple modes of engagement with ecclesial structures?" (SCE 2014). Indeed, what about ecclesial engagement? Are we missing significant opportunities for collaboration and learning? When we restrict our vision to where academic Christians ethicists are rather than where Christian ethics could be (and in many cases, already is), we suffer from a failure of imagination.

What would it look like for a professional guild, such as SCE, to reorient itself to the wider field of Christian ethics rather than the narrow purview of academic advancement? To my academic colleagues, I offer several thoughts for consideration. Instead of defining the borders of our terrain, perhaps we should map uncharted territory—places of messy collaboration and solidarity. Instead of engaging in

---

[5] I thank Matthew Bersagel-Braley for this insightful observation.

reconnaissance to determine the possible "negative impact" of emerging fields of study threatening the turf of Christian ethics and then sighing in relief when realizing that they "seem not to engage ethical studies very much at all" (SCE 2014), perhaps we should lament the dearth of ethical attention in other fields and seek to partner with them. Instead of worrying about PhD programs producing too many graduates for the number of academic jobs available, perhaps we should equip and encourage Christian ethicists with PhD training to embed themselves in the social fabric and institutional lives of our communities—taking on diverse roles, responsibilities, and forms of employment. Instead of scholarly guild meetings focusing almost exclusively on scholarship within the academy, perhaps we should focus guild meetings on learning from and with Christian ethicists and practitioners who work primarily outside of academic institutions. To really see "the future prospects for, the field of 'Christian ethics'" (SCE 2014), scholars need to practice, and hear from others who practice, Christian ethics in churches, school boards, hospitals, and many other locations within the pluralistic communities in which we live.

To see beyond Christian ethics as an academic endeavor only, we must reenvision this field as contributing to every aspect of life. To put it differently, which aspects of life would we want devoid of Christian ethical thought, reflection, and practice? I believe that Christian ethics needs to expand beyond the academy and even beyond the Christian if we are truly to partner with all members of global society for the common good, shared justice, and full flourishing of all of creation. We need, always and everywhere, to engage with and reflect on the shared journey of being good neighbors in this "world house" (King 1968). As I reenvision Christian ethics, I see an awe-filled, discerning, responsive, participatory, and hopeful task. I invite you to join in!

Funding: This research received no external funding.

Conflicts of Interest: The author declares no conflict of interest.

References

Benhabib, Seyla. 1992. *Situating the Self: Gender, Community, and Postmodernism in Contemporary Ethics*. New York: Routledge.

Block, Elizabeth Sweeny. 2019. White Privilege and the Erroneous Conscience: Rethinking Moral Culpability and Ignorance. *Journal of the Society of Christian Ethics* 39: 357–74. [CrossRef]

Cannon, Katie G. 1988. *Black Womanist Ethics*. American Academy of Religion Academy Series, no. 60. Edited by Susan Thistlethwaite. Atlanta: Scholars Press.

Curran, Charles. 2018. Humanae Vitae: Fifty Years Later. *Theological Studies* 79: 520–42. [CrossRef]

De La Torre, Miguel A. 2014. *Doing Christian Ethics from the Margins: 2nd Edition Revised and Expanded*. Maryknoll: Orbis.

De La Torre, Miguel A. 2017. *Embracing Hopelessness*. Minneapolis: Fortress Press.

Edwards, Elise M. 2014. Response to SCE 2020 Committee Report on the Future of Christian Ethics. January 10. Available online: https://scethics.org/about-sce/current-officers-and-committees/committees/2020-future-christian-ethics-committee (accessed on 5 February 2020).

Gustafson, James M. 1981. *Ethics from a Theocentric Perspective: Volume One: Theology and Ethics*. Chicago: University of Chicago.

Gustafson, James M. 1996. Conclusion: The Relation of Other Disciplines to Theological Ethics. In *Intersections: Science, Theology, and Ethics*. Cleveland: Pilgrim, pp. 126–47.

Habermas, Jürgen. 1990. *Moral Conciousness and Communicative Action*. (Studies in Contemporary German Social Thought). Translated by Christian Lenhardt, and Shierry Weber Nicholsen. Cambridge: MIT Press.

Harris, Melanie L. 2017. *Ecowomanism: African American Women and Earth-Honoring Faiths*. Ecology and Justice Series; Maryknoll: Orbis.

Hauerwas, Stanley. 1983. *The Peaceable Kingdom: A Primer in Christian Ethics*. Notre Dame: University of Notre Dame Press.

Hollenbach, David S. J. 2003. *The Global Face of Public Faith: Politics, Human Rights, and Christian Ethics*. Washington: Georgetown University Press.

Isasi-Díaz, Ada María. 2004. *En La Lucha / In the Struggle: Elaborating a Mujerista Theology, 10th Anniversary Edition*. Minneapolis: Fortress.

Jenkins, Willis. 2013. *The Future of Ethics: Sustainability, Social Justice, and Religious Creativity*. Washington: Georgetown University Press.

Jung, Patricia Beattie, Aana Marie Vigen, and John Anderson, eds. 2010. *God, Science, Sex, Gender: An Interdisciplinary Approach to Christian Ethics*. Urbana: University of Illinois Press.

Junker-Kenny, Maureen. 2019. *Approaches to Theological Ethics: Sources, Traditions, Visions*. New York: T & T Clark.

James Keenan, S. J. 2020. Vulnerable to Contingency. Washington, DC: SCE plenary address, January 10.

Kim, Grace Ji-Sun, and Susan M. Shaw. 2018. *Intersectional Theology: An Introductory Guide*. Minneapolis: Fortress.

King, Martin Luther, Jr. 1968. *Where Do We Go from Here: Chaos or Community?* Boston: Beacon Press.

Lovin, Robin W. 2008. *Christian Realism and the New Realities*. Cambridge: Cambridge University Press.

Lovin, Robin W., and Joshua Mauldin, eds. 2017. *Theology as Interdisciplinary Inquiry: Leaning with and from the Natural and Human Sciences*. Grand Rapids: Eerdmans.

Lovin, Robin, Peter Danchin, Agustín Fuentes, Friederike Nüssel, and Stephen Pope. 2017. Introduction: Theology as Interdisciplinary Inquiry: The Virtues of Humility and Hope. In *Theology as Interdisciplinary Inquiry: Leaning with and from the Natural and Human Sciences*. Edited by Robin W. Lovin and Joshua Mauldin. Grand Rapids: Eerdmans.

Martens, Paul. 2014. Comments on the 2020 SCE Committee Report: The Future of Christian Ethics: Informal Reading Draft. January 10. Available online: https://scethics.org/about-sce/current-officers-and-committees/committees/2020-future-christian-ethics-committee (accessed on 5 February 2020).

Moe-Lobeda, Cynthia D. 2013. *Resisting Structural Evil: Love as Ecological-Economic Vocation*. Minneapolis: Fortress Press.

Niebuhr, H. Richard. 1970. *Radical Monotheism and Western Culture: With Supplementary Essays*. New York: Harper & Row. First published 1943.

Niebuhr, H. Richard. 1978. *The Responsible Self: An Essay in Christian Moral Philosophy*. New York: HarperSanFrancisco. First published 1963.

Niebuhr, Reinhold. 1960. *Moral Man and Immoral Society: A Study in Ethics and Politics*. New York: Charles Scribner's Sons. First published 1932.

Rasmussen, Larry L. 1996. *Earth Community, Earth Ethics*. Ecology & Justice series. Maryknoll: Orbis.

SCE. 2014. 2020 SCE Committee Report on 'The Future of Christian Ethics'. Available online: https://scethics.org/about-sce/current-officers-and-committees/committees/2020-future-christian-ethics-committee (accessed on 5 February 2020).

Scharen, Christian, and Aana Marie Vigen. 2011. *Ethnography as Christian Theology and Ethics*. New York: Continuum.

Soto Albrecht, Elizabeth, and Darryl W. Stephens, eds. 2020. *Liberating the Politics of Jesus: Renewing Peace Theology through the Wisdom of Women*. T&T Clark Studies in Anabaptist Theology and Ethics. New York: T&T Clark.

Stephens, Darryl W. 2016. *Methodist Morals: Social Principles in the Public Church's Witness*. Knoxville: University of Tennessee Press.

Thurman, Howard. 1980. The Sound of the Genuine. *The Spelman Messenger*. Edited by Jo Moore Stewart. 96, no. 4 (Summer). pp. 14–15. Available online: https://www.uindy.edu/eip/files/reflection4.pdf (accessed on 5 February 2020).

Townes, Emilie M. 2006. *Womanist Ethics and the Cultural Production of Evil*. Black Religion/Womanist Thought/Social Justice Series. Edited by Dwight N. Hopkins and Linda E. Thomas. New York: Palgrave Macmillan.

West, Traci. 2006. *Disruptive Christian Ethics: When Racism and Women's Lives Matter*. Louisville: Westminster John Knox.

© 2020 by the author. Licensee MDPI, Basel, Switzerland. This article is an open access article distributed under the terms and conditions of the Creative Commons Attribution (CC BY) license (http://creativecommons.org/licenses/by/4.0/).

Article

Transformational Ethics: The Concept of Obedience in Post-Conciliar Jesuit Thinking

Antje Schnoor

Department of Equity, Diversity and Inclusion, Hochschule Hannover (HsH), Bismarckstraße 2, 30173 Hannover, Germany; antjeschnoor@gmx.de

Received: 2 April 2019; Accepted: 23 May 2019; Published: 27 May 2019

Abstract: The paper sheds light on the change in the concept of obedience within the Society of Jesus since the 1960s. In the aftermath of the Second Vatican Council, a so-called crisis of authority and obedience took place in the Catholic Church and the religious orders. As a consequence, the notions of responsibility and conscience came to the fore in the Jesuit definition of obedience. The religious concept of obedience, that is the obedience towards God, was reassessed as a service to humanity. The paper analyzes how the change in the concept of obedience gave rise to the promotion of social justice, which the Society of Jesus proclaimed at General Congregation 32 in 1974/75. By including the promotion of social justice into their central mission, Jesuits not only fundamentally transformed their self-conception, but also their ethical values. The paper argues that the pursuit of social justice became a form of religious obedience.

Keywords: obedience; ethics; Jesuits; social justice; intellectual history; conceptual history; authority; identity, Catholic Church

---

1. Introduction

In October 2016, Jesuit delegates from all over the world came to Rome for General Congregation 36. This supreme governing body of the Society of Jesus set the agenda for the Jesuit mission for the following years, laid down in two decrees. In Decree 1 the delegates of General Congregation 36 declared that Jesuits see themselves as companions in a mission of reconciliation and justice.[1] The promotion of justice has been an important aim of the Society of Jesus since General Congregation 32 in 1974/75. Previously, the Jesuit mission was unequivocally the spread of faith, but in Decree 4 of General Congregation 32, Jesuits declared the promotion of justice in addition to evangelization as the basic mission of Jesuits. In the 1970s this new mission not only became a political issue within the Catholic Church, but also meant a fundamental change of Jesuit ethics and in Jesuit self-conception.

The intention of this paper is to examine the change in Jesuit self-perception in a broader context of conceptual history and to show that it resulted last but not least from the so-called 'crisis of obedience and authority' in the aftermath of the Second Vatican Council. The idea of obedience changed to the effect that the notions of initiative, responsibility and conscience came to the fore in the definition of obedience. I analyze how the promotion of social justice, proclaimed by General Congregation 32 in 1974/75, resulted from the change in the concept of obedience. My argument is that the pursuit of justice became a new form of religious obedience.

Approaches of conceptual history as the German *Begriffsgeschichte* and the Cambridge School of intellectual history have in common to ask for interrelations between change and innovations of

---

[1] See General Congregation (GC) 36, Decree (D.) 1. Decrees of General Congregation 36 of the Society of Jesus. Available online: http://www.mdsj.org/gc36decrees.

concepts and social and political reality.[2] Whereas these approaches are usually connected to the history of social and political concepts, I use this approach to analyze the change of a concept in the religious field, namely obedience. Nevertheless, the concept of obedience is characterized both by its religious and its political meaning. Therefore, the history of the concept of obedience cannot be told independently of the political and religious conflicts in which the concept was shaped.

A central difference between the Cambridge School of intellectual history according to Quentin Skinner and John Pocock and the German *Begriffsgeschichte* according to Reinhart Koselleck refers to the relationship of reality and language. According to Skinner and Pocock the terms and concepts referred to in the public discourse cannot be understood as a mirror of political reality, they rather believe that reality originates from language. Koselleck in contrast holds another view: Although he believes in an interrelation of language and reality, he is convinced that a linguistic transformation may also result from a change of reality. The present article shows that this was true for the concept of obedience as it was transformed in consequence of a changing political reality.

The methodological approach of conceptual history illustrates that theological thinking is embedded in a historical context. The potential of conceptual history for the field of Christian ethics lies in its contribution to deeper understanding of ethical values as time-dependent. A historical perspective also contributes to the recognition of cultural and regional differences of Christian ethics and theological thinking as a whole. During the military dictatorships in Latin America in the 1970s and 1980s, Jesuits, but also other representatives of the Catholic Church and lay people, promoted justice and human rights in several countries. Not least, their engagement was driven by the significant shift of the concept of obedience, as I will highlight in the present paper.

My analysis is particularly based on legal documents from the Society of Jesus, which stipulate the goals of action and rules of conduct. The members of the Jesuit order are subject to canon law as well as to the order's own law. Among the legal documents of the Jesuit's own law are counted the constitutions of the order, legal norms enacted by the General Superiors and the decrees of the General Congregations. The latter two are especially important sources for the present paper. In addition, I refer to letters and speeches of the General Superiors, which illustrate and inspire the way of life of Jesuits, but are not laws in a narrow sense.

Since the 1960s, Jesuits themselves published several studies on their concept of obedience. Most of these studies can be understood as an attempt to adapt the Ignatian concept of obedience—that is obedience according to Ignatius of Loyola, the founder of the Jesuit order—to new social requirements.[3] These studies do not *examine* the change in the concept of obedience since the 1960s, but *realize* and promote it. Therefore, they serve here as sources to describe the discourse on obedience within the Society of Jesus. These sources offer valuable clues to the perception and way of thinking of individual Jesuits and thus complement the legal documents of the order, which give information about the fixed norms. By referring to documents and writings of a specific religious congregation in a concrete historical context—instead of consulting central theological and legal writings—I examine how the concept of obedience was shaped and transformed within a concrete religious discourse. This approach corresponds to the demand for contextuality of the Cambridge School of intellectual history.

The present paper begins by discussing the specific Ignatian concept of obedience. It then moves on to briefly review the conceptual history of obedience since the age of Enlightenment and to outline the crisis of authority and obedience in the Catholic Church. Within this historical context the paper analyzes the change of the concept of obedience within the Jesuit order at General Congregations 31 in 1965/66 and 32 in 1974/75. Finally, I show that the concept of obedience was reassessed as a service to human beings and thus became oriented towards the promotion of justice.

---

[2] See (Koselleck 1978; Skinner 2010; Hampsher Monk et al. 1998; Van Gelderen 1998; Bevir 2010).
[3] See for example (Palmés 1963; O'Gorman 1971; Knight 1974; Rahner 1980). Especially in the United States many articles have been published about obedience, authority and leadership. A central journal for these topics was and is *Studies in the Spirituality of Jesuits*.

2. The Ignatian Concept of Obedience

As a basic principle, two different forms of obedience in Catholic thinking can be distinguished, namely the canonical or institutional obedience and the religious obedience. The Ignation concept of obedience belongs to the latter. Canonical or institutional obedience refers to the subordination to ecclesiastical authority and is regulated by canon law. Therefore, it is a form of obedience that in this context serves as a means to an end, namely for maintaining order. Religious obedience on the other hand, along with the vows of poverty and chastity, is central to life within religious orders.[4] Religious obedience is closely linked to Christian faith; it is obedience to God's will. The most important example of religious obedience in religious thinking is Jesus carrying the cross in obedience to his father. Jesus adopts the will of his father, obeys him and does not rebel against the father even though he suffers carrying the cross. In contrast to canonical obedience, religious obedience does not refer to a certain order, but to a way of life. It is an end in itself for the obeying person and theologians considered it for a long time to be the quintessence and the core attitude of Christian existence.[5] Freedom—which is given by God—is the prerequisite for religious obedience. It is precisely this voluntariness, which makes this form of obedience different from imposed coercion. In other words, freedom is a central precondition for obeying from a theological perspective. Within the life of Catholic orders, it was a goal to renounce self-determination, a renunciation, which would equate to a full obedience to God. Unlike canonical, institutional obedience, religious obedience was conceptualized as loving obedience towards God.

The idea of religious, mystic obedience is especially shaped by the concept of obedience of Ignatius of Loyola. As for the Jesuits, Ignatius considered obedience to be the core virtue.[6] From the beginning of the 1960s the Ignatian concept of obedience became problematic, as will be shown later. The main strategy for resolving this problem consisted of a reinterpretation of the concepts of both obedience and authority. This reinterpretation was generally defined as a return to tradition and legitimated by the letters and attitudes of Ignatius.[7] The conceptual change of obedience and authority became important not only for the concrete relationship between superiors and subordinates within the Society of Jesus, but also for the identity of the Jesuits and their sociopolitical self-perception.

In the Ignatian concept of obedience one should obey his or her superior, because he or she represents Jesus Christ. To obey the decision of the superior was the equivalent of obeying the will of God and of devoting oneself to God. Religious obedience is therefore based on the love to God and on the desire to be directly connected to him. From Ignatius' point of view obedience to God can be expressed only in the obedience to a human being, namely to the superior. This is to say, the concrete obedience to the superior was the only way to demonstrate and prove obedience to God.

Ignatius distinguished between three degrees of obedience, namely the obedience of execution, the obedience of will and the obedience of mind. The first degree refers only to the external execution of the command. The second degree, the obedience of will, refers to the internal conformity of the will of the obedient person with the will of the superior. The second degree implies the effort of a Jesuit to harmonize his will with the will of the superior and by doing so, he wishes to act on the given order and does not try to change the will of the superior in the direction of his own will. The third degree of obedience, the obedience of mind, is according to Ignatius the highest degree of obedience. The obedient person shall exert him- or herself to subordinate not only his or her will, but also his

---

[4] See (Müller 1968, p. 233f).
[5] See (Hilpert 1996, pp. 360–62).
[6] See (Conference of Provincials 1991, p. 75f).
[7] Hugo Rahner explained, for example, that the joint responsibility of the subordinates was already stated in the constitutions, referring among other sources to Const. III, 2a. See (Rahner 1980, p. 26). Another perspective in this debate was suggested by the Jesuit Robert Harvanek. He rejected the assumption of an essence of Jesuit obedience and by doing so recognized the historic inconstancy of the idea of obedience. Nowadays there is a broad agreement within the academic community about the problem of essentialism, however this idea was quite radical at the time of publication. See (Harvanek 1978, p. 172).

or her intellect to the superior, that is to consider best the commands of the superior. Ignatius in fact explained that the mind is not as free as the will and naturally tends to accept what seems to be true. However, if the mind is not obliged by the 'evidence of the perceived truth' to think in another way then the superior, the obedient person shall be apt to accept his superior's opinion as true.[8]

Ignatius was aware that a superior may be mistaken and his commands may be factually wrong. Nevertheless, he explained: We must not '[...] look at the person whom we obey, but see Christ, our Lord, for whose sake we obey'[9] in the person. As long as the superior's order does not present an obvious sin, Jesuits shall adhere to it, because even an improper command may be the expression of God's will.[10] Moreover, by following orders—even poor orders—the obedient person gets the opportunity to prove his or her surrender to God. For achieving obedience of mind, it is helpful according to Ignatius to believe that everything commanded by the superior is God's command and constitutes his will, which should be obeyed blindly. The outcome of putting the superior's will with God's will on the same level is that the superior's will shall likewise be obeyed blindly.[11] The term 'blind obedience' is based on the Ignatian concept of obedience.

3. The Challenge of Obedience

Both in- and outside the Church, obedience was understood for a long time as a virtue, as an ethical value in itself. The concept of obedience changed after the end of the 18th century as a consequence of the Enlightenment, which placed emphasis on reason and the autonomy of the individual. In the history of philosophy, obedience was increasingly linked to the authority of reason. Immanuel Kant exerted a strong influence on the debate about the term obedience by redefining the relation between obedience and autonomy.[12] According to Kant, obedience is an expression of ethical freedom. In this context, we find the terms law and duty in the center of his thinking. To adhere to the law—understood as moral law—was according to Kant an imperative of practical reason and at the same time a moral duty. For him, this was not in contradiction to autonomy since the subjective will of any human being should tend to conform to the objective, general moral law, according to his categorical imperative. Obedience, resulting from the recognition of moral law, was according to Kant an expression of autonomy.[13] As a consequence of the Enlightenment, the question of the *telos*, of the aim of obedience, became increasingly important. The moral value of obedience became dependent on what obedience was related to. That is to say, it became dependent on its aim. This implied that the *telos*, the aim for which obedience was asked for, had to be assessed by the obedient person. Against this development, theologians after the First World War tried to link obedience more closely to the authority of God and thereby to emphasize the religious dimension of obedience.[14] It was precisely this religious dimension, which suspended the connection between obedience and reason, which had been made before. Therefore, it is important to understand that there is no linear and consistent development in the conceptual shaping of the nexus between obedience and reason.

---

[8] See (Ignatius of Loyola 1993, MI Epp. IV, p. 463). The letter 'To the Jesuits in Portugal', written on the 26th of March in 1553, is also known as the 'Letter on obedience' in which Ignatius reveals his general concept of obedience. This perspective was recently questioned by Mark Rotsaert, SJ, who argues that the idea of obedience described in the letter 'To the Jesuits in Portugal' has to be interpreted in close connection with the concrete situation of the addressees and should not be understood as the general concept of obedience. See (Rotsaert 2008). However Rotsaert, a Jesuit himself, seems to assume a historic constancy between the contemporary concept of obedience in the Society of Jesus and the Ignatian concept.
[9] (Ignatius of Loyola 1993, MI Epp. IV).
[10] See (Knauer 1993, p. 458).
[11] (Ignatius of Loyola 1993, MI Epp. IV, p. 467). The most important example of the obedience of mind is the obedience of Abraham sacrificing his son Isaac.
[12] See (Walther 1984, p. 152).
[13] See (ibid., p. 152).
[14] See (ibid., p, 153).

In conjunction with fascism and totalitarianism in the 20th century, obedience was fundamentally challenged.[15] Along with these experiences, the danger of obedience as 'blind' and as lack of attention to individual responsibility became obvious.[16] This historic experience was also highly significant for the notion of obedience within the Christian churches. In 1968, Dorothee Sölle argued that after National Socialism, after Auschwitz, it was no longer possible to talk about obedience as a theologically innocent term and as a basic principle of Christian ethics, and by doing so, she articulated the feeling of many Christians.[17] Furthermore, she asked a question that was crucial at that time: 'Can the Christian education to obedience be held partly responsible for the quiet conscience of the desk murderers?'[18] Obedience not only lost its virtue, but it became suspicious for its possible sinfulness.

4. *Humanae Vitae* as the Crisis's Trigger

The debate about the concepts authority and obedience became more dynamic in the Catholic Church after the Second World War, and ended after the Second Vatican Council in the so-called crisis of authority and obedience, which became apparent in all sectors of the Church.[19] This came along with a move away from a mere legalistic understanding of morality towards a more person-centered understanding of morality. Although the change of concepts had already begun several decades before the Second Vatican Council, it became visible only during the Council. The participants of the Council criticized the ecclesiastical concept of authority, but did not examine the authority issue in detail. This omission created wide room for maneuvering, which could be used in the aftermath of the Council for developing of new ideas about authority.[20]

The encyclical *Humanae Vitae* (1968), which established the continued prohibition of artificial contraceptives, was a watershed in the relation of authority between lay Catholics and the Vatican, as well as between clerics and the Vatican. The encyclical caused an uproar in the Catholic world since the prohibition disappointed many Catholics. Since numerous lay Catholics perceived the encyclical *Humanae Vitae* as an obvious error, they began to disobey the ecclesiastical authority openly. A large number of clerics shared this feeling. Hugh McLeod vividly describes aged priests remembering what they were doing the moment they learned that Paul VI was continuing to ban contraceptives, as aged Americans remember what they were doing the moment they heard about the assassination of John F. Kennedy.[21] At least in the United States, according to Leslie Tentler, the encyclical was more significant to priests then to lay people.[22] The clergy were obliged to defend the encyclical and to convince lay people comply with it, although not all priests fulfilled that obligation. Many priests and theologians—numerous Jesuits among them—criticized *Humanae Vitae* and by doing so legitimized the possible disobedience of lay people. The opposition of many Jesuits resulted not only from the content of the encyclical, but also from the way it came into being, which was incompatible with the modified idea of authority in the 1960s. Pope Paul VI established a committee to reconsider the position of the Catholic Church on birth control. The committee reasoned that the Church should lift the ban on contraceptives in reference to married couples. In the encyclical *Humanae Vitae*, Pope Paul VI ignored the judgment of the committee and disregarded the arguments, which favored lifting the ban. This led eventually to a weakening of the 'papal authority' of Pope Paul VI.[23] The criticism within the Catholic

---

[15] See in this context the preface of (Floristán 1980, pp. 603–4).
[16] Without doubt significant for this debate: (Adorno et al. 1950).
[17] (Sölle 1988, p. 13). Unless otherwise indicated, translations are those of the author.
[18] (Sölle 1988, p. 13). "Kann man die christliche Erziehung zum Gehorsam mitverantwortlich machen für das gute Gewissen der Schreibtischmörder?"
[19] See (Hanmer 1977).
[20] (Neumann 1970, pp. 142ff, 168). Among the participants who criticized the ecclesiastical concept of authority have been among others cardinal Augustin Bea, cardinal Franz König and bishop Wilhelm Josef Duschak. With reference to their concrete criticism see (ibid., p. 142ff).
[21] See (McLeod 2007, p. 193).
[22] See (Tentler 2004, p. 268).
[23] See (Eschenburg 1976, pp. 240–42).

Church of the encyclical of Pope Paul VI was at the same time a criticism of the management structures in the Church.

What did the modified concepts of obedience in the Society of Jesus and other parts of the Church look like? Numerous clerics and theologians defended the concept of responsible obedience, which, unlike 'blind obedience', was linked with the question of the obedience's *telos*, of the aim of obedience.[24] The obedient person who was considered responsible for his or her deeds should assess the objective pursued by obedience. Translated into Max Weber's terms, ethics of responsibility became more important, while at the same time the meaning of the ethics of conviction persisted and did not cease. The demand for responsible obedience—that is obedience, which was ethically justified—could hardly be reconciled with the religious concept of obedience in Catholic orders, which understood obedience as a way of life. However, this was exactly what many Jesuits tried to do. Because of the central religious connotation of obedience, it was impossible for Jesuits to refuse obedience, or, more precisely, if they did so they had to question their whole faith. Therefore, they began to rethink their concept of obedience, which led to a modification of Ignatius' definition of obedience in the Society of Jesus. A Jesuit joke, originating probably in the post-conciliar era, demonstrates this modification:

> At a conference about religious obedience, the Jesuit representative is asked, "Your Order places great emphasis on the vow of obedience. How do you ensure that Jesuits remain faithful to this vow?" He replies, "It's simple. Our superiors first ask us what we want to do, and then they mission us to do it. Thus, we never have any problems with obedience."
>
> Another conference participant then asks the Jesuit, "But aren't there some members of your Order who don't know what they want to do? What do you do with them?" The Jesuit replies, "We make them the superiors!" [25]

The joke ascribes influence to the individual Jesuit on his superior's orders. Thereby it reflects the modification of the concept of obedience towards more autonomy and responsibility of the individual, which led at the same time to a modification of the concept of authority and leadership and to new forms of giving orders.

5. The Problematization of the Ignatian Concept of Obedience

The problem, which the Jesuits confronted since the 1960s becomes especially evident in the concept of obedience of mind. To retain Ignatian obedience some Jesuits tried to reconcile it with the principle of acting on one's own responsibility. While the term 'blind obedience' seems to contradict this principle, some theologians in the 20th century connected it to the self-will of the obedient person. According to this idea, 'blind obedience' did not mean to switch of the mind while obeying, but to have a 'blind' spot regarding one's own self-will and self-interest and to try to understand the superior's judgment as God's will.[26] However, the interpretation of 'blind obedience' without doubt depended on the position taken up within the debate about obedience. It could serve the persons involved as a strategy to promote their ideal construction of obedience. In the letter of obedience, Ignatius connects 'blind' to the examination the obedient person is supposed to abstain from. For this reason, 'blind' can be understood as clearly connected to the intellect. To abstain from an examination of the superior's judgment correlates—contrary to the interpretation put forward since the 1960s—to not making full use of one's reason. The statement on the 'obedience of mind' on the 31st General Congregation can be interpreted in different ways. Decree 17 defines:

---

[24] The debate about responsible obedience was not specifically Catholic, but was also current in other confessions and had its equivalent outside the religious sphere.
[25] Jesuit Jokes compiled by Felix Just, SJ. Available online: http://catholic-resources.org/JesuitJokes.htm (accessed 28 July 2018).
[26] See for example (Knauer 1990, p.144; Müller 1964, p. 146f).

For obedience of judgment does not mean that [...] one should assent to the superior's will against reason, rejecting the evidence of truth. For the Jesuit, employing his own intelligence, confirmed by the unction of the Holy Spirit, makes his own the will and judgment of superiors, and with his intellect endeavors to see their orders as more conformed to the will of God. [27]

It is questionable how the expression 'more conformed', which is of vital importance for the declaration, should be interpreted. If the order of the superior is interpreted as corresponding more to the will of God then the judgment of the subordinate, he may have no choice but to endorse the will of the superior. The relativization of obedience of mind made by Decree 17 had in the end no consequences for the subordinate.

From a theological perspective, 'blind obedience' to God's will was ethical. However, the Jesuit theologian Karl Rahner put the underlying problem concisely, when he asked, 'How do I know that the instruction of my superior is God's will?'[28] The mere submission to an external will is not an ethical act, according to Rahner, but may be even immoral. Additionally, he goes on:

Neither does it help to point to the example of Jesus. Of course, he was obedient; he asserted that the obedience to his father was the form and strength, the substance of his life. Of course, we have to follow Jesus Christ. But the question is precisely how we can know that we are obedient to God in the most radical way by submitting to human authority. This is exactly what Jesus did *not* do. [29]

This question, already raised by Rahner in 1956, was of central importance for the debate within the Society of Jesus during the following decades.[30]

The distinction between religious and canonical obedience, presented at the beginning of this article, is abrogated in the Ignatian concept of obedience. By claiming that obedience to God has to be demonstrated by obedience to the concrete superior—whether he is benevolent and qualified or not—Ignatius transferred religious obedience into canonical obedience.[31] According to Raimund Schwager, the Ignatian concept of obedience is therefore contrary to that of Luther. Luther criticized the authority of the Church in the name of an unconditional obedience to God, Ignatius, on the contrary, demanded a radical obedience to the ecclesiastical authority.[32] The special obedience to the pope, which distinguishes Jesuits from other religious congregations, must be understood in this context. The implementation of obedience to the pope has to be seen in regard to the foundation of the Society of Jesus. The main objective of the Jesuit order, founded in 1540, was the propagation and defense of Catholic faith. Jesuits played a decisive role in the counter-reformation.[33]

According to the philosopher and Dominican priest Joseph Bocheński, Ignatius confused epistemic with deontic authority regarding the religious superior.[34] Whereas deontic authority is the authority of a boss giving instructions, Bocheński defines epistemic authority as the authority of a prudent person making statements. Statements indicate what is given; instructions state what should be given, and therefore what somebody should do. In questions of faith, the Church is, according to Bocheński an epistemic authority, the religious superior is, in contrast, only a deontic one. The deontic authority is delegable; the epistemic is not. According to Bocheński, Ignatius' confusion between epistemic and

---

[27] GC 31, D. 17, n. 11. Decrees of General Congregations 31 to 35. Available online: https://jesuitportal.bc.edu/research/general-congregations/.
[28] See (Rahner 1955–1956, p. 260).
[29] (Ibid., p. 261). The italics are mine.
[30] The fact that Rahner raised this question already in 1956 indicates that the so-called crisis of authority was not a result of the Second Vatican Council, but that the discussion about the concepts of authority and obedience had already begun before. According to Klaus Schatz the vast of majority of the younger generation of Jesuits in Germany appreciated the article by Rahner, whereas some Jesuits of the older generation harshly criticized it. See (Schatz 2013, vol. IV).
[31] See (Böckle 1968, p. 245).
[32] See (Schwager 1996, pp. 359–60). For the church conception of Ignatius of Loyola see (Schwager 1970).
[33] For the role and the development of the Jesuit order in the 16th century, see for example the general survey by (Banger 1986).
[34] See (Bocheński 2004, p. 105).

deontic authority becomes evident in his argument for an obedience of mind. If Ignatius demands that the will of the superior be accepted as the will of God, he erroneously believes that the epistemic authority of God is delegable to the superior. However, the religious superior, as already said, has primarily deontic authority; he may or may not also possess epistemic authority. With the distinction between epistemic and deontic authority, Bocheński describes—and this is the essential element of his concept—two completely different types of authority relationships. The deontic authority is a kind of mandatory authority and thus insists on obedience. The epistemic authority on the contrary would never do this. Therefore, Bocheński also specifies two different types of obedience. The epistemic authority seems to become authority only by being chosen by the obedient person.

In the era after the Second World War, Jesuits perceived the concept of obedience derived from Ignatius's *Letter to the Jesuits in Portugal* as increasingly outmoded and unfit. Nevertheless, it was read out once a month in the refectories of Jesuit communities.[35] In a letter about obedience and humility written on 8 December 1963, General Superior Juan Bautista Janssens explained that Jesuits should not understand the text of Ignatius as a legal and dogmatic text, but rather turn their attention to the prudence and practical psychology of the text.[36] This can be interpreted as an initial relativization of some of Ignatius' demands.

Just a few years later, Pedro Arrupe, elected General Superior at General Congregation 31 in 1965/66, spoke about a 'Crisis of obedience'. On 1 October 1966, during the second period of the Congregation Arrupe stated that Jesuits have to incorporate the 'new elements of today's Society' into their characteristic obedience.[37] He named the problems of obedience as follows:

> There is a conflict between the apostolic *dynamism* and the aspect of *passivity* or receptivity; between the *guidance of the Holy Spirit* and a rule exercised by man; between *dialogue* looking toward discussion of what is to be done and the *strictly personal character of decision-making* or of the laying down of a directive. There is, moreover, the conflict between the *responsibility* which *each* religious [...] is aware of in his own conscience and the *responsibility of the superior as such* [...]. [38]

In this quotation, Arrupe contrasts different elements of Jesuit self-conception. Except for 'dialogue' these elements were not new, but they seemed to be decreasingly compatible. On the one hand, Jesuits should pursue apostolic goals on their own initiative, on the other hand, they should passively follow orders. On the one hand, the Holy Spirit should lead Jesuits, on the other hand this leadership was concretely assumed by a superior. On the one hand, they should seek the will of God through community dialogue, on the other hand, decisions should not be taken collectively, but by a superior. On the one hand they should bear responsibility, on the other hand obey the superior.

6. The Change of the Obedience Concept

Obedience was questioned in connection with the fascistic and totalitarian regimes in the 20th century, since it was seen as the basic cause for the lack of individual sense of responsibility. This development accompanied a theological-ethical reassessment of conscience.[39] Linked with that trend was a stronger emphasis on the individual person, the call for more participation and the recognition of the individual's autonomy. Henceforth it was one's conscience that was to be obeyed. This implied the personal responsibility for one's own actions and thus an examination of the goals obedience was asked for.

---

[35] See (Tollenaere 2001, p. 1693).
[36] See (Ibid., p. 1693).
[37] See (Arrupe 1966, p. 62)
[38] (Ibid. p. 63). Italics in original.
[39] See (Hilpert 1996, p. 360).

This change of discourse resulted in a reform of the dictate of obedience at General Congregation 31 in 1965/66. Decree 17 highlights several times the responsibility of the obedient person for his own action.[40] Whereas Ignatius allowed non-compliance with instructions only in the case that an instruction was an obvious sin,[41] Decree 17 made it possible to suspend the execution of an order due to reasons of conscience.[42] In preparation of a General Congregation the Jesuit Provinces all over the world sent postulates to Rome which made suggestions for the agenda of the General Congregation. In the run-up to the meeting in Rome in 1965/66, the Provinces asked either for a confirmation of the principles of obedience, or for a clarification of the connection between these principles and new insights from Bible studies, psychology and sociology. Decree 17 on obedience could only be passed after adding passage 10, which contained the possibility of suspending the execution of an order.[43] However, this did not mean that an order of a superior could be disregarded, but it meant that a Jesuit who could not follow an order due to reasons of conscience, could speak to his superior and achieve that the order was *temporarily* suspended. Thereupon the superior had to decide—if necessary after consulting a higher superior—in favor of the good of the religious order and the individual. Furthermore, it was possible to ask other persons for consultation even from outside of the Society of Jesus, if both the subordinate and the superior agreed to it. In any case, should it happen frequently that a Jesuit could not follow an order for reasons of conscience, he should, according to the decree, consider leaving the Jesuit order. This passage 10 of Decree 17 can be understood as a kind of extension of the Jesuit *repraesentatio*. The *repraesentatio* describes the principle that a subordinate is allowed and even supposed to inform his superior about problems and objections regarding a given order. The *repraesentatio* constituted an old principle in the Society of Jesus, but did not include the option—as Decree 17 did—to suspend an order temporarily.[44]

Nevertheless, Decree 17 did not mean that obedience lost importance. Quite the contrary, the decree aimed at conserving the significance of obedience as a central feature of the Jesuit order. The introduction of the decree mentions the freedom and responsibility of the individual as well as the 'excessively critical attitude' towards obedience.[45] The idea that a superior represents Christ was maintained in Decree 17. It was this point especially which more and more Jesuits considered to be wrong. The keyword describing the doubt about this kind of conception was 'demythologization'. In an article of 1974 the Jesuit David Knight asked: 'Is it theologically defensible, in this age of demythologization, to speak of "God's will" for an individual being expressed authentically through any human authority [...]?'.[46] The demythologization of faith launched by the protestant theologians Rudolf Bultmann and Paul Tillich characterized first and foremost the attempt to reconcile the New Testament with the modern scientific world view.[47] However, as mentioned before, Knight's question had been raised in a similar way almost 20 years earlier by Karl Rahner.[48] Despite the lasting doubt about this belief, the Jesuit order also maintained it at General Congregation 32 in 1974/75—though using a more cautious formulation. Decree 11 states:

---

[40] GC 31, D. 17, n. 1 and 9–12. Decrees of General Congregations 31 to 35. Available online: https://jesuitportal.bc.edu/research/general-congregations/.
[41] See (Gioia 2001, p. 2854).
[42] GC 31, D. 17, n. 10. Decrees of General Congregations 31 to 35. Available online: https://jesuitportal.bc.edu/research/general-congregations/.
[43] See (Padberg 1994, p. 14).
[44] At General Congregation 32 an explanation was added to passage 10 of decree 17 of General Congregation 31. This explanation explicitly refers to the *repraesentatio* as a way of conflict resolution. The fact that the explanation was added afterwards shows that in previous years Jesuits interpreted the decree in different ways. See GC 32, D. 11, n. 55. Decrees of General Congregations 31 to 35. Available online: https://jesuitportal.bc.edu/research/general-congregations/.
[45] GC 31, D. 17, n. 3. Decrees of General Congregations 31 to 35. Available online: https://jesuitportal.bc.edu/research/general-congregations/.
[46] (Knight 1974, p. 139).
[47] See also on this issue Sydney Ahlstrom, who calls the theological change in the USA accompanying demythologization as 'theological radicalism' (Ahlstrom 1970).
[48] See (Rahner 1955–1956, p. 260).

> Vowed obedience [...] is always an act of faith and freedom whereby the religious recognizes and embraces the will of God manifested to him by one who has authority to send him in the name of Christ. [49]

The formulation 'by one who has authority to send him' implies the possibility that the superior is not necessarily seen as the *representative* of Christ, but nevertheless has the power to give orders to a subordinate *in the name* of Christ. The increasing challenge to religious myths provoked counterforces, which boosted the religious aspect against reason and rationality. As a reaction to demythologization, a certain 're-religiousization' took place in the Society of Jesus. The introduction of the obedience decree at General Congregation 31 claims that the grace of Jesuit vocation cannot be understood exclusively by philosophers, psychologists and sociologists, but that it requires the insight of faith.[50] Over and above the emphasis on responsibility and the conscience of the obedient person, it was argued that the superior is not always and necessarily supposed to explain to his subordinate the reasons for his instructions and that a Jesuit should act in religious obedience knowing that he was sent by his superior.[51] This means on the one hand that despite the conceptual change, the superior could justify any lack of willingness for dialogue on his part by referring to the decree. On the other hand, it demonstrates the attempt to conserve the faith as a fundament of obedience. Jesuits tried in a sense to reanimate the mysticism, which was connected to obedience and authority within Christian thinking. The emphasis on the religious element could furthermore serve as a unifying factor with regard to the deep conflicts of the post-conciliar era.

6.1. Obedience as a Service

The challenge to obedience in the Society of Jesus led on the one hand to a reflection about what obedience should not and must *not* be, on the other hand it also led to a constructive redefinition of the term. The ethical dispute about the concept of obedience emerging with the Enlightenment and reaching a milestone after National Socialism in the 20th century took two courses. Firstly, obedience was linked to reason and to the responsibility of the obedient person. The question of the *telos*, of the aim of obedience became central and the virtue of obedience depended unequivocally on the aim to be achieved. Jesuits integrated this critical element stemming from the philosophical discussion on obedience into their own specific concept of obedience and by doing so their religious obedience lost its characteristic trait of being unconditional. This loss was a tremendous shock for their concept of faith. Despite the religious fundament of obedience, it ceased being always and without conditions 'good'. Therefore, the Christian tenor, which was embodied in obedience lost its sharp contour. As explained before, the Jesuit order responded to this development at General Congregation 31 by passing Decree 17, which allowed an order to be temporarily suspended for reasons of conscience.

The second course within the ethical dispute about obedience consisted of describing obedience as a service.[52] In Christian thinking, obedience acquired a new constructive meaning by being linked to a selfless service following Christ. In this understanding obedience was more than just being subjected to somebody and acting under orders. A characteristic trait of this form of obedience consisted of '[...] a conscious step out of the sphere of privacy into the public in which obedience was demonstrated in a concrete political and social way namely as a *service to the right to live of every human being*.'[53] In this

---

[49] GC 32, D. 11, n. 31. Decrees of General Congregations 31 to 35. Available online: https://jesuitportal.bc.edu/research/general-congregations/.
[50] See GC 31, D. 17, n. 1. Decrees of General Congregations 31 to 35. Available online: https://jesuitportal.bc.edu/research/general-congregations/.
[51] See GC 31, D. 17, n. 11. Decrees of General Congregations 31 to 35. Available online: https://jesuitportal.bc.edu/research/general-congregations/.
[52] For these two aspects of the obedience term within theological ethics, see (Walther 1984, p. 155).
[53] (Ibid., p. 155). Italics in Original.

spirit, the Jesuit promotion of justice, which became, in addition to the service of faith, the central task of Jesuits at General Congregation 32 in 1974/75, can be understood as a new form of religious obedience.

6.2. Apostolic and Ascetic Obedience

At the time of its foundation the Society of Jesus defined itself basically according to its apostolate, that is to say according to its activity in the world. The ideal of Jesuits was therefore not a secluded life seeking their own spiritual healing, but on the contrary an active life. The apostolic element played a central role in the construction of Jesuit identity. Hence the question of which apostolate to follow and how much value to attach to the respective apostolates touched the (felt) core of being a Jesuit. Since the Jesuit order was founded precisely because of the apostolate, any consideration of how to structure the Society of Jesus, including the specific definition of 'Jesuit obedience', tended to serve the apostolate.[54] At General Congregation 31, the apostolic element implemented in Jesuit obedience was particularly emphasized and it was stated: 'Now through the vow of obedience our Society becomes a more fit instrument of Christ in His Church, unto the assistance of souls for God's greater glory.'[55]

As mentioned before, canonical and religious obedience can be differentiated. Furthermore, religious obedience can be sub-classified into ascetic and apostolic obedience.[56] Asceticism refers to a field within theology dealing with spirituality. Asceticism describes the practice of abstinence and austerity from wordly pleasures in order to achieve greater spirituality. Ascetic obedience therefore means obedience as an ascetic discipline for its own sake. Apostolic obedience in contrast refers to a form of obedience as a means to a more effective apostolate. The apostolic obedience is part of religious obedience insofar as the fulfillment of the apostolate corresponds to the fulfillment of God's will. In any case, since apostolic obedience is issue-related, it does not have the characteristic trait of being unconditional, as ascetic obedience has. It *is not* the fulfilling of God's will *in its own terms*, but it is the *means* to the fulfillment of God's will. For this reason, apostolic obedience met the ethical requirement that obedience must be evaluated in relation to its *telos*, as defined in the 1960s. The ethical value did not result from the obedience in itself, but from its aim. That is to say that the objective to be achieved became more significant than the attitude. Hence it becomes apparent that Decree 4 at General Congregation 32, which redefined the apostolate by declaring the promotion of justice to be a central goal, has to be understood in connection to the concept of obedience.

7. The Promotion of Justice as a New Form of Religious Obedience

The change of the apostolate and Jesuits' self-conception in relation to their social role was of course not only due to the change in the concept of obedience, but also due to the growing liberation theology movement and the redefinition of the idea of mission. The change of the concept of mission was on the one hand a consequence of secularization, defined here as a declining commitment to the Church, particularly in Western Europe. Subsequently, the opposition between 'sending' Christian nations and 'receiving' nations became obsolete or rather Western European countries became receiving nations.[57] On the other hand, the idea of mission also changed in consequence of decolonization, which originated a discussion about the role and the methods of the Church in the process of colonization.[58] These developments demanded a reevaluation and redefinition of mission, which was found in the link between the service of faith with the promotion of justice. The introduction of Decree 4 at General Congregation 32 reads as follows: 'The mission of the Society of Jesus today is the service of faith,

---

[54] See (O'Gorman 1971, p 15).
[55] GC 31, D. 17, n. 2. Decrees of General Congregations 31 to 35. Available online: https://jesuitportal.bc.edu/research/general-congregations/.
[56] See (Knight 1974, p. 135f).
[57] In 1974 General Superior Pedro Arrupe named this change explicitly. See (Arrupe 1982, p. 230). The conceptual change of mission already began at General Congregation 31. See (Bisson n.d.).
[58] See (Gruber 2018, pp. 14–25).

of which the promotion of justice is an absolute requirement. For reconciliation with God demands the reconciliation of people with one another.'[59]

Several parts of Decree 4 demonstrate the perceived connection between faith and justice. Further down it is stated: 'Since evangelization is proclamation of that faith which is made operative in love of others, the promotion of justice is indispensable to it.'[60] The connection between faith and justice led both previously and in the following decades to severe theological disputes.[61] The Holy See vehemently criticized the combination of faith and justice made in Decree 4, arguing that the promotion of justice should be unequivocally subordinated to evangelization. In any case, in the opinion of Pope Paul VI the changing of social structures with the objective to achieve more social justice could not be the mission of priests, but should be the task of lay Catholics. The Vatican's criticism of the Society of Jesus because of their amalgamation of faith and justice correlated with criticism of liberation theology. Whereas liberation theologians hold the Church responsible for the promotion of social justice, the Holy See defined the mission of the Church within the context of other-worldly salvation, but not with reference to a this-worldly liberation from social, economic and political repression. Theologians of liberation criticized that according to the Church's official attitude poor and oppressed people could only hope for salvation after death, but not for the Church's support for a better life in this world. The development of liberation theology certainly played an important role in the reorientation of the Jesuit order.[62] The important point is that according to Jesuits who supported Decree 4 the service of faith was no longer possible without the promotion of justice. Regarding this matter, the Jesuit und theologian Ignacio Ellacuría explained:

> [...] who ever denies that justice is an essential part of faith does not have a derogatory and dismissive opinion of what is supposed to be justice, but a derogatory and dismissive opinion of what is supposed to be faith. A faith which continues to be faith without sanctifying grace, without love and without justice can't have top priority within Christianity. [63]

For Ellacuría, justice was a form of Christian love. In his opinion, the love towards God could not be separated from the love towards human beings, which means that faith could not be separated from justice.[64]

The significance of Decree 4 also lies in the fact that it did not refer solely to the social apostolate—as was the case in former General Congregations—but that it was all-encompassing. Whether they were teachers, spiritual directors or staff of a relief organization, Jesuits should reflect on the social significance of their actions. For this reason, the Jesuit Peter Bisson calls the decree an intended reconstruction of religious identity of Jesuits.[65] To take this thought up it could be stated that justice was linked to faith by understanding the promotion of justice as the fulfillment of God's will. To promote justice was the equivalent of being obedient to God. Therefore Decree 4 resulted from the transformation of the concept of obedience and implied the new understanding of this concept, namely the promotion of social justice. In this context, the transformation of the concept of obedience changed ethical values within the Jesuit order.

---

[59] GC 32, D. 4, n. 2. Decrees of General Congregations 31 to 35. Available online: https://jesuitportal.bc.edu/research/general-congregations/.
[60] GC 32, D. 4, n. 28. Decrees of General Congregations 31 to 35. Available online: https://jesuitportal.bc.edu/research/general-congregations/.
[61] This becomes in particular evident in the study of Decree 4 written by Walter Kerber, SJ, Karl Rahner, SJ, and Hans Zwiefelhofer, SJ, which aims to prove theologically the 'and' between faith and justice. See (Kerber et al. 1976).
[62] See (Schnoor 2011).
[63] (Ellacuría 1977, p. 28). "[...] si [...] se niega que la justicia es parte esencial de la fe, no se ha disminuido o depreciado lo que es la justicia sino que se ha disminuido y depreciado lo que es la fe. Una fe que puede seguir siendo fe sin gracia santificante, sin amor y sin justicia no puede ser lo que tenga la máxima prioridad en el cristianismo."
[64] See (Ellacuría 1977, p. 29).
[65] See (Bisson n.d.).

8. Conclusions

This examination of the link between justice and obedience in Jesuit thinking aims to illuminate the horizon of meaning and motivation of the acting persons. This does not mean that the same action could not have been realized in the context of another horizon of meaning. On the contrary, the promotion of social justice was at the same time the objective of different social movements, in particular left-wing ones. Therefore, Decree 4 may be interpreted as an answer to the demand to justify one's own religious character. The reference to Karl Marx in Decree 4 is to be understood in this spirit, stating that it has to be shown that, 'Christian hope is not a dull opiate, but a firm and realistic commitment to make our world other than it is.'[66] This mixing of religion and politics evident in a religiously justified promotion of justice—not only observable in the Jesuit order—was definitely a religious development, which resulted most significantly from the challenge to the concept of religious obedience.

Since Decree 4 belonged to the legislation of the Jesuit order, it had important social and political consequences, as for example during the military dictatorships in Latin America in the 1960s and 1970s. During this era numerous individuals have been persecuted, tortured and murdered. In several Latin American countries Jesuits promoted human rights and were engaged against political repression.[67] This was true for example for Chile during the military dictatorship of Augusto Pinochet (1973–1990), where the Jesuit journal *Mensaje* criticized since 1975 the violation of human rights by the military regime.[68] This promotion for human rights and social justice resulted last but not least from the transformation of the concept of obedience. Notwithstanding, the promotion of social justice and human rights did neither result monocausally from the change of the concept of obedience, nor did the transformation of the concept and in consequence Decree 4 have the same effect on all Jesuits. There are indications that some Jesuits who served in Chile as prison chaplains knew about the systematic torture in the military prisons, but denied it.[69]

Nevertheless, the change of the concept of obedience in the Society of Jesus had a strong impact on the objective of action and was tightly interwoven with the social apostolate and therefore with the sociopolitical self-image of the religious congregation. The change of the concept of obedience represents also a transformation of Christian ethics. During General Congregation 34 in 1995, the self-conception as stated in Decree 4 at General Congregation 32 was both reinforced and enhanced.[70] Ever since then, the 'service of faith' is not solely linked to the promotion of justice, but is also closely connected to the terms culture and interreligious dialogue. According to Decree 2 of General Congregation 34, the service of faith presupposes, in addition to the promotion of justice, dialogue with other cultures and openness to other religious experiences.[71] General Congregation 35 in 2008 discussed the term 'reconciliation' intensely as an apostolic response to new challenges. It eventually became prominent in the last General Congregation 36 in October and November of 2016 which stated that Jesuits see themselves as having a mission of reconciliation and justice. However, the fundamental change of Jesuit identity and ethical values in Decree 4 of General Congregation 32 has not since been contradicted, but rather refined.

Both the history of Decree 4 at General Congregation 32 and the enhancement of this idea at General Congregation 34 prove the significance of the historical and cultural context in the definition of ethical values. The named decrees served the Jesuit order for answering to historical developments,

---

[66] GC 32, D. 4, n. 30. Decrees of General Congregations 31 to 35. Available online: https://jesuitportal.bc.edu/research/general-congregations/.
[67] See (Klaiber 2007).
[68] See (Schnoor 2012).
[69] See (Schnoor 2015, pp. 263–67).
[70] GC 34, D. 2–5. Decrees of General Congregations 31 to 35. Available online: https://jesuitportal.bc.edu/research/general-congregations/.
[71] See GC 34, D. 2, n. 19. Decrees of General Congregations 31 to 35. Available online: https://jesuitportal.bc.edu/research/general-congregations/.

this is to social, cultural and political transformations. The present paper aimed to contribute to a reenvisioning of the field of Christian ethics by raising the awareness of the meaning of the concrete historical context for the shaping of ethical values. Using the method of conceptual history, the paper showed how social, cultural and political developments gave birth to new theological thinking and in consequence to the transformation of the concept of obedience. Therefore, it serves as an illustration of the usefulness of this methodological approach as a partner-discipline for the Christian ethics.

Taking into account the entanglement of social and theological developments it should be mentioned that the influence between these fields is bidirectional. It would be fruitful for example to ask for the links between the transformation of the religious concept of obedience and new forms of leadership in organizations. Since the 1960s Jesuits developed a new culture of leadership in consequence of the crisis of authority and obedience within the Catholic Church. They changed their own organizational structures. The modification of the Jesuit concept of leadership may have an impact in particular on the business sector, since Jesuits are known as coaches of leadership-skills and for training business leaders.[72]

As a closing remark, it should be addressed what happened to the basic Ignatian idea of obedience in the long term. The idea that the superior represents Jesus Christ, which was understood as the religious reason for the obligation to obey to him, was finally abandoned at General Congregation 35 in 2008. The decree on obedience promulgated at this General Congregation states with reference to the *Constitutions* that a formed Jesuit should obey to the commands of the superior, 'as if they came from Christ because it is for love of Christ that he obeys'.[73] Thus this concept does not attribute the same role to the person of the superior as previous documents did, because a Jesuit should obey his orders *as if* they come from Christ, but the superior does not *represent* Christ. There is no judgment on the quality of the superior's commands, which had been previously understood as an expression of God's will. Another paragraph warns that the exercise of authority may be degraded to an exercise of power.[74] An individual Jesuit had the opportunity to react to possible problems in the *account of conscience*, in which he could reveal to the superior his doubts and reservations in reference to a given command, in order to allow the superior to send him 'more prudently and confidently'.[75] However, the decree does not give an answer to the question raised in the 1960s and 1970s of how to react if a problem cannot be solved in the potential case that the superior is lacking prudence.

Without doubt, the emphasis on responsibility and conscience will endure in the Jesuit concept of obedience, even though conflicts in concrete relationships of Jesuits and their superiors may continue. Obedience was obviously of no relevance at General Congregation 36, since the term appears in the decrees just one time without adding new elements to the concept.[76] However, the way the concept of obedience will be discussed at future General Congregations remains to be seen.

Funding: This research was funded in part by the Cluster of Excellence "Religion and Politics in Pre-Modern and Modern Cultures" of the University of Münster.

Conflicts of Interest: The author declares no conflict of interest.

---

[72] The Jesuit Georgetown-University in Washington, D.C. for example was one of the first universities which offered a program for leaders and leadership-coaches.

[73] GC 35, D. 4, n. 8. Decrees of General Congregations 31 to 35. Available online: https://jesuitportal.bc.edu/research/general-congregations/.

[74] See GC 35, D. 4, n. 21. Decrees of General Congregations 31 to 35. Available online: https://jesuitportal.bc.edu/research/general-congregations/.

[75] GC 35, D. 4, n. 24. Decrees of General Congregations 31 to 35. Available online: https://jesuitportal.bc.edu/research/general-congregations/.

[76] See GC 36, D. 1, n. 8. Decrees of General Congregation 36 of the Society of Jesus. Available online: http://www.mdsj.org/gc36decrees.

References

Adorno, Theodor W., Else Frenkel-Brunswik, Daniel J. Levinson, and R. Nevitt Sanford, eds. 1950. *The Authoritarian Personality. Studies in Prejudice Series*. New York: Harper & Brothers.
Ahlstrom, Sydney. 1970. The Radical Turn in Theology and Ethics. Why it occurred in the 1960's. *The Annals of the American Academy of Political and Social Science* 387: 1–13. [CrossRef]
Arrupe, Pedro. 1966. A Talk on Obedience. *Letters and Notices* 342: 62–69, Archivum Romanum Societatis Iesu (ARSI), Rome.
Arrupe, Pedro. 1982. Evangelización y promoción humana. In *La iglesia del hoy y del futuro*. Bilbao: Mensajero, pp. 229–33.
Banger, William. 1986. *A History of the Society of Jesus*. St. Louis: Institute of Jesuit Sources.
Bevir, Mark. 2010. Geist und Methode in der Ideengeschichte. In *Die Cambridge School der Politischen Ideengeschichte*. Edited by Martin Mulsow and Andreas Mahler. Berlin: Suhrkamp, pp. 203–40.
Bisson, Peter. n.d. Social Justice Activism as Religious Experience. The Transformation of the Jesuits. Available online: http://web.295.ca/gondolkodo/talalkozo/irasok/BissonEN04.html (accessed on 15 February 2017).
Bocheński, Joseph. 2004. *Autorität, Freiheit, Glaube. Sozialphilosophische Studien*. München: Philosophia Verlag.
Böckle, Franz. 1968. Zur Krise der Autorität. Randbemerkungen aus Anlass eines Buches. *Theologisches Jahrbuch*, 239–49.
Conference of Provincials. 1991. *Jesuit sein heute. Formel des Instituts, Satzungen, Dekrete der Gesellschaft Jesu*. Brussels: Conference of Provincials of the Central European Assistance.
Ellacuría, Ignacio. 1977. Fe y Justicia, Parte I, *Christus. Revista Mensual de Teología* 501: 26–33.
Eschenburg, Theodor. 1976. *Über Autorität*. Frankfurt am Main: Suhrkamp.
Floristán, Casiano. 1980. Der christliche Gehorsam. *Concilium*, 603–4.
Gioia, Mario. 2001. Obediencia. In *Diccionario Histórico de la Compañía de Jesús (DHCJ)*. Rome: Institutum Historicum Societatis Jesu, vol. III, pp. 2852–55.
Gruber, Judith. 2018. *Intercultural Theology. Exploring World Christianity after the Cultural Turn*. Göttingen: Vandenhoeck & Ruprecht.
Rahner, Hugo. 1980. *Über den theologischen Sinn des Gehorsams in der Gesellschaft Jesu*. Geistliche Texte SJ Nr. 1. München: Provinzialkonferenz der Deutschen Assistenz SJ.
Hammer, Felix. 1977. *Autorität und Gehorsam*. Düsseldorf: Patmos.
Hampsher Monk, Iain, Karin Tilmans, and Frank van Vree, eds. 1998. *History of Concepts. Comparative Perspectives*. Amsterdam: Amsterdam University Press.
Harvanek, Robert. 1978. The status of Obedience in the Society of Jesus. *Studies in the Spirituality of Jesuits* 10: 169–215.
Hilpert, Konrad. 1996. Gehorsam. III. Theologisch-Ethisch. In *Lexikon für Theologie und Kirche (LThK)*, 3rd ed. Freiburg: Herder, vol. 4, pp. 360–62.
Ignatius of Loyola. 1993. An die Mitbrüder in Portugal, 26 March 1553; 3304. In *Ignatius of Loyola: Briefe und Unterweisungen*. Edited by Peter Knauer. Translated by Peter Knauer. Würzburg: Echter, pp. 458–69.
Rahner, Karl. 1955–1956. Eine ignatianische Grundhaltung. Marginalien über den Gehorsam. *Stimmen der Zeit (StdZ)* 158: 253–67.
Kerber, Walter, Karl Rahner, and Hans Zwiefelhofer. 1976. *Glaube und Gerechtigkeit. Überlegungen zur theologischen Begründung von Dekret 4 der 32. Generalkongregation*. Frankfurt am Main: Library of Phil.-Theol, Hochschule Sankt Georgen, unpublished manuscript.
Klaiber, Jeffrey L. 2007. *Los Jesuitas en América Latina, 1549–2000. 450 años de Inculturación, Defensa de los Derechos Humanos y Testimonio Profético*. Lima: Pueblo Libre.
Knauer, Peter. 1990. *Unsere Weise voranzugehen* nach den Satzungen der Gesellschaft Jesu. In *Ignatianisch. Eigenart und Methode der Gesellschaft Jesu*. Edited by Michael Sievernich and Günter Switek. Freiburg: Herder, pp. 131–48.
Knauer, Peter. 1993. Erläuternde Einleitung zu Ignatius von Loyola, An die Mitbrüder in Portugal, 26 March 1553. In *Ignatius of Loyola: Briefe und Unterweisungen*. Edited by Peter Knauer. Translated by Peter Knauer. Würzburg: Echter, p. 458.
Knight, David. 1974. Joy and Judgement in Religious Obedience. *Studies in the Spirituality of Jesuits* 6: 131–67.
Koselleck, Reinhart. 1978. *Historische Semantik und Begriffsgeschichte*. Stuttgart: Klett-Cotta.

McLeod, Hugh. 2007. *The Religious Crisis of the 1960s*. Oxford: Oxford University Press.

Müller, Alois. 1964. *Das Problem von Befehl und Gehorsam. Eine pastoraltheologische Untersuchung*. Einsiedeln: Benziger.

Müller, Alois. 1968. Autorität und Gehorsam in der Kirche. *Theologisches Jahrbuch*, 227–38.

Neumann, Johannes. 1970. Die Autorität auf dem II. Vatikanischen Konzil. In *Die päpstliche Autorität im katholischen Selbstverständnis des 19. und 20. Jahrhunderts*. Edited by Erika Weinzierl. Salzburg and München: Universitätsverlag Anton Pustet, pp. 141–69.

O'Gorman, Thomas. 1971. *Jesuit Obedience from Life to Law. The Development of the Ignatian Idea of Obedience in the Jesuit Constitutions 1539–1556*. Manila: Loyola House of Studies.

Padberg, John. 1994. *Together as a Companionship. A History of the Thirty-Fist, Thirty-Second, and Thirty-Third General Congregations of the Society of Jesus*. Saint Louis: Institute of Jesuit Sources.

Palmés, Carlos. 1963. *La Obediencia Religiosa Ignaciana*. Barcelona: Eugenio Subirana.

Rotsaert, Mark. 2008. L'obéissance religieuse dans les Lettres d'Ignace de Loyola, les Constitutions de la Compagnie de Jésus, et le Décret de la 35ᵉ Congrégation générale de la Compagnie. *Gregorianum* 96: 365–94.

Schatz, Klaus. 2013. *Geschichte der deutschen Jesuiten (1814–1983)*. Münster: Aschendorff Verlag, vol. IV, pp. 1945–83.

Schnoor, Antje. 2011. Zwischen jenseitiger Erlösung und irdischem Heil. Die Rezeption der Befreiungstheologie in der Gesellschaft Jesu. *Archiv für Sozialgeschichte* 51: 419–43.

Schnoor, Antje. 2012. Mehrstimmig, aber im Chor. Jesuiten und Erzbistum Santiago in Pinochets Chile, 1975. *Schweizerische Zeitschrift für Religions- und Kulturgeschichte (SZRKG)* 106: 413–33.

Schnoor, Antje. 2015. Jesuitas bajo Pinochet. Actitudes frente al orden político y a las violaciones de los derechos humanos. *Jahrbuch für die Geschichte Lateinamerikas (JbLA)* 52: 249–69. [CrossRef]

Schwager, Raimund. 1970. *Das dramatische Kirchenverständnis bei Ignatius von Loyola. Historisch-Pastoraltheologische Studie über die Stellung der Kirche in den Exerzitien und im Leben des Ignatius*. Köln: Benziger.

Schwager, Raimund. 1996. Gehorsam II, Systematisch theologisch. In *Lexikon für Theologie und Kirche (LThK)*, 3rd ed. Freiburg: Herder, vol. 4, pp. 359–60.

Skinner, Quentin. 2010. Bedeutung und Verstehen der Ideengeschichte. In *Die Cambridge School der politischen Ideengeschichte*. Edited by Martin Mulsow and Andreas Mahler. Berlin: Suhrkamp, pp. 21–78.

Sölle, Dorothee. 1988. *Phantasie und Gehorsam. Überlegungen zu einer künftigen christlichen Ethik*, 12th ed. Stuttgart: Kreuz Verlag.

Tentler, Leslie. 2004. *Catholics and Contraception: An American History*. New York: Cornell University Press.

Tollenaere, Maurice De. 2001. Los generales de la CJ: Janssens, Juan Bautista. In *Diccionario Histórico de la Compañía de Jesús (DHCJ)*. Rome: Institutum Historicum Societatis Jesu, vol. II, pp. 1690–96.

Van Gelderen, Martin. 1998. Between Cambridge and Heidelberg. Concepts, Languages and Images in Intellectual History. In *History of Concepts. Comparative Perspectives*. Edited by Iain Hampsher Monk, Karin Tilmans and Frank van Vree. Amsterdam: Amsterdam University Press, pp. 227–38.

Walther, Christian. 1984. Gehorsam. In *Theologische Realenzyklopädie (TRE)*. Berlin: De Gruyter, vol. 12, pp. 148–57.

 © 2019 by the author. Licensee MDPI, Basel, Switzerland. This article is an open access article distributed under the terms and conditions of the Creative Commons Attribution (CC BY) license (http://creativecommons.org/licenses/by/4.0/).

Article

The Scales Integral to Ecology: Hierarchies in *Laudato Si'* and Christian Ecological Ethics

Kevin J. O'Brien

Department of Religion, Pacific Lutheran University, Tacoma, WA 98447, USA; obrien@plu.edu

Received: 29 June 2019; Accepted: 24 August 2019; Published: 3 September 2019

Abstract: Pope Francis's *Laudato Si'* advocates for an "ecological conversion" to the ideal of "integral ecology". In so doing, it offers insights into different scales of moral attention, resonating with sophisticated thinking in scientific ecology and environmental ethics. From the encyclical, Christian ecological ethicists can learn about the importance of identifying spatial and temporal scales in moral terms and the usefulness of hierarchical levels that distinguish between local, community, and global concerns. However, the encyclical assumes some hierarchical relationships—among genders, among species, and with the divine—that it does not question. Scalar thinking is a key strength of *Laudato Si'* and also a signal of the work it leaves undone regarding the constructedness and limitations of all hierarchical assumptions.

Keywords: Christian ethics; ecology; scale; hierarchy; integral ecology; *Laudato Si'*; Pope Francis

1. Introduction

In his 2015 encyclical *Laudato Si'*, Pope Francis calls for and seeks to inspire an "ecological conversion" in human hearts that will help people to live more justly with one another and with all other creatures. This is introduced as a personal conversion, in which people recognize the harms their sins cause to other creatures and start behaving more charitably, justly, and sustainably. But Francis emphasizes that private actions and attitudes will be insufficient on their own, and so also calls for "a community conversion" of social contexts that will habituate people to live differently together. Ultimately, he argues, both personal and community changes require a global conversion, a move toward a broad community of human and non-human creatures based on "a loving awareness that we are not disconnected from the rest of creatures but joined in a splendid universal communion".[1]

In a few paragraphs, Pope Francis connects three distinct levels of moral work, calling for personal change, communal reform, and global awareness of interconnection. Such thinking across scales, I argue, is both a key strength of the encyclical and a signal of the work it leaves undone. Drawing on insights from scientific ecology and environmental ethics, this essay demonstrates that the encyclical captures the importance of scalar thinking and the heuristic value of hierarchical levels, but then argues that future work in Christian ecological ethics can build on this with more attention to the ecological understanding that all hierarchical levels are social constructions.

Laudato Si' was issued by the Roman Catholic Pope, and so carries authority for many within that tradition. An obedient Catholic approach to this document might involve reading it as a set of teachings to be learned from, with its validity assumed as a first principle. This would mean accepting the encyclical's authority based on its provenance in the Church as God's instrument in the world, and so would put the text primarily into conversation with other authoritative Catholic teachings.

---

1 (Francis 2015, paras. 218–20).

My approach is different. I am impressed by the substantial accomplishment of the document, but I also have critiques and believe that serious and respectful engagement can include dissent from some aspects of an encyclical. I acknowledge the particular ecclesial context from which the text comes but am confident that discourse will be strengthened by a broader conversation that also includes other environmental and religious texts.

Pope Francis invites just such a reading by addressing the encyclical to "every person living on this planet" and emphasizing that all people must collaborate to preserve the health of the planet, "our common home".[2] While the document is very clearly a work of Catholic Social Teaching, it explicitly seeks conversation with other faith traditions, with indigenous peoples, with scientists, and with others. Thus, I believe it is respectful to understand the encyclical in the context of not only Catholic theology but also a diverse range of other efforts to think morally about the environmental and social challenges of the 21st century.

The next section introduces scalar concepts from ecological science and environmental ethics. I then turn to note appreciatively the sophisticated use of scale and hierarchical levels in *Laudato Si'*, which contributes to the document's rhetorical power. Finally, I offer my critique that the encyclical too readily assumes the reality of certain hierarchies—between God and the world, between male and female, and between humans and other animals—and that Christian ecological ethics should work to advance a form of integral ecology that does not take these assumptions for granted.

2. Scale and Hierarchy as Scientific and Moral Concepts

The primary conversation partners I want to bring into discussion with *Laudato Si'* are ecological theory and environmental ethics that learns from it, particularly insofar as both develop tools to think about scale. Scale refers to the size or extent of something relevant to a measurement. The concept calls attention to the relative orientation of an observer or actor in both space and time and helps to clarify what is central and what is peripheral in any measurement or assessment.

2.1. Scale in Scientific Ecology

In an influential 1992 essay, ecologist Simon Levin argued that scale is "the fundamental conceptual problem in ecology, if not in all of science". Understanding how a natural system works, Levin argues, requires deliberate attention to and balance among different scales of attention, which allows scientists to identify patterns and develop models of understanding and prediction.[3]

The science of ecology studies living organisms in their contexts, and the concept of scale allows ecologists to differentiate the spatial and temporal levels at which living organisms interact with one another and the non-living world. The concept offers a vocabulary by which ecologists communicate how they are studying the world. Most specialize at a relatively small scale, studying a particular species or group of species in a particular habitat or region. Others, who work on theoretical connections, ecological education, or public science tend to prioritize broader, more global trends. The two groups depend on one another: those who work at small scales are informed by trends across regions (e.g., migratory patterns), across the globe (e.g., climate change), across decades (e.g., pollution patterns), and across millennia (e.g., evolution). Those who work at large scales depend upon more focused studies to inform and test their ideas.

An example of the various ways scale is approached in scientific ecology can be drawn from a recent issue of *Ecology*, the official journal of the Ecological Society of America. One article developed a hypothesis of how temperature impacts the behavior of four ant species in central Kenya, and another reported on the migratory habits of giant Galápagos tortoises. These are relatively small-scale articles, with primary attention on a specific species or category of species in a particular region. Other articles

---

[2] (Ibid., para. 3).
[3] (Levin 1992, pp. 1944–45). Twenty years later, ecologist Chave (2013) reviewed and affirmed Levin's argument.

are far broader, such as one that offers a more general theory of how herbivores influence plants' relationships to pollinators or another that offers tools to combine disparate datasets to model the distribution of species. These are more generalized, broad-scale articles. Each research project can only be fully understood when one grasps the scale at which it was conducted.[4] The giant tortoises were studied exclusively on a particular archipelago, while data on herbivores and pollinators were gathered from across the world. Additionally, each project depends upon cross-scalar understanding: researchers who study African ants look for connections between the behavior they observe and that of other social animals in symbiotic relationships with plants, and those who work with species distribution data depend on field ecologists gathering that data on specific organisms.

2.2. Scale in Environmental Ethics

Environmentalists and environmental ethicists have learned from ecological theorists to take scale seriously as a moral as well as ecological concept. Just as scientists must make choices about their scales of attention when they seek to describe natural systems, so must activists and moral thinkers make scalar choices about the spatial and temporal dimensions of moral attention. To sustain a healthy ecosystem for the next week is different from sustaining it for our children's lifetimes, which is different from sustaining it for seven generations. To protect a watershed is different from protecting an entire national park, which is different from protecting the entirety of the world's oceans and atmosphere. Scale makes a moral difference.

Aldo Leopold, an early twentieth-century forester whose writings have shaped the environmental movement, famously called for an "expansion of ethics" so that human beings learn to care for and to understand our own fate as dependent upon the non-human systems around us. Leopold believed that human beings, who had learned to care for one another, could learn to extend that care outward to other species with whom we share our habitats. He proposed that people should learn to "think like a mountain" in order to consider broader temporal and spatial scales than those that come naturally at the human scale. In light of environmental degradation, Leopold argued, such an expansive moral vision that encompasses other species and ecosystems must be embraced as "an evolutionary possibility and an ecological necessity".[5]

A generation later, the economist E. F. Schumacher influenced environmental ethics with a very different scalar argument. In the book *Small is Beautiful*, Schumacher argued that human beings in contemporary cultures have become distracted and ungrounded by life in a global economy and, as a result, have great difficulty acknowledging the particulars of our own communities. Schumacher, therefore, called for an ethics focused on a more immediate scale as a corrective to the "almost universal idolatry of giantism" in global culture. His thesis was that the most vital contemporary ethical project is "to insist on the virtues of smallness". He argued that global ideas and systems are too complicated and too grand for real people ever to understand them, much less feel morally responsible for what they do to the natural environment. As an alternative, he called for technologies and political policies designed and enacted on a more local, familiar, "human scale".[6]

Leopold and Schumacher came to different conclusions about scale, and ethicists continue to negotiate between attempts to scale moral attention upward and downward.[7] But the shared premise

---

[4] "Left Out in the Cold: Temperature-Dependence of Defense in an African Ant-Plant Mutualism", "Migration Triggers in a Large Herbivore: Galápagos Giant Tortoises Navigating Resource Gradients on Volcanoes", "A Meta-Analysis of Herbivore Effects on Plant Attractiveness to Pollinators", and "Resolving Misaligned Spatial Data with Integrated Species Distribution Models" from *Ecology*, Volume 100, Issue 6 (June 2019).

[5] "The Land Ethic" in Leopold (1949). For a thoughtful response to the ways Leopold overestimated the human capacity to care for one another in a world still beset by racism and oppression, see "Alien Land Ethic" in Savoy (2015).

[6] (Schumacher 1973).

[7] In recent Christian ecological ethics, for example, consider Harris (2017) argument that the concrete experience of black women should shape moral arguments in contrast to Appolloni (2018) argument that moral arguments should be shaped by a more comprehensive and integrated approach to global knowledge.

behind both arguments is that there are moral implications to ecological scale; the ways people spatially and morally attend to the world shape our ability to care about and act on behalf of endangered neighbors, communities, ecosystems, and the planet as a whole.

2.3. Thinking in Hierarchies

In both ecological science and environmental ethics, scalar thinking tends to be organized into discrete hierarchical levels. While scale is a blanket term for all spatial and temporal measurements, levels are attempts to categorize scales, to define and distinguish among different kinds of scalar thinking. In scientific ecology, the most important such levels refer to the spatial scale of what is studied, distinguishing between organisms, ecosystems, landscapes, and biomes. These levels are hierarchically organized in the sense that the smaller are contained within the larger. So, multiple organisms interact in an ecosystem, landscapes are made up of more than one ecosystem, biomes contain landscapes, and the planetary system as a whole is structured with biomes. One common metaphor suggests that these hierarchical levels are "nested" like a Russian doll, with each smaller scale existing entirely inside the one above.[8]

Such hierarchies help to remind ecologists to pay attention to the ways structured bodies like ecosystems or complex organisms are made up of sub-structures. Furthermore, any part of a system likely plays multiple roles within it. So, an ant colony represents a subsystem nested within a larger structure (a forest ecosystem) and is also itself made up of subsystems (e.g., ants, aphids, and plant matter).[9] The world is understood as a set of bounded entities that contain and are contained within entities at other levels of scale.

Ethicists, too, think hierarchically. This has been most explicitly developed by philosopher Bryan Norton, who developed a set of three nested levels for moral thinking about environmental issues. The first and narrowest level of moral attention is the local, an ethics that focuses on individuals, their contexts, and their needs within a few years. A local ethics asks what will serve a particular entity or particular place in the near future. The next level up is community-oriented, including a system of individuals organized into social and ecological structures, with temporal concern extending across a full century. Thinking on the community level, an ethicist asks what will be good for a society or species for the next century. The third and broadest level is global, which attends to the entire planetary community over indefinite time. Ethical questions raised at this level concern the good of Earth and all life thereon for the foreseeable future and beyond.[10]

Norton's levels help to characterize debates in environmental ethics. One can observe, for example, that Leopold's "mountain" appeals to a community-oriented scale, while Schumacher's "human" level is more local. Norton argues that this kind of disagreement is foundational to the field: "Environmental problems are, most basically, problems of scale", and so it is vital for ethicist to debate the levels of attention at which we will engage such problems.[11] Norton's own pragmatic philosophy tends to emphasize the need to scale up from local to community-oriented morality,[12] but his main emphasis is

---

[8] Ecologists draw this attention to "nested hierarchies" from the broader findings of "hierarchy theory", a study of "how a system of discrete functional elements or units linked at two or more scales operates". See Forman (1995).

[9] For many ecologists, the most immediate question about such hierarchies is why they have proven adaptive and thus evolved. The behavioral scientist Simon (1973) suggests that such a system of "nested hierarchies" is an expedient to evolution: when more complex systems can incorporate simpler systems as part of their make-up, they will be more likely to function (pp. 7–8). Hierarchies also create fail-safes within evolutionary change: while different units within a hierarchy might adapt or maladapt, as long as the majority remain stable, catastrophe is unlikely.

[10] (Norton 2003, pp. 67–72); (Norton 2005, pp. 230–31). He refers to these three categories as "scales", but based on the terms I have adopted from ecological theory, I identify them as levels because they concern the categories of observation that govern our attention rather than the particular measurements.

[11] (Norton 2005, p. 311).

[12] For example, "The second level of the spatiotemporal hierarchy is especially important because it is the level at which humans shape their own culture and multigenerational community through individual and cooperative acts that, at the same time, impact the landscape in which they will make future decisions. This is the level on which a human cultural

on the need to integrate multiple levels of attention and to be self-conscious about what is included and excluded in any given moral argument.[13]

3. Scale and Hierarchy in *Laudato Si'*

Pope Francis's encyclical does not cite ecological theory, Aldo Leopold, E.F. Schumacher, or Bryan Norton. But it shows considerable attention to scalar issues. As demonstrated in the first paragraph above, the call for ecological conversion requires the integration of scales, seeking changes at the personal, community, and global levels.

3.1. Integral Ecology

Such conversion is best understood in the context of "integral ecology", a central concept in the encyclical. The second word suggests a scientific approach, but here "ecology" is also normative, suggesting moral consideration of the non-human context that makes human life possible. Such ecology becomes integral when it embraces a synthetic view of the world and humanity's place in it, uniting attention to environmental degradation and social injustice. Perhaps the most important argument in the entire document is that "the human environment and the natural environment deteriorate together", and so people must learn to connect human justice to environmental health. In other words, there is no adequate response to environmental degradation that does not account for social degradation, no effective response to social problems that does not also attend to ecological issues.[14] Humans are called to action, to conversion, that integrates our social systems with the non-human world.

Integral ecology also informs the methodology of *Laudato Si'*, which insists that multiple ways of knowing and engaging the world must converge if human beings are to respond morally to the challenges of the 21st century. A key example is the integration of science and religion, each of which Pope Francis insists have an incomplete understanding of the world without the other. "With their distinctive approaches to understanding reality", he argues, science and religion "can enter into an intense dialogue fruitful for both". So, the encyclical calls for careful attention to scientific data about the climate and ecological system, insists that such research should not be unduly influenced by economic interests, and also encourages scientists to "take into account the data generated by other fields of knowledge, including philosophy and social ethics".[15] This integration of methods suggests that the project of this essay—to use ecological theory and environmental ethics to better understand the theology of *Laudato Si'*—fits the spirit of the document.

Integration among human communities, between human and non-human systems, and among different ways of knowing are all essential to integral ecology. Pope Francis is confident that such connections are possible on theological grounds, insisting that human beings were created as part of an interrelated world: "everything is interconnected" and all of life is "a web of relationships". Human beings, the image of the trinitarian God, "were made for love", and so every person "grows more, matures more and is sanctified more to the extent that he or she enters into relationships". Francis, therefore, has faith that integration is possible, that moral people in moral societies can build a better world by finding harmony among different communities, between the social and the environmental, and between science and religion.[16]

---

unit, a population or a human community interacts with the other species that form with it a larger ecological community, or place" (Norton 2005, p. 230).
[13] For an application of these concepts to the issue of biodiversity conservation, see O'Brien (2010), especially Chs 4 and 5.
[14] (Francis 2015, para. 48).
[15] (Ibid., para. 62).
[16] (Ibid., para. 240, 258).

3.2. Hierarchical Arguments

While Aldo Leopold argued for "thinking like a mountain" at the community level and E.F. Schumacher advocated "the virtues of smallness" at the local level, Pope Francis's integral ecology is a powerful example of global environmental ethics. *Laudato Si'* contrasts the "risk of rampant individualism" in our modern world with "a new and universal solidarity" through which all human beings can "work together in building our common home".[17] This explains why the document is addressed to "every person living on this planet", all of whom are understood to have common cause in a global environmental project.

Ultimately, Pope Francis's appeal is best understood as even broader than the global level, because his calls for human unity are based on an understanding that we all share our origin and ultimate meaning from God, the creator of the cosmos who is greater than the entirety of creation. The encyclical characterizes a basic mistake of contemporary societies as thinking too small by "worshiping earthly powers" and "ourselves usurping the place of God". The solution is a spiritual understanding of "God as all-powerful and Creator" and an understanding of the world as a creation, "a gift from the outstretched hand of the Father of all" and "a reality illuminated by the love which calls us together into universal communion".[18] Thus, the call for a united humanity to care for the entire world is nested in a cosmic vision of all that exists as God's generous creation. This is cosmically large-scale thinking, a basis for universal morality.

Interestingly though, *Laudato Si'* also demonstrates the importance of other levels, balancing the push to broader morality with attention to particular communities and local thinking. This is consistent with the Catholic doctrine of subsidiarity, which emphasizes a preference for local communities over national and international systems. Introduced in Pope Pius XI's 1931 encyclical *Qaudragesimo Anno*, subsidiarity insists that:

> Just as it is gravely wrong to take from individuals what they can accomplish by their own initiative and industry and give it to the community, so also is it an injustice and at the same time a grave evil and disturbance of right order to assign to a greater and higher association what lesser and subordinate organizations can do.[19]

In other words, that which can be accomplished at a smaller scale of human organization should be, and large-scale organizations—communities, nations, international collectives—should take responsibility only for what cannot be handled more locally.

Pope Francis cites subsidiarity in part to argue against excessive market control, noting that international corporations too often take over things that could be managed more locally by nation-states or communities. When local control is possible, it is better. On this basis, Francis insists that the highest priority should be given to "the family, as the basic cell of society", the smallest level at which individuals cooperate with one another.[20] He further argues that local and indigenous cultures should be consulted so that environmental and social problems are understood on human terms rather than entirely through abstractions.[21] Thus, the call for global and cosmic attention to "our common home" is balanced by a recognition of genuine local differences among people and the importance of particular communities in shaping moral life.

This is consistent with Pope Francis's theme of integral ecology because he argues that attention at each level is required in order to connect environmental concerns with social justice. The push toward the global and the cosmic insists that every person and every ecosystem deserves our moral

---

[17] (Ibid., paras. 162, 14, 13).
[18] (Ibid., paras. 75, 76).
[19] (Pope Pius XI 1931, para. 79) My previous work applying this principle to environmental issues is most fully developed in O'Brien (2008).
[20] (Francis 2015, paras. 196, 157).
[21] (Ibid., paras. 143, 146).

attention, that such a "sense of responsibility for our fellow men and women" is the basis "upon which all civil society is founded". At the same time, the call of subsidiarity insists that not all women and men have the same moral duties in an unjust world: "regarding climate change, there are *differentiated responsibilities*" through which rich countries and peoples owe a debt to the poor, weak, and marginalized who already suffer the effects of climate change disproportionately.[22]

While less prominent, temporal scale is also discussed in *Laudato Si'*. As with spatial scale the key use is to contrast integral ecology with the logic of the market, characterizing the latter as "looking for quick and easy profit" which creates a "more intensified pace of life and work which might be called rapidification". The corrective to this is longer-term thinking, "far-sightedness" embracing a "notion of the common good [that] extends to future generations". Francis also insightfully connects temporal and spatial scales to emphasize his integrative argument, asserting that "our inability to think seriously about future generations is linked to our inability to broaden the scope of our present interests and to give consideration to those who remain excluded from development".[23]

So, *Laudato Si'* offers a sophisticated use of scalar hierarchies, appealing to a universal and global morality in order to justify political and economic systems that favor local and community control. It achieves what Bryan Norton calls for in environmental ethics: sophisticated engagement with multiple hierarchical levels and self-aware choices about which levels to favor.[24]

Using these levels, the encyclical offers a nuanced argument to "every person living on this planet" while also distinguishing between the rich and powerful, who have overwhelmingly caused environmental problems, and the poor and marginalized, who overwhelmingly suffer the consequences. *Laudato Si'* uses scalar awareness to nuance its advocacy of integral ecology and its critique of market logic.

4. Questioning Hierarchies

While hierarchical thinking is incredibly useful in constructing and understanding moral arguments, it is also limited and, without careful attention to those limits, dangerous. Scientific ecology and environmental ethics offer tools for building humility about any human-constructed hierarchy, and I turn now to use those tools to question some aspects of *Laudato Si'*.

4.1. The Social Construction of Hierarchies

Ecological theorist Simon Levin, who advocates careful attention to scale, also argues that good science requires awareness that any hierarchical models we create have limitations. Any understanding of the world is, at best, "a low-dimensional slice through a high-dimensional cake". Our understandings may capture some sense of the ways the natural world works, but they are always only approximations. It is never possible to observe and account for every scale; something is always missed.[25]

So, a coherent and useful explanation of an ecosystem requires attention to what is happening in the landscape of which it is a part and the organisms nested inside it, but no one can fully account for all these levels at once. Ecologists are human beings with biases and predispositions; every research project is shaped by the temporal and spatial scales that come naturally to the researcher.[26]

Other ecological theorists go further to emphasize that even the levels between which ecologists work are socially constructed. The concepts "ecosystem", "species", and "biome" may be based on the real world, but these are constructed names and concepts. There are no simplistic or clear boundaries between levels, and so distinguishing them inevitably turns attention away from some nuances and

---

[22] (Ibid., paras. 25, 51, 52). Emphasis in original.
[23] (Ibid., paras. 18, 36, 159, 162). For an insightful commentary on how *Laudato Si'* addresses temporal issues, see Keller (2015).
[24] Interestingly, this also connects the encyclical to the movement of "Critical Environmental Justice", which scholar Pellow (2018) argues requires "multiscalar" work.
[25] (Levin 1992, pp. 1945, 1947).
[26] See especially Allen and Hoekstra (1992).

complexities. Ecologists who work at the ecosystem level inevitably miss some details occurring at other levels or between them. Philosopher Angela Potochnik and ecologist Brian McGill use this point to argue that ecology should reject any simplistic hierarchical understanding of the world at discrete levels. Good science, they argue, allows only "quasi-hierarchical representations" with "no expectation that a successful demarcation of quasi levels has ontological significance".[27]

Whether hierarchical categories have ontological significance is a controversial question in ecological theory, but the broader point is not: researchers make choices about the scales and levels of their attention, and those choices limit what they see and understand. All ecological research and explanations involve choices about which hierarchical levels to emphasize and which to de-emphasize. Thus, all ecological research and explanations are partial and imperfect.

The environmental ethicist Bryan Norton, who has worked closely with ecological theory, is well aware that every hierarchical level is a social construction. He emphasizes that his distinction between local, community, and global thinking is a "model" and a "representation". As a pragmatist philosopher, he suggests that these levels are useful rather than insisting that they are true in any objective sense.[28]

For this reason, Norton's hierarchical model leaves open the possibility of tweaks, adjustments, and alternatives. For example, he links temporal and spatial scales in his model, emphasizing that local ethics works at short-term time scales while global ethics works with indefinite time scales. This is a helpful way to grasp the concept of scale, but it does not always reflect all moral arguments. A different approach is implied by the Potawatomi scholar Kyle Powys Whyte, who emphasizes that long-term moral thinking can be the product of local attention to particular places. Because the indigenous peoples of the Great Plains in North America have spent millennia in a place with variable weather patterns, he argues, they deeply understand "the concept that society must be organized to constantly adapt to environmental change". Whyte's argument for long-scale temporal thinking is based upon a local spatial scale. By contrast, he understands settler colonial thinking as dangerously short-sighted in part because it is spatially global, believing that "one can simply transplant cultural practices to a new territory".[29] Temporal and spatial scale are here in tension rather than straightforwardly aligned. I find Whyte's argument powerful, and I am convinced by the critique he suggests of expansive, colonial thinking as inevitably short-sighted precisely because it seeks to control a global scale. For the present argument, though, what is important is to note that this is a very different use of scalar concepts from Norton's. Both are constructed ideas coming from particular social contexts.

The fact that scalar concepts are always human constructions also offers cautions to the classic environmental arguments of Aldo Leopold and E.F. Schumacher. Leopold's proposal that we learn to "think like a mountain" and Schumacher's argument for "a human scale" both imply that there is an accessible, natural indicator of the proper level of moral attention. While the ideas of thinking at the level of a mountain or the human are helpful, neither is straightforward or obvious. Humans and mountains exist at many different scales and so ethicists and activists who embrace these ideas still need to carefully consider the multiple ways attention might be focused across and among those scales.

Whyte's, Norton's, Leopold's, and Schumacher's ideas are incredibly useful tools for ethical analysis. But moral approaches to hierarchy, like ecological perspectives, are constructions and inevitably limited. Ecological theory and environmental ethics therefore remind us that it is important always to consider alternatives, to humbly note what a particular model or image includes and what it precludes. We are always making choices about how to focus attention based on limited information, in moral arguments as much as in scientific research.

---

[27] (Potochnik and McGill 2012, pp. 133–36). An even stronger critique of hierarchical scale is developed in the field of human geography. For the critique, see especially Marston (2000) and Marston et al. (2005). For a more constructive account of scale in the discipline, see Herod (2011).
[28] (Norton 2003, p. 68).
[29] (Whyte 2016, pp. 91, 99).

4.2. Assumed Hierarchies in Laudato Si'

Pope Francis's encyclical does not consistently consider alternatives to its own hierarchical assumptions, and so I turn now to three hierarchies in *Laudato Si'* that I believe should be questioned: between male and female, between human and animals, and between God and the world.

4.2.1. Gender Hierarchies

Building on its assertion that the family is "the basic cell of society", *Laudato Si* is filled with familial metaphors. It follows St. Francis in labeling the earth a "mother" and a "sister" and referring to other human beings as "brothers and sisters". Pope Francis repeatedly stresses his global argument by appealing to "the whole human family". However, the document maintains traditional Roman Catholic assumptions about what a family is, most particularly in assuming without question that the human species can be divided simplistically between two genders and that there is a legitimate power distinction between them.

Ivone Gebara notes that Francis's approach to women is charitable but not ultimately empowering: "In *Laudato Si'*, women do not speak in their own voice about their life situations, their sufferings, and their demands. The pope speaks for them".[30] Nicole Flores similarly observes that "our sister, Mother Earth, is cast as the feminine victim" while the church "is cast as the father, a *paterfamilias* responsible for the direction of the family". *Laudato Si'* thus continues "a gender binary inscribed by modernity's drive to divide, define, and conquer, the salvation of the earthly, bodily feminine remains dependent on masculine governance".[31] Hierarchical understandings of the masculine as over and broader than the feminine are maintained without question.

These assumptions about gender may not be surprising in the context of a church that doctrinally insists on complementarity between men and women and reserves the priesthood for men alone. Magisterial Catholic Social Teaching has consistently affirmed the moral significance of gender distinctions. However, these ideas are not the only possibility within the Catholic faith; Nicole Flores and Ivone Gebara are both Catholic thinkers who argue for revisions in their church's teachings about gender.[32] It need not be a foregone conclusion that Pope Francis accept his tradition's assumed attitudes toward gender and gender roles; and it is certainly not a given that such attitudes are useful and true for "every person living on the planet". So, it is unfortunate that the encyclical does not clearly articulate nor defend its assumptions about gender, much less consider alternatives to them.

4.2.2. Species Hierarchies

A similar approach is taken to the relationship between human beings and other species. Daniel Dombrowski observes that "there is an unresolved tension regarding non-human animals" in *Laudato Si'* and that "Francis is more of an anthropocentrist than he is willing to admit".[33] Francis insists that non-human animals are not merely "resources" and that "the Bible has no place for a tyrannical anthropocentrism unconcerned for other creatures".[34] But he also asserts that human beings "possess a uniqueness which cannot be fully explained by the evolution of other open systems" and decries those who are more interested "in protecting other species than in defending the dignity which all

---

[30] (Gebara 2017, p. 76).
[31] (Flores 2018, p. 474). Flores also helpfully distinguishes this gender binary from other ways to incorporate family, which she suggests could be a strong foundation for an intimately integral ecology and a powerful reflection of the importance of family in Latin American and Latinx communities.
[32] See also Johnson (2002).
[33] (Dombrowski 2015, p. 32).
[34] (Francis 2015, paras. 33, 68). Jenkins (2018) argues the "deepest theological shift" in *Laudato Si'* is its break from previous Catholic thought through the assertion that human dominion is based not on distinction from other species, but rather "respect for the goodness of other creatures". Jenkins notes, however, that this idea is "underdeveloped" in the encyclical.

human beings share in equal measure". The encyclical insists without question that human beings have power over other species as "God's stewards of other creatures".[35]

Again, this is consistent with Magisterial Catholic Social Teaching, but it is not the only possibility, even within Catholicism. Saint Francis, after whom Pope Francis named himself, is honored as the patron saint of animals and of environmentalism precisely because he offered a far less hierarchical view of other species interrelated with human beings. Stories recount St. Francis preaching to birds just as he preached to human beings, freeing animals from hunter's traps and angler's lines, and reasoning with a wolf to stop its attacks on the town of Gubbio.[36] Saint Francis regularly referred to all animals as his brothers and sisters. By contrast, Pope Francis in *Laudato Si'* only uses "brother" or "sister" to refer to human beings or the earth as a whole.[37] The encyclical ultimately maintains and does not question the hierarchy of human beings over other creatures on earth.

4.2.3. The Hierarchy of God

Ultimately, the most central hierarchy in *Laudato Si'* is the hierarchy of God over creation. As noted already, Pope Francis's central argument that humans should protect the non-human world is justified by the ultimate authority, power, and generosity of a God who is understood as above and beyond all of creation:

> A spirituality which forgets God as all-powerful and Creator is not acceptable. The best way to restore men and women to their rightful place, putting an end to their claim to absolute dominion over the earth, is to speak once more of a figure of a Father who creates and who alone owns the world.[38]

In this document, power and authority rest ultimately and singularly in God.

This contextualizes the hierarchies of gender and species as part of an even more foundational hierarchy. For Pope Francis, human beings have a "rightful place" as stewards of the Earth that we understand when we respect the ultimate authority of God over humans. A system of levels has been established with God unquestionably at the top, non-human animals below, and human beings in between, with male humans implied to be closer to the power of the "Father".

Again, such a hierarchical view of reality is not the only option, even within theological context of Catholicism. Liberation theology, a resource for other parts of the encyclical, includes emphases on God's particular presence with the poor and suffering and more frequently identifies God in terms of the incarnation of Jesus among humans than as distant creator. The Divine can be understood in the midst of rather than beyond all human activity, the immanence of God can be emphasized rather than or instead of transcendence.[39] Using the language of Catholic Social Teaching, we might say that it is possible to have an idea of God that is more informed by subsidiarity, stressing divinity at small scales at least as much as large scales. *Laudato Si'* does not openly consider this possibility; it emphasizes the transcendence of God far more than the immanence.

Throughout the encyclical, hierarchies between God, humans, and creation are assumed without question. In the latter two cases, the encyclical goes further than previous Catholic Social Teaching toward exploring limits, cracking the door open to a more inclusive approach to gender and other species. But in both cases, it stops short of genuinely questioning tradition, ultimately assuming the hierarchical relationship of Magisterial Catholic thinking. The third hierarchy seems most crucial and least questioned. *Laudato Si'* puts humans over other animals and the masculine over the feminine

---

[35] (Francis 2015, paras. 33, 68, 81, 90, 116).
[36] See, especially, Boff (1982).
[37] The discussion of St. Francis is in (Francis 2015, para. 11), quoting Bonaventure. To my reading, every other use of "brothers and sisters" in the document refers to human beings broadly or the poor more specifically.
[38] (Francis 2015, para. 75).
[39] See for example Gutiérrez (1988), chp 10; Leonardo Boff (1997), chp 7; and Sobrino (2004).

because it connects God, "the Father", to the human and the masculine, because it assumes that reality is a nested hierarchy in which everything is created by, smaller than, and less important than the divine. God is the universal and eternal scale by which everything else is measured.

4.3. Questioning Hierarchies in Laudato Si'

While I have pointed out limitations in *Laudato Si'*, I believe that the encyclical's central idea, integral ecology, can be extended to include the potential of integrating the divine with creation, the human with other creatures, and of more diverse gender expressions and power relations within humanity. The encyclical powerfully critiques some assumed hierarchies, most notably the authority of market logics over other forms of knowing and the priority of technological progress over other concerns of human communities. It is possible to bring the same critical approach to the hierarchies of gender, species, and divinity, and doing so will allow for an exploration of whether and how theology and ethics might need to change alongside politics and economics in response to the contemporary moral challenges of climate change and inequality.

While the encyclical does not offer an explicit defense of its assumed hierarchies (my primary critique is, after all, that they are assumed without explanation), I find such a defense implied in the document's consideration of relativism. Pope Francis argues that a "culture of relativism" is one of the roots of environmental and social degradation. He writes that relativism is a disorder which "drives one person to take advantage of another, to treat others as mere objects", leading to "the sexual exploitation of children and abandonment of the elderly". Relativism justifies those who "allow the invisible forces of the market to regulate the economy, and consider their impact on society and nature as collateral damage". At the root of this thinking is the fact that "objective truth and universally valid principles are no longer upheld". The solution is to insist that there are "objective truths" and "sound principles other than the satisfaction of our own desires and immediate needs".[40]

Laudato Si' insists that certain facts are immutable, and so would likely dispute my assertion that the hierarchies of gender, species, and divinity are social constructions. The ideas I have questioned are, instead, treated as "objective truths". The evidence of these truths can be found in the Magisterial teachings that came from a church ordained and sustained by God: Divinity is all-powerful and beyond human experience; human beings are called to be stewards over the rest of creation; humanity is made up of two genders with distinct and complementary roles. Affirming these truths is, by the logic of the encyclical, a way to oppose the brokenness and selfishness of dominant culture in the 21st century.

Building on ecological theory and its application to environmental ethics, I disagree. I have argued above that it is best to treat every hierarchy as a construction, and, so, to test rather than assume its usefulness and applicability in a given situation. So, while the encyclical suggests that questioning immutable truths is a sign of societal corruption, I argue instead that social cohesion is threatened when truths are believed to be immutable and beyond question, perhaps especially when those truths are stated as hierarchies. So, I argue that the deep questioning Pope Francis offered to political and economic structures should also be applied to social and theological structures. Doing so will lead to a more rather than less integral ecology.

Fully developing this argument would require a contrasting systematic theology and ethics, which is far beyond the scope of the present paper. Instead, I want to more modestly point out that the immutability or objective truth of hierarchies is not essential to the encyclical's most fundamental argument, which is the moral challenges of the 21st century call for a multi-scalar, ecological conversion to an attitude of integral ecology. One could advocate integral ecology in less foundational or structuralist terms, insisting that integration is most possible when the world is understood to be based on evolving processes rather than immutable principles.[41] Or, if one accepts the need for foundational

---

[40] (Francis 2015, para. 123).
[41] This is the emphasis of many responses to the encyclical in Cobb and Castuera (2015).

moral principles, one could still appeal to less controversial ideals like the common good and universal human rights that do not assume all the hierarchies affirmed by the Magisterial Catholic Church. One can learn from and affirm the central argument of the encyclical without accepting the nested power dynamics it assumes between genders, species, and with the divine.

Laudato Si' does impressive and important work deconstructing and challenging the hierarchies that many people in the wealthy world make about economics and political scales. Those of us learning from the encyclical and supporting its goal of integral ecology should bring the same critical perspective to its assumptions about theological and social scales.

5. Conclusions—Toward an Inquisitive Integral Ecology

Scalar thinking reminds us that human beings are always making choices in how we measure and compare the systems and structures around us and that these choices shape what we see and what we prioritize. The construction of hierarchical levels offers language by which these choices can be articulated, communicated, and standardized. But ecological theory also teaches that these levels are always social constructions, and so calls for a humble willingness to question our assumptions about them.

Laudato Si' uses scalar and hierarchical concepts effectively in its inspiring call for an integral ecology that will convert people, communities, and global civilization toward a more just and sustainable world. Scalar thinking helps to integrate social and environmental concerns, calling attention to the common root of 21st century challenges in a short-sighted but globally expansive economic system and advocating a more expansive and global ethic. The doctrine of subsidiarity also facilitates attention to hierarchical levels, noting that any global organization must continue to allow whatever autonomy and self-direction is possible to nation-states, communities, and families.

However, I have argued that not all the hierarchical assumptions in the document are essential to the encyclical's central idea. Pope Francis invites all people into the work of integral ecology, and he encourages us to explore the intersections of science and religion in response to the moral challenges of the 21st century. In taking up that invitation, Christian ecological ethicists should do more than he has to understand the constructedness and limitations of all the scales and hierarchies we use to think about morality.

This will be a challenging process, but environmental ethics will ultimately be most effective the more it builds on a sophisticated, scientific understanding of reality. Ecological theory demonstrates the power of unpacking and questioning assumptions about scale, and so the most integral ecology will come from moral work that insists on inquiring about such assumptions. The path forward is to learn from *Laudato Si'* while also more fully embracing the limited scale of all human understanding.

Funding: This research received no external funding.

Conflicts of Interest: The author declares no conflict of interest.

References

Allen, Timothy F. H., and Thomas W. Hoekstra. 1992. *Toward a Unified Ecology*. New York: Columbia University Press.
Appolloni, Simon. 2018. *Convergent Knowing: Christianity and Science in Conversation with a Suffering Creation*. Montreal: McGill-Queen's University Press.
Boff, Leonardo. 1982. *Saint Francis: A Model for Human Liberation*. Translated by John W. Diercksmeier. New York: Crossroad.
Leonardo Boff. 1997. *Cry of the Earth, Cry of the Poor*. Maryknoll: Orbis Books.
Cobb, John J., and Ignacio Castuera, eds. 2015. *For Our Common Home: Process-Relational Responses to Lduato Si'*. Anoka: Process Century Press.
Chave, Jérôme. 2013. The Problem of Pattern and Scale in Ecology: What Have We Learned in 20 Years? *Ecology Letters* 16: 4–16. [CrossRef] [PubMed]

Dombrowski, Daniel A. 2015. A Liberal, Catholic Response. In *For Our Common Home: Process-Relational Responses to Laduato Si'*. Edited by John Cobb Jr. and Ignaio Castuera. Anoka: Process Century Press, pp. 30–34.

Flores, Nichole M. 2018. Our Sister, Mother Earth: Solidarity and Familial Ecology in *Laudato Si'*. *Journal of Religious Ethics* 46: 463–78. [CrossRef]

Forman, Richard T. T. 1995. *Land Mosaics: The Ecology of Landscapes and Regions*. New York: Cambridge University Press.

Francis, Pope. 2015. *Laudato Si': On Care for Our Common Home*. Vatican City: Encyclical Letter.

Gebara, Ivone. 2017. Women's Suffering, Climate Injustice, God, and Pope Francis's Theology: Some Insights from Brazil. In *Planetary Solidarity: Global Women's Voices on Christian Doctrine and Climate Justice*. Edited by Grace Ji-Sun Kim and Hilda P. Koster. Minneapolis: Fortress Press, pp. 67–79.

Gutiérrez, Gustavo. 1988. *A Theology of Liberation: History, Politics, and Salvation*. Maryknoll: Orbis Books.

Harris, Melanie L. 2017. *Ecowomanism: African American Women and Earth-Honoring Faiths*. Maryknoll: Orbis Books.

Herod, Andrew. 2011. *Scale*. New York: Routledge.

Jenkins, Willis. 2018. The Mysterious Silence of Mother Earth in *Laudato Si'*. *Journal of Religious Ethics* 46: 441–62. [CrossRef]

Johnson, Elizabeth A., ed. 2002. *The Church Women Want: Catholic Women in Dialogue*. New York: Crossroad.

Keller, Catherine. 2015. Encycling: One Feminist Response. In *For Our Common Home: Process-Relational Responses to Laudato Si'*. Edited by John Cobb Jr. and Ignaio Castuera. Anoka: Process Century Press, pp. 175–86.

Leopold, Aldo. 1949. *A Sand County Almanac, and Sketches Here and There*. New York: Oxford University Press.

Levin, Simon A. 1992. The Problem of Pattern and Scale in Ecology: The Robert H. Macarthur Award Lecture. *Ecology* 73: 1943–67. [CrossRef]

Marston, Sallie A. 2000. The Social Construction of Scale. *Progress in Human Geography* 24: 219–42. [CrossRef]

Marston, Sallie A., John Paul Jones III, and Keith Woodward. 2005. Human Geography Without Scale. *Transactions of the Institute of British Geographers* 30: 416–32. [CrossRef]

Norton, Bryan G. 2003. *Searching for Sustainability: Interdisciplinary Essays in the Philosophy of Conservation Biology*. New York: Cambridge University Press.

Norton, Bryan G. 2005. *Sustainability: A Philosophy of Adaptive Ecosystem Management*. Chicago: University of Chicago Press.

O'Brien, Kevin J. 2010. *An Ethics of Biodiversity: Christianity, Ecology, and the Variety of Life*. Washington, DC: Georgetown University Press.

O'Brien, Kevin J. 2008. Thinking Globally and Thinking Locally: Ecology, Subsidiarity, and a Multiscalar Environmentalism. *Journal of the Society for the Study of Religion, Nature, and Culture* 2: 218–36. [CrossRef]

Pellow, David N. 2018. *What is Critical Environmental Justice*. Medford: Polity Press.

Pope Pius XI. 1931. *Quadragesimo Anno: On Reconstruction of the Social Order*. Vatican City: Encyclical Letter.

Potochnik, Angela, and Brian McGill. 2012. The Limitations of Hierarchical Organization. *Philosophy of Science* 79: 120–40. [CrossRef]

Savoy, Lauret E. 2015. *Trace: Memory, History, Race, and the American Landscape*. Berkeley: Counterpoint.

Schumacher, Ernst F. 1973. *Small is Beautiful: Economics as if People Mattered*. New York: Harper & Row.

Simon, Herbert A. 1973. The Organization of Complex Systems. In *Hierarchy Theory: The Challenge of Complex Systems*. Edited by H. H. Pattee. New York: G. Braziller.

Sobrino, Jon. 2004. *Where Is God? Earthquake, Terrorism, Barbarity, and Hope*. Maryknoll: Orbis Books.

Whyte, Kyle Powys. 2016. Is it Colonial Déjà Vu? Indigenous Peoples and Climate Injustice. In *Humanities for the Environment: Integrating Knowledges, Fording New Constellations of Practice*. Edited by Joni Adamson, Michael Davis and Hsinya Huang. New York: Earthscan Publications, pp. 88–104.

© 2019 by the author. Licensee MDPI, Basel, Switzerland. This article is an open access article distributed under the terms and conditions of the Creative Commons Attribution (CC BY) license (http://creativecommons.org/licenses/by/4.0/).

Article

Taking Children's Moral Lives Seriously: Creativity as Ethical Response Offline and Online

Kate Ott

Theological School, Drew University, Madison, NJ 07940, USA; kott@drew.edu

Received: 31 July 2019; Accepted: 9 September 2019; Published: 12 September 2019

Abstract: Core Christian ethics concepts are affected by assumptions related to the primary subject or moral agent and the social context in which moral encounters take place. This article asks: Are children full moral agents? If so, what can Christian ethics, which predominantly focuses on adult subjects, learn from a focus on children? A small group of Christian ethicists has asked this very question in conversation with psychologists, child development theorists, educators, theologians, and philosophers. Centering children requires attention to age and ability differences and inclusion of their voices. Children as ethical subjects focus attention on issues of particularity, a decentering of rational individualism, and debunking linear moral developmental assumptions. The research on children's moral lives points toward ethics as creativity in forms of play or improvisation. Given children's digitally saturated lives, their creative use of critical digital literacies also helps Christian ethics begin to map a response to the impact of digital technologies.

Keywords: children; childhood; ethics; play; improvisation; moral imagination; moral agency; digital literacies; digital technology

---

1. Introduction

The discipline of Christian ethics has imbedded assumptions about the primary subject or moral agent and the social context in which moral encounters take place. For example, are children full moral agents? Can children or infants make moral-decisions? If so, what can Christian ethics, which predominantly focuses on adult subjects, learn from a focus on children? A small group of Christian ethicists has asked this very question in conversation with psychologists, child development theorists, educators, theologians, and philosophers. Ethicists join a variety of scholars within religious studies fields, often in the fields of biblical studies or practical theology, who have made the methodological shift to centering children (Bunge 2001, 2012; Browning and Miller-McLemore 2009; Browning and Bunge 2011; Fewell 2003; Mercer 2005; Miller-McLemore 2019). The shift to centering children requires attention to authentic representation and inclusion of children. Many scholars use first hand child narratives or direct participant research to bring the voices of children into conversation with their research. They then ask, how does centering children affect Christian ethics concepts and assumptions? The response is a reimagining of moral agency away from historically dominant criteria like rational individualism and a debunking of linear moral development.

The research on children's moral lives points toward ethics as a creative response. Ethics as a creative response does not completely replace ethics as a system of norms, duties, or principles. Rather, moral imagination exhibited in practices of play or improvisation more closely align with children's (and adults) moral decision-making and the expansive growth of their moral selves interpersonally and communally. After addressing the shift in ethics that centers children and its effect on redefining ethics, I invite the reader to consider the radical social shift of the digital revolution. In a digital age, ethics as creative response matches well with the networked and co-produced nature of digital technology. Given our digitally saturated world, children evidence creative ethical response through critical digital literacies.

This article contributes to the field of childist ethics in particular, and childism as an advocacy movement in academia, public policy, and education more broadly. Religious ethicist John Wall proposes "the concept of 'childism' in this particular sense: not as an ethical or social ideology, but as a methodology for social change, albeit one that should revise basic ethical norms in the process" (Wall 2012, pp. 136–37). Scholars who focus on childism often share a commitment to eliminate the oppression of children (Young-Bruehl 2011; Wells 2009). Thus, the childist ethics approach significantly raises the profile of one of the most vulnerable and diverse segments of our population (children) as well as attending to an experience and state-of-being that all of us share (childhood). The specific investigation of moral agency and children in this article suggest a number of new directions for Christian ethics. A centering of children's moral lives opens Christian ethics to theological imagination and ethical response as a creative act. It affirms an on-going process of moral growth, rather than an age of reason or goal of moral completion. In addition, it may provide the necessary clues needed to live ethically in a rapidly changing digital society.

2. Christian Ethics and Children

The shift to children as the subject in Religious studies is a few decades old. In the field of Christian ethics, it is a relatively new phenomenon. That is not to say that past theologians and ethicists have not addressed the lives of children (Bunge 2001; Ridgely 2011). In fact, narratives about children and theological responses to and for children have been part of the Christian tradition since its earliest beginnings (Fewell 2003; Browning and Bunge 2011). Historically, theologians address children as objects or not-yet-adults rather than address them in their full humanity at whatever age they are. It is also rare for past theologians to represent children's voices in their works. In this section, I outline the effect of centralizing children's lives—capturing their voices, interpretation, activity, and participation—and the new insights this brings to moral agency, a central concept in ethics.

Western Christian formulations of agency view the moral actor as rational, independent, and experienced, while overwhelmingly discounting affective or emotional knowing, interdependence, and inexperience. Intentionality has played a significant role in the formulation of moral agency. That is to say, a moral agent should have a level of rationality measured by the ability to explain and analyze one's decision, be independent and able to act autonomously, and have a level of experience to predict consequences. Women, people of color, the disabled, and the elderly have at different historical times been left out of this definition or been treated as less capable moral agents due to constructions of gender, race, and mental capacity.

If one must be experienced, independent, and rational to be a moral agent, then how would one describe children? Are they pre-moral or amoral given they do not have these capacities? John Wall argues that most historical theologies put children into three ethical categories (Wall 2010, chp. 1). The first is children as little devils, evil and corrupted by original sin in need of harsh obedience training. The second is children as innocent, in need of protection from the sinful world. The third view sees children as empty vessels in need of developmental training to shape these blank slates into morally good adults. Wall suggests that these absolutes are part of the problem. Instead we might think of children's moral status as shaped by all three, considering children from as "diverse of ethical angles" as we do adults (Wall 2010, p. 32). He eschews the notion of a "magical time of adulthood in which moral capability is completed" (Wall 2012, p. 147). The proposed new understanding of moral agency values children as complete moral agents—as they are now—rather than waiting for what they will become. In addition, it engages the diversity and complexity of children's moral lives rather than seeing them as completely evil, completely innocent, or amoral.

The Christian imagination related to children, or babies, and ethics often references back to Augustine's confessions. In an infamous passage, Augustine describes his own remembrance of his infant cries and grasping for milk as evidence of original sin and self-centeredness (Augustine

2009, Book 1 chp. 7). Cristina Traina revises Augustine's reading of infantile behavior: "To begin with, crying for milk is an obvious expression of appropriate dependency that others must honor an expression that Augustine himself implies cannot be communicated to inattentive adults except through the language of tears. If this is the act of a dependent moral agent, it is an act of necessary and appropriate self-preservation" (Traina 2009, pp. 31–32). Augustine leans on the first model of children and ethics that Wall names—the infant as corrupt and sinful. In response, Traina balances the ways in which children (even infants) react out of diverse moral sensibilities within dependent relationships (Traina 2011).

Current research in cognitive sciences and childhood studies with infants as young as three months old has shown that babies express a moral sense or "capacity to make certain types of judgements" (Wynn and Bloom 2013, pp. 437–38). A variety of scholars, referenced in and collaborators of Karen Wynn and Paul Bloom have demonstrated that babies "have prosocial tendencies that influence their social actions and interactions; in some circumstances at least, they care about others, and this motivates certain positive actions" (Wynn and Bloom 2013, p. 437). Babies not only communicate about their own desires making claims on those who care for them as Traina points out. They can interpret social meanings of actions and how actions influence others (Wynn and Bloom 2013, p. 447), including in some cases the difference between intention and outcome. Wynn and Bloom conclude, that "infants' and toddlers' social judgements and responses bear a strong resemblance to those of adults" (Wynn and Bloom 2013, p. 450). Given this research, Traina's revision of infant Augustine's cry as evil to a moral sensing or relational call is not only theologically helpful, but scientifically accurate.

In response to views of children as born innocent or as blank slates, Wall argues the linear and inevitable progress of time built into these theories implies passivity and generalizability of the child (Wall 2010, p. 80). Interdisciplinary scholars engaging queer theory, also dismiss a romanticized or linear developmental view of children (Cornwall 2017; Ott 2015, 2019). Moving the child to the subject, a queer subject in this case, disrupts seeing childhood as a stage on the way to adulthood or children as some proposed future hope of humanity (Halberstam 2011, p. 27; Cornwall 2017; Ott 2015, 2019). Kathryn Bond Stockton calls childhood "growing sideways" (Stockton 2009). Children are moral agents with full humanity to be valued as they are, rather than for a teleological adulthood. Susannah Cornwall, in her latest book, *Un/Familiar Theology*, engages a queer approach to the "alterity and otherness of the child" (Cornwall 2017, p. 146). She uses José Muñoz and Stockton to counter Lee Edelman's use of child reproductive futurity. She writes, "Childhood is not, then, what Edelman constructs as a permanent deferral to the future, rather, the child, as queer, as natal, already has agency and influence to generate in the present" (Cornwall 2017, p. 148). The child is both now and not-yet which characterizes an eschatological hope. The child in this version of queer theology lives in "back-and-forth reciprocity" rather than downward transmission (Cornwall 2017, p. 147). This is another example of the child understood contextually, interdependently, and theologically as an "already complete person" (Cornwall 2017, p. 147). Children are striving for wholeness, a narrative wholeness, which is expansive rather than linear or inevitable (Wall 2010, p. 80).

For example, a three year old child who defends another child on the playground from teasing is a full moral agent. An affective and empathetic moral knowing undergirds her actions. She may provide limited interpretation of her actions, like "I was helping a friend who was sad when another child was mean." She may also have intervened because appeals to adults were unhelpful or they were not present. The children who choose not to help are also making a moral choice. Whether the moral agent is three years old or fifty years old, no human is completely independent and uses only rational knowledge. Cristina Traina writes, "Children's behavior in situations of dependency is still moral agency even though it is not fully autonomous. Agency is not a zero-sum game ... Children are neither marionettes nor mere conduits for powerful adults' actions. They possess moral freedom even when that freedom is (sometimes rightly) circumscribed" (Traina 2009, p. 24). Traina directly engages a crucial connection between moral agency, freedom of choice, and accountability. If the three year old who ends the bullying is a moral agent, so too is the one bullying. This raises the question of how to hold a three year old accountable for immoral actions. When moral agency is no longer a "zero-sum game" equal measures of accountability need not be either. Traina is not arguing that because children have full moral agency they must be penalized in a similar fashion to adults. Rather when a child (or anyone) is dependent, responsibility for her actions should be determined by a mix of contextual factors that account for her dependent status. Some feminist scholars, like Traina, have argued for a decoupling of one-to-one measurements of moral agency and social or legal accountability.

Critics suggest childist ethicists romanticize the child, their agential abilities, and freedom from adult influence. Of course, like all human beings, children are influenced by those around them. With children, we tend to assume they are parroting adult ethical standards even when evidence strongly suggests otherwise as in cases, for example, where preschoolers engage in racist behavior (Van Ausdale and Feagin 2001 and see also Ott 2014). Additionally in studies with children from preschool to tenth grade, researchers found that children's status as a victim or perpetrator influence their moral understandings (Wainryb et al. 2005, p. 2). That is to say, children's beliefs or personal interpretations, like adults, influence their moral judgements. When children recognize themselves as a perpetrator, they often "depicted themselves as being engaged in pursuing their own goals or interests, rather than intending to hurt someone else" (Wainryb et al. 2005, p. 37). Children's recognition of harm and consequences is nuanced exhibiting complex morally agential responses.

While infants exhibit moral behavior that leans toward valuing the helper, as children grow older they encounter more complex ethical circumstances. Children's own awareness of their agency affects social and relational encounters. Jennifer Beste, a Christian Ethicist who uses sociological quantitative research notes, her "research findings indicate that, not only are Catholic second graders social actors, but their perceived sense of agency when receiving Reconciliation (a Roman Catholic sacrament) greatly affects their overall experiences and its effects" (Beste 2011, p. 347). Her research validates "children as actively co-constructing meaning and reality as opposed to merely absorbing and internalizing the teachings" (Beste 2011, p. 346). The children in Beste's study demonstrate creative synthesis and ethical reflection. Their sacramental experience deepened through social participation that recognizes their agency.

Integrating the revised notion of children's moral agency with a human rights framework, Wall argues that we need to expand children's right beyond provision and protection, which objectifies them. He argues children, like those in Beste's study, deserve avenues for social participation that honor their agency (Wall 2012, p. 150). Bonnie Miller-McLemore articulates an example of children's right to participation related to child labor (Miller-McLemore 2012). If we consider child labor from a global perspective, we can see that for some families children's paid labor is a necessity even though it is often exploitative. Many child advocates using a human rights framework focused on provision and protection argue for the elimination of child labor. However, child labor (when not abusive and exploitative) is a form of social participation not for future gain or a return on investment, but part of children's call and flourishing. Miller-McLemore advocates for efforts related to increased wages, safety, and fair practices (Miller-McLemore 2012, p. 182). Understanding the value of child's work as social participation includes seeing it "as an obligation, a crucial part of formation, a contribution to the common good, and a demonstration of love of God" (Miller-McLemore 2012, pp. 185–86).

The methodological commitment to centralizing children as moral subjects in ethics yields a revised conceptualization of moral agency, including treating the child for who they are now, acceptance of their diverse and complex moral leanings, and the need for their increased social participation. The scholars noted in this section establish that children have richer moral capacities than previously thought. As John Wall writes, "it is clear that children do not just passively absorb the narratives that are fed to them by adults. Rather, each child is a full human being who both is narrated by her world and narrates it anew for herself" (Wall 2010, p. 152). Children exercise their moral agency even when they cannot explain reasons for their actions, when they are dependent on others, and when they lack experience with social codes or moral norms.

3. Children's Moral Lives and Creativity

In my experiences with leading Christian Education ministries, coaching sports teams, and running communities programs, I am amazed at how children puzzle through moral-decisions in community contexts. Below is an example of this, one that has shaped me over the years as I reflect on children's moral agency and what it might teach us about moral-decision making and ethical practices.

In 2003, my partner, Brian Hill and I led a children's program in Bridgeport, CT called Coaching Kids. The program served about 25 children aged 5–12 twice a week in an after-school program. The children learned about healthy eating habits, physical fitness, and social skills like resolving conflict, dealing with aggression, and asking others for assistance. The 21st Century Lighthouse grant received by Fairfield University School of Nursing funded the program. The majority of participants were elementary school age and identified as African American or Latinx. In the first few months of the program, the children were vocal about what hindered their personal health and relationships. For example, playing games like kickball, tag, or jump rope in the neighborhood was difficult given safety issues, such as broken glass and drug paraphernalia littering the open field, sidewalks in disrepair, or car traffic. We often played indoors at the high school where we rented space. The children only had access to this space when the program met.

The children's astute assessments of their environment lead to conversations about desired change. Given the social, economic, and environmental problems in the city, how would the children envision a different space? What values would guide them? How would they organize themselves? What was needed in such a community? We challenged the children to design a new community. The process of designing a community requires evaluation, imagination, and cooperation. As part of the project, the children negotiated the ethics of group dynamics in addition to the ethical vision of change for their community. We created the community out of a 12-foot-long piece of plywood, cardboard boxes, paint, and popsicle sticks (Figure 1). After designing parks, stores, living spaces, hospital, police station, firehouse, and beaches, the kids decided what employment they would have. There were pilots, bankers, firefighters, restaurateurs, and music producers. A priority for the children was that this community be clean and safe. From a newspaper story about the project, Shanitza said, "It's a lot of fun to go swimming ... But I don't swim here in Bridgeport. It's much too cold and dirty. The water at our Ocean Shores is warm and clean." Jennifer Concino noted, "Our community has a lot of places to go ... There's a lot of different stores and it's real safe" (Meshberg 2003). Additionally each child created a magazine page describing a different aspect of the community and enticing travelers to visit.

As adult group leaders, we facilitated the activity by helping with supplies, mediating disagreements, and asking questions to encourage reflection on their ethical choices. For example, how would we keep the ocean shores clean? Is the recording studio open to all types of music or only the kind the owner likes? What food options would Jose Corcino offer at his restaurant that would be unique and welcoming? One of the magazine pages "features Jose's Famous Restaurant. 'I'm a good cook,' said 12 year old Jose Corcino, who specializes in burgers and seafood. 'But I'll cook whatever anybody wants'" (Meshberg 2003). During the course of the project, all of the children engaged in various sorts of ethical decisions related to community design and lived these ethics in the way they related to each other during the building of the project.

I share this story as a low-tech engagement of children's moral evaluation, decision-making, and vision. These children ranging from 5 to 12 years old had wise insights about community development and design. Similar to the interviews with Catholic second graders preparing for reconciliation (albeit without the rigorous sociological research method), the children in Coaching Kids demonstrated creative ethical response. They answered and implemented fundamental questions of ethics: who ought we to be and how ought we to act as a community? They named the values that guided design—safety, cleanliness, hospitality, inclusion, diversity—and used the same values to negotiate intergroup dynamics. The youngest participant was Eva Ott Hill, 18 months old, a daughter of the leaders. Following their values, the kids added a daycare center to the community given the challenges and needs posed by a toddler trying to help paint during construction!

Figure 1. Photo from Connecticut Post article, 1 June 2003. (Abraham 2003)

4. Ethics and Creativity

The research related to children and Christian ethics warrants changes in the dominant approaches to moral agency and ethical response. Or as Wall argues, it is time "to ask the difficult question of how the ways in which children think ethically should transform how to understand ethical thinking as such" (Wall 2010, p. 168). Children's formation of self and relational engagement happens most often through play and social interaction as encounters with otherness (Ryall et al. 2013; Qvortrup et al. 2009). The community building activity in the Coaching Kids program was both a critical thinking opportunity to articulate shared values and vision *and* an immediate opportunity to test these values. We creatively built together, played at a craft activity, and negotiated our otherness together. While some might characterize this play as moral education in a process of development, I claim it was that, *and* it was the "doing of ethics" as full moral agents who participated across our differences of age, ethnicity, race, gender or ability. Ethical response, as Wall puts it, "creates received historical and social meanings into new worlds of meaning over time and in response to others. It deals in moral tension and disruption as selves confront their own narrative diversity and the otherness of others" (Wall 2010, p. 169). In this section, I will argue that the centering of children's moral responses shifts ethics from a practice of thinking and doing through logical, independent rationality to an interdependent encounter that requires imagination and creative practices like play or improvisation.

In Christian ethics, we often rely too heavily on socially imposed, normative rules and expectations that obscure the moral opportunity of encounter with another in mundane everyday situations. Wall worries that, "Fixed principles, laws, and virtues have ever since dominated over children in particular and over imagination, interdependence, and change in general" (Wall 2010, p. 169). This does not mean we should completely jettison moral rules or principles. Rather we need an approach that does not use the rules and expectations to foreclose creative discernment or imply a preference for independent, rational reasoning exempting children's moral agency. Such an approach would value moral response that includes the use of imagination exhibited in play or improvisation as a reaction to or engagement with otherness.

Thelathia Nikki Young, in *Black Queer Ethics, Family, and Philosophical Imagination*, argues that imagination is "a significant part of moral subjectivity and moral agency that contributes to social transformation" (Young 2016, p. 152). Her turn toward imagination stems from in-depth interviews with black queer family members, some are youth but most are adults. Many black queer people experience a moral erasure or judgement that resonates with the moral dismissal of children. As I have already noted, many queer theorists view the child as a queer subject. Christian ethics use of dominant constructions of moral agency that preference rationality and independence, socially and theologically elevate whiteness, heterosexuality, and adulthood. Blackness and queerness have resulted in characterizations of people as immoral or morally inferior. I am not equating histories of violence against black and/or queer bodies with that of all children. Rather, Young's insights specifically generated from conversations with black queer families provides an example of moral imagination that disrupts dominant notions of moral agency similar to those discussed above. Young demonstrates how black queer families use imagination in survivalist, prophetic, subversive, and generative ways (Young 2016, pp. 153–54).

Thinking back to the example from Coaching Kids, these predominantly black and brown children's moral imagination created a different possibility for community. Their creative moral response was not naïve to their current daily survival, it was in response to it, subversive of it, and generative of new possibilities. Young suggests that "imagination helps us to see and classify the consequences of policies, to see what it is like for people to be in certain situations, and to relate moral ideas to pragmatic considerations" (Young 2016, p. 157). Thus, moral imagination is both aware of current realities and seeking a new vision or world, which Young characterizes as "queer world making" (Young 2016, p. 158). She notes the role of improvisation and a building capacity like play that utilize "culture's normative discourse" as "raw material" for these new visions or expansive worlds (Young 2016, p. 159, see p. 156 on improvisation). "Moral imagination also features this element of now and not-yet and allows moral agents to occupy spaces that are projections (of) future possibilities," writes Young (Young 2016, p. 161). Young points to the power of relationality and micro-communities where these possibilities become realities. Young's black queer family ethic shares eschatological resonances with imaginative practices like John Wall's description of play and Samuel Wells' notion of moral improvisation.

Engaging Christian notions of mystery and creation, Wall looks to phenomenological understandings of play as co-creational examples of self-expansion and "an ever fuller imitation over time of humanity's Creator" (Wall 2012, p. 147). This human activity is one in which we all participate, not only children. From a phenomenological perspective, "Play is ultimately impossible to explain because it is not a meaning but, rather, the very condition for the possibility of meaning as such. It could be called the impossible possibility: able to be experienced, evoked, even symbolized but not finally containable within the playground of play itself" (Wall 2010, pp. 53–54). Play involves the imagination in ways that acknowledge reality and seek to alter it toward new forms of meaning. Wall says ethical thinking is "inherently artful or poetic . . . in the sense that it creates more imaginatively expansive relationships" (Wall 2010, p. 169). Children participate in constructing their worlds in and through the relationships around them, first with family, and then friends, broadening out as the meet new people (Wall 2010, pp. 152–53). The practice of play provides the forum for moral imagination to contribute to self-transformation and world making.

The communal nature and open-endedness of improvisation employs moral imagination in similar ways to children's play. Samuel Wells writes, "Improvisation means a community formed in the right habits trusting itself to embody its tradition in new and often challenging circumstances" (Wells 2012, p. 12). Wells draws on Shannon Craigo-Snell's incorporation of embodied and communal notions of performance in worship and theology to develop his theo-ethics of improvisation (Wells 2012, p. 61). He argues that discipleship or Christian moral formation as a performance akin to theater with a script can be limiting even when rehearsal is the primary mode of new interpretations and roles (Wells 2012, p. 62). Wells suggests that, "improvisation is concerned with discernment. It is about hearing God speak through renewed practice and attending to the Spirit through trained listening. It is corporate ... (and) ... concerned with engaging with the world" (Wells 2012, p. 66). He situates his notion of improvisational listening in a communally pre-formed habit or Christian virtue, similar to Young's concept of using "culture's normative discourse" as "raw material" (Young 2016, p. 159).

In relation to children, Sandy Eisenberg Sasso shares an example that reflects aspects of play and improvisation. She describes children learning Midrash as an engagement with the dominant narrative (in this case the Torah) and creating new meaning through the conversational practice (Sasso 2012, p. 47). Sasso observes the need for both a story that provides meaning and expansive narration of children's selves. She advocates for "children as partners in telling the story" (Sasso 2012, p. 47). This requires imagination on the part of all involved. Sasso adds a helpful reminder that being a communal partner, engaging personal and collective religious imaginations may like queer theorist Jack Halberstam suggests, involve failure (Halberstam 2011). In the Jewish practices Sasso describes, she notes, "It is the process of a child's seeking and learning, trying and even failing, that is valued over accuracy" (Sasso 2012, p. 46). Engagement and response to the encounter constitute outward, swelling moral change and growth.

Whether we focus on practices like improvisation, play, storytelling, or art, imagination is core to moral response. The role of imagination is central in responding to otherness as each person and community presents itself anew, and we morally constitute and reconstitute ourselves. In the Coaching Kids example, the children were not going to lobby lawmakers and civic leaders to revamp the whole city. With increased community investment in children's social participation that might happen. The economically disadvantaged, black and brown children in Coaching Kids were living into possibilities that allowed for immediate shifts in their everyday interactions and visions of a new future. With their moral agency centered, the world as they (and I) knew it shifted through each other's visions. We used our moral imagination to make community, relationships, and our sense of selves anew in the now and the yet-to-come.

5. Children in a Digital Society

For many of today's children, community building and encounters with otherness take place in both analog spaces like afterschool programs and online like gaming and social networks. I wonder how the Coaching Kids community building exercise would be different now that digital devices and software are ubiquitous. In 2003, most schools and homes had internet and many people used mobile phones to call and text. But, no one had our current smart phones (iPhone was released in 2007), no Wi-Fi centers in public places, and no social media networks (Myspace started in August 2003). Digital technology has shifted the way we communicate, form relationships, and participate in society (Ott 2018). Most children, today, grow-up digital. Factors like ownership of hardware, online access, and stability of one's country or local community affect the digitization of a child's life. Even with these qualifications, only a few rare locations escape directly interacting with digital technology, indirectly they are mapped by global GPS systems, populations quantified for government measures, and so on.

Does this radical growth in digital technology affect children's use of imagination as central to moral response? I have argued against a linear and inevitable moral development model that views children as not-yet-adults. Rather than preferencing rationality, independence, and experience, imagination and creativity are important elements in children's moral response. Similarly, the structure of digital technology "as responsive, adaptive, and networked" moves us away from an analog, linear way of knowing and being in the world (Ott 2018, p. 2). Children's moral responsiveness shares a way of operating with digital technology that can teach us how ethical response may need to shift in our new digital landscape. John Dyer, a technologist and theologian, says "when it comes to using technology, the ability to imagine and tell stories is awakened even in adults" (Dyer 2011, p. 32). Technologies allow us to imagine new ways of doing things as well as being in the world.

Wearing a watch, for example, transforms me into a human time-teller. Not just digital technology, all technology "is a bridge from this world to the imagined one" (Dyer 2011, p. 34). Though humans often create the technology; it recreates us as we interact with it. Digital media has an even greater impact than wearing a watch given the avenues for self-expression and experimentation. Luci Pangrazio notes, "informal digital writing involves play and communication" as well as "complex identity performances" (Pangrazio 2019, p. 15). It is a space to meet otherness and respond. The digital self becomes another part of the embodied self; one is not fake and the other real. It is more accurate to describe ourselves as "digitally embodied spirits" (Ott 2018, p. 58). Pangrazio explains, "While the audience might know the offline identity of the individual, the online identity that is presented through a digital profile works in an aspirational way" (Pangrazio 2019, p. 15). Moral imagination fuels the recreation of the self and community as a now and not-yet.

The centralization of children also provides insights for the overall approach and openness needed to address digital technology (Ott 2018). Charles Ess notes, that digital technology similar to a centralization of childhood displaces the rational, independent self. He writes, "the emergence of networked communications as facilitated via the internet and instantiated in social networking technologies, correlate with the (re)turn to more *relational* emphases in our conception of selfhood and identity" (Ess 2016, p. 310). Because digital technology democratizes participation with a delimiting of time and geographic barriers as well as shifts in authority of knowledge production and dissemination, "there is a blurring and distribution of the ethical *agencies* and *responsibilities*" (Ess 2016, p. 310). The agencies and responsibilities are no longer held by "those who know" or "those who have been trained" (read: adults or authority figures like digital developers). Instead, agency to participate, reshape, and create via digital technology exists regardless of age and sometimes background knowledge.

Digital technologies require more fluidity in how we characterize moral agency and moral response. Similar to the centering of children as the subject of ethics, we should ask: "Do such new [digital] technologies require new ethical frameworks, norms and processes of decision-making, and/or will extant norms, processes, and frameworks prove to be adequate in confronting the new behavioral and thus ethical possibilities evoked by these technologies?" (Ess 2016, p. 309). Talking specifically about digital literacies and young children, educational theorists Douglas Thomas and John Seely Brown, want to "make play, questioning, and imagination the bedrocks of our new culture" specifically related to digital learning and I would argue related to ethics (Thomas and Brown 2011, p. 20). Digital technology changes at a rapid pace. "Wonder, imagination, and creativity are the genesis of digital technology, they must also be its constant moral companion" (Ott 2018, p. 144). We can take a clue from childist ethics as we both observe and learn from children's interaction with digital technology. If we overlook the impact of digital technology on ethics the same way we have overlooked children's contribution, we will be a generation behind in formulating Christian ethics relevant to a digital world.

Children engage in a variety of imaginative moral responses to otherness in digital spaces. On a daily basis, they use multiplayer video games to create new social landscapes. Whether it is Minecraft or Fortnite, children have the tools to build communities from scratch or manipulate existing structures (Minecraft 2019; Fortnite 2019). As Fortnite suggests, "Build your Fortnite: Imagine a place where you make the rules, filled with your favorite things and your favorite people. Claim your own personal island and start creating!" or "Design your own games: Invent games with friends, and build your dream Fortnite experiences" (Fortnite 2019). This is one example of the many ways children are prosumers (producers + consumers) in a digital landscape. They may also be creating relationships with people across the world in ways that break down geographic and time barriers that once limited encounters with others (and otherness). This is not to say that the game platform is value free. The medium of the game has more built in values than the Coaching Kids example using plywood and cardboard. For starters, these games require a form of survival that includes fighting others to preserve one's community. When Young reminds us that moral imagination is survivalist, she does not mean it in this sense. Rather, she is pointing toward survival amidst systems of oppression and the need for prophetic moral alternatives (Young 2016). A creative moral response along these lines define "winning" as or building a world to end the oppression of others.

Moral imagination also has a connection to physical realities and current circumstances while imagining hoped for futures. Likewise, digital networks exist beyond, and yet, connected to physical realities of embodiment. Heidi Campbell and Stephen Garner write,

> "The idea of the network highlights not only how we encounter various people and relationships but also the variety of ways in which those relationships are organized. The network can promote flattened rather than hierarchical structures, along with relationships that allow more dynamic interaction rather than being unresponsive and static. This creates sources of creativity and participation that promote connectedness within Christianity Community". (Campbell and Garner 2016, p. 14)

Networked Theology, the title of Campbell's and Garner's work, describes the way in which interdependence and interaction—constant engagement with otherness—characterize faith communities in a digital landscape. They view the impact of digital technology on Christian community formation as an opportunity to democratize participation and invite moral imagination.

For example, youth are leading international movements made possible by digital technology. In 2018 Bana Alabed, at eight years old, used a Twitter account to raise awareness of the daily violence in Syria. She used the platform to "broadcast the nightmarish experience of living in Aleppo during the siege, airstrikes, and hunger" (Pimentel et al. 2018). Alabed creatively deploys the technology (for which she is too young to legally have an account) to highlight social and political vulnerabilities that needed an immediate response. Additionally, she exploits the viral, democratizing affordance of the technology to up-end social systems that grant authority to journalist over citizens.

A group of students who survived the mass shooting at Marjory Stoneman Douglas High School in Parkland, Florida engaged in similar digital activities (Pimentel et al. 2018). They used their online influence to draw attention to and pressure companies who supported gun manufacturers and sellers. They used online organizing tactics to generate a national march in Washington DC to end gun violence. Akin to Bana Alabed, these students exploited the affordances of digital technology for social good. In both examples, children engage their moral imagination when responding to social forms of otherness that lead to death and destruction albeit on different scales. The prophetic and generative moral response became possible via digital spaces and connection. Unlike the cardboard and plywood out of which a new moral vision of community arose in Coaching Kids, the digital technologies employed by Alabed and the students of Marjory Stoneman yielded embodied communities in real time.

Of course, some children exploit the creative, connected, and networked opportunities of digital technology for immoral purposes. Some prominent child hackers, like Ittai and Ruben Paul, demonstrate their skills live for cybersecurity conferences to show the ease with which many children can hack toys, company networks, or social media accounts (Bell 2018). They also do this as a way of promoting digital literacies and cybersecurity education. Digital literacies can be used for moral good or evil. Similarly, children's practices of play and improvisation can promote moral good or evil (Bell 2018). The examples of Alabed and students and Marjory Stoneman demonstrate the best of children as moral agents acting in their fullness, responding to complex moral circumstances, and engaging social participation that transforms communities. Of course, we cannot expect the same from every child who logs onto Minecraft or Fortnite, Twitter or Instagram. Children have complex and nuanced moral lives, like adults. Digital technologies provide a space and place for moral harms as well as moral good. This is the reality of all worlds we inhabit and why we desperately need moral imagination to envision the now and not-yet. Digital literacies used for creative moral response can be one of these practices of ethical imagination.

6. Christian Ethics as Creative Moral Response

Centering children and childhood as the subject of Christian ethics helps us to see how imagination is a central characteristic of a moral response. Whether it is online or offline, creativity is the process by which we (adults and children) morally grow through narrative expansion when we encounter otherness. The social act of painting cardboard together or building a digital world with players across the globe are examples of this process. Childist methods highlight the ways Christian ethics can be enriched by centering the subjectivity of children.

The recognition of creativity as a moral response begins with a revision of the ethical concept of moral agency. Moral agency is not something that one gets at a certain age or with certain capacities. The rational, independent, and experienced self has no more moral agency than an interdependent, pre-verbal, vulnerable self. They have different levels of ability to socially enact their moral choices and how we judge accountability should also differ (Traina 2009). In general, the proposed revision of moral agency also begs the question of the existence of any independent and rational self. Humans have always been relational and reliant on various forms of knowing—cognitive, affective, embodied, and now digital. We need to move beyond ethical theories that denigrate these qualities and seek to erase the moral agency of particular populations of people.

The Coaching Kids children employed imagination and creativity as moral response in the process of both designing new community and becoming community with each other. Childist ethics reminds us to encounter these children as they are, at the age they are, as complete moral beings. They are dependent and relational, yet capable of social participation that enriches community and contributes to the Christian story. Like adults, children have diverse and complex moral lives. We should not romanticize them as exempt from or affected by evil. And still, children lead rich moral lives that highlight imagination as moral response. Christian ethics can learn a great deal from a childist turn. We can and should use these insights to navigate pressing ethical issues raised by digital technologies.

Funding: This research received no external funding.

Conflicts of Interest: The author declares no conflicts of interest.

References

Abraham, Christian. 2003. Photo in "Children Offer Vision of Hope, Community". *Connecticut Post*, June 1.
Augustine. 2009. *Confessions*. Translated by Henry Chadwick. Oxford: Oxford University Press.
Bell, Sara. 2018. Child Hackers Encourage Ethical Use of Skills at UMSL's STLCyberCon. *USMLDaily*. November 19. Available online: https://blogs.umsl.edu/news/2018/11/19/stlcybercon-18/ (accessed on 24 August 2019).
Beste, Jennifer. 2011. Children Speak: Catholic Second Graders' Agency and Experiences in the Sacrament of Reconciliation. *Sociology of Religion* 72: 327–50. [CrossRef]
Browning, Don S., and Marcia Bunge, eds. 2011. *Children and Childhood in World Religions: Primary Sources and Texts*. Piscataway: Rutgers University Press.
Browning, Don S., and Bonnie J. Miller-McLemore, eds. 2009. *Children and Childhood in American Religions*. Piscataway: Rutgers University Press.
Bunge, Marcia, ed. 2001. *The Child in Christian Thought*. Grand Rapids: Eerdmans.
Bunge, Marcia, ed. 2012. *Children, Adults, and Shared Responsibilities: Jewish, Christian, and Muslim Perspectives*. New York: Cambridge University Press.
Campbell, Heidi, and Stephen Garner. 2016. *Networked Theology: Negotiating Faith in Digital Culture*. Grand Rapids: Baker Press.
Cornwall, Susannah. 2017. *Un/Familiar Theology: Reconceiving Sex, Reproduction and Generatvity*. New York: Bloomsbury.
Dyer, John. 2011. *From the Garden to the City: The Redeeming and Corrupting Power of Technology*. Grand Rapids: Kegel Publications.
Ess, Charles M. 2016. Ethics—and—Emancipation for the Rest of Us? In *Controversies in Digital Ethics*. Edited by Amber Davisson and Paul Booth. New York: Bloomsbury, pp. 308–19.
Fewell, Danna Nolan. 2003. *The Children of Israel: Reading the Bible for the Sake of Our Children*. Nashville: Abingdon.
Fortnite. 2019. Creative. Available online: https://www.epicgames.com/fortnite/en-US/creative (accessed on 31 July 2019).
Halberstam, Judith Jack. 2011. *The Queer Art of Failure*. Durham: Duke University Press.

Mercer, Joyce Ann. 2005. *Welcoming Children: A Practical Theology of Childhood*. St. Louis: Chalice.
Meshberg, Ronald. 2003. Children Offer Vision of Hope, Community. *Connecticut Post*, June 1.
Miller-McLemore, Bonnie J. 2019. *Let the Children Come: Reimagining Childhood from a Christian Perspective*. Minneapolis: Fortress Press. First published 2003 by John Wiley & Sons.
Miller-McLemore, Bonnie J. 2012. Work, Labor and Chores: Christian Ethical Reflection on Children and Vocation. In *Children, Adults, and Shared Responsibilities: Jewish, Christian, and Muslim Perspectives*. Edited by Marcia Bunge. New York: Cambridge University Press, pp. 171–86.
Minecraft. 2019. What Is Minecraft. Available online: https://www.minecraft.net/en-us/what-is-minecraft/ (accessed on 31 July 2019).
Ott, Kate. 2014. Children as An/other Subject: Redefining Moral Agency in a Postcolonial Context. *Journal of Childhood and Religion* 5. Available online: http://childhoodandreligion.com/issues/volume-5/ (accessed on 15 July 2019).
Ott, Kate. 2015. "Animating Children" for Syndicate, Roundtable on Queer Art of Failure. Available online: https://syndicate.network/symposia/literature/the-queer-art-of-failure/ (accessed on 15 July 2019).
Ott, Kate. 2018. *Christian Ethics in a Digital Society*. Lantham: Rowman & Littlefield.
Ott, Kate. 2019. Orgasmic Failure: Ethical ReVisions of Adolescent Sexuality. In *Theologies of Failure*. Edited by Roberto Sirvento and Ducan Reyburn. Eugene: Cascade Books, pp. 107–29.
Pangrazio, Luci. 2019. *Young People's Literacies in the Digital Age: Continuities, Conflicts, and Contradictions*. New York: Routledge.
Pimentel, Julia, Carolyn Bernucca, and Khal. 2018. 20 Young Activists Who Are Changing the World. *Complex*, December 22. Available online: https://www.complex.com/life/young-activists-who-are-changing-the-world/ (accessed on 26 August 2019).
Qvortrup, Jens, William Corsaro, and Michael-Sebastian Honig, eds. 2009. *The Palgrave Handbook of Childhood Studies*. New York: Palgrave.
Ridgely, Susan, ed. 2011. *The Study of Children in Religions: A Methods Handbook*. New York: NYU Press.
Ryall, Emily, Wendy Russell, and Malcolm MacLean, eds. 2013. *The Philosophy of Play*. New York: Routledge.
Sasso, Sandy Eisenberg. 2012. Children's Spirituality in Jewish Narrative Tradition. In *Children, Adults, and Shared Responsibilities: Jewish, Christian, and Muslim Perspectives*. Edited by Marcia Bunge. New York: Cambridge University Press, pp. 39–58.
Stockton, Kathryn Bond. 2009. *The Queer Child or Growing Sideways in the Twentieth Century*. Durham: Duke University Press.
Thomas, Douglass, and John Seely Brown. 2011. *A New Culture of Learning: Cultivating the Imagination for a World of Constant Change*. Lexington: CreateSpace Publishing.
Traina, Cristina. 2009. Children and Moral Agency. *Journal of the Society of Christian Ethics* 29: 19–37. [CrossRef]
Traina, Cristina. 2011. *Erotic Attunement: Parenthood and the Ethics of Sensuality between Unequals*. Chicago: University of Chicago Press.
Van Ausdale, Debra, and Joe R. Feagin. 2001. *The First R: How Children Learn Race and Racism*. Lanham: Rowman & Littlefield.
Wainryb, Ceclia, Beverly A. Brehl, and Sonia Matwin. 2005. *Being Hurt and Hurting Others: Children's Narrative Accounts and Moral Judgments of Their Own Interpersonal Conflicts*. Boston: Blackwell Publishing.
Wall, John. 2010. *Ethics in Light of Childhood*. Washington: Georgetown University.
Wall, John. 2012. Imagining Childism: How Childhood should Transform Religious Ethics. In *Children, Adults, and Shared Responsibilities: Jewish, Christian, and Muslim Perspectives*. Edited by Marcia Bunge. New York: Cambridge University Press, pp. 135–51.
Wells, Karen. 2009. *Childhood in Global Perspective*. Oxford: Polity.
Wells, Samuel. 2012. *Improvisation: The Drama of Christian Ethics*. Grand Rapids: Brazos Press.
Wynn, Karen, and Paul Bloom. 2013. The Moral Baby. In *Handbook of Moral Development*. Edited by Melanie Killen and Judith G. Smetana. Abingdon: Routledge, pp. 435–53.
Young, Thelathia Nikki. 2016. *Black Queer Ethics, Family, and Philosophical Imagination*. New York: Palgrave.
Young-Bruehl, Elisabeth. 2011. *Childism: Confronting Prejudice against Children*. New Haven: Yale University.

© 2019 by the author. Licensee MDPI, Basel, Switzerland. This article is an open access article distributed under the terms and conditions of the Creative Commons Attribution (CC BY) license (http://creativecommons.org/licenses/by/4.0/).

Article
Reconstructing an Ethics of Credit in an Age of Neoliberalism

Ilsup Ahn

Department of Philosophy, North Park University, Chicago, IL 60625, USA; iahn@northpark.edu

Received: 30 July 2019; Accepted: 16 August 2019; Published: 17 August 2019

Abstract: One of the most formidable socio-economic challenges which Christian communities are facing today is the growing dominance of neoliberalism. From wheat fields in Brazil to Wall Street in New York City, neoliberalism is marching on everywhere with its massive credit (or credit money). The purpose of this paper is to address a key structural injustice of neoliberalism—the deepening colonization of "social capital" by "financial capital." Since the 1980s, a new economic process known as "financialization" has structurally changed the global economic system entailing an extreme income and wealth gap between the haves and the have nots. It has also rendered a countless number of ordinary people vulnerable to various types of debt entrapment while destroying the environment on a global scale. Behind all these forms of social and natural disintegration lies a crucial neoliberal apparatus fueled by credit. This paper engages in such problems by attempting to reconnect the lost link between social capital and financial capital. In doing so, it first analyzes the genealogical origin of the separation between financial capital and social capital. The author then comes up with ethical principles to re-anchor financial capital in social capital through a critical and interdisciplinary exploration.

Keywords: social capital; financialization; financial capital; ethics of credit; neoliberalism; colonization; Christian ethics

1. Introduction

Without a doubt, one of the most formidable socio-economic challenges which Christian communities are facing today is the growing dominance of neoliberalism. From wheat fields in Brazil to Wall Street in New York City, neoliberalism is marching on everywhere with its massive credit. In his book, *A Brief History of Neoliberalism*, David Harvey describes the concept of neoliberalism as follows: "Neoliberalism is in the first instance a theory of political economic practices that proposes that human well-being can best be advanced by liberating individual entrepreneurial freedoms and skills within an institutional framework characterized by strong private property rights, free markets, and free trade" (Harvey 2007, p. 2). As Harvey correctly points out in the book, by the time the worst financial crisis since the Great Depression hit the global society in the late 2000s, neoliberalism had already taken over the world by becoming hegemonic as a mode of discourse. He writes, "the advocates of the neoliberal way now occupy positions of considerable influence in education (the universities and many 'think tanks'), in the media, in corporate boardrooms and financial institutions, in key state institutions (treasury departments, the central banks), and also in those international institutions such as the International Monetary Fund (IMF), the World Bank, and the World Trade Organization (WTO) that regulate global finance and trade" (Harvey 2007, p. 3). What is alarming about the rise of neoliberalism is that it has become so influential that many of us are now accustomed to "interpret, live in, and understand the world" from its perspective (Harvey 2007).

What, then, has happened to our world and to its inhabitants after forty years of its global dominance? Many scholars and researchers report that the socio-economic situations of our world and the quality of life have been worse off rather than better off during this period. In his book, *Capital in the Twenty-First Century*, French economist Thomas Piketty has discovered that an unhealthy economic trend has settled in during this period. For instance, according to Piketty, since the late 1970s, wealth (not income) has been increasingly reasserting itself, reminiscing about the unequal socio-economic situations of the eighteenth- and nineteenth-century western European society. He writes, "from 1977 to 2007, we find that the richest 10 percent appropriated three-quarter of the growth. The richest 1 percent alone absorbed nearly 60 percent of the total increase of US national income in this period. Hence for the bottom 90 percent, the rate of income growth was less than 0.5 percent per year" (Piketty 2014, p. 297). While economists address the ever-widening economic gap between the rich and the poor, other social scientists such as sociologists point out the gradual erosion of "social capital" (such as social networks, norms of reciprocity, and trustworthiness) during this period. Although we shall shortly discuss this notion further, and its implication later, let me briefly illustrate some of the unmistakable evidence we are witnessing today.

Sociologist Matthew Desmond, in his book *Evicted: Poverty and Profit in the American City*, uncovers an unstated yet important aspect of American society. According to him, "the majority of poor renting families in America spend over half of their income on housing, and at least one in four dedicates over 70 percent to paying the rent and keeping the lights on. Millions of Americans are evicted every year because they can't make rent" (Desmond 2016, p. 4). Desmond estimates in his interview with NPR (National Public Radio) that 2.3 million evictions were filed in the U.S. in 2016 (Gross 2018). Let us turn to another alarming issue of our time—rising student debt. As of today (July 2019), the current U.S. student loan debt surpasses $1.53 trillion dollars, and an estimated 44.7 million people have student loan debt with the average amount of $37,000.[1] We should note that the total number of student loan borrowers has increased by 89 percent from 2004 to 2014 as two-thirds of student loan balances are held by borrowers (Haugwout et al. 2015). It seems right for Italian sociologist Maurizio Lazzarato to argue in his book, *Making of the Indebted Man*, that the birth of the indebted man (a type of dehumanized debtor) has become a key moral issue in an increasingly neoliberalized society (Lazzarato 2011, pp. 38–39).

Above, we have seen briefly how the rise of neoliberalism has coincided with the deterioration of our society and its social fabric to the core. The purpose of this paper is to address one of the key structural injustices of our world—the deepening colonization of "social capital" by rising "financial capital"—which is pervasively undergoing in many parts of the world. Since the 1980s, a new economic process known as financialization has structurally changed the global economic system entailing extreme income and wealth discrepancies. It has also rendered a countless number of ordinary people vulnerable to various forms of debt entrapment while destroying the environment on a global scale. Behind all these forms of social and natural disintegration lies a crucial neoliberal apparatus enabled by the deployment of the various types of credit. In this paper, thus, I attempt to develop a much-needed, yet largely obscure ethical idea—ethics of credit—by reconnecting the lost link between social capital and financial capital. An ethics of credit is possible when we begin to see that credit is not a mere obverse of debt, but a form of societal gift whose purpose is not only to increase financial capital but also to enhance social capital without thereby discriminating or denying anyone who is eligible to access to it.

2. Neoliberalism and the Colonization of Social Capital by Financial Capital

What is the notion of neoliberalism, and what does it specifically have to do with the colonization of social capital by financial capital? According to Harvey, neoliberalism as an ideology is a creation of a small and exclusive group of passionate advocates (mainly academic economists, historians, and philosophers) who gathered around the renowned Austrian political philosopher and economist

---

[1] This statistics can be found at: https://www.nitrocollege.com/research/average-student-loan-debt.

Friedrich von Hayek by creating the Mont Pellerin Society in 1947 (Harvey 2007, p. 20). From the beginning, they opposed state interventionist theories such as those of John Maynard Keynes while holding onto Adam Smith's notion of the invisible hand as the best device to motivate a human desire for wealth and power even though they attempted to displace the classical theories of Adam Smith, David Ricardo, and Karl Marx (Harvey 2007). Neoliberalism as an ideology became a new economic orthodoxy regulating public policy at the state level in the U.S. and Britain in the late 1970s. For instance, in May 1979, when Margaret Thatcher was elected in Britain, she deserted Keynesianism by adopting monetarist "supply-side" solutions to the lingering problem of stagflation that had characterized the British economy during the 1970s (Harvey 2007, p. 22). This ideological change subsequently brought the following structural transformations to Britain such as "confronting trade union power, attacking all forms of social solidarity that hindered competitive flexibility, ... dismantling or rolling back the commitments of the welfare state, the privatization of public enterprises, reducing taxes, encouraging entrepreneurial initiative, and creating a favorable business climate to introduce a strong inflow of foreign investment" (Harvey 2007, p. 23).

Across the Atlantic Ocean, Ronald Reagan's victory over Carter in 1980 also entailed a new era of neoliberalism in the U.S. We should note that in the U.S., as well as in Britain, the turn to neoliberalism depended not only on adopting a new monetarism but also on the unfolding of government policies in many other arenas (Harvey 2007, p. 24). For instance, as is the case for Britain, the Reagan administration also provided the requisite political backing for the full deployment of neoliberalism "through further deregulation, tax cuts, budget cuts, and attacks on trade union and professional power" (Harvey 2007, p. 25). Regarding the rise of neoliberalism, what we should particularly attend to is that it effectively induced a new age called financialization resulting in a huge growth of the financial market and its profits. As Harvey points out succinctly, increasingly freed from the regulatory constraints and legal barriers (such as the 1933 Glass-Steagall legislation) that had successfully confined the volatile financial markets, the financial sector could flourish as never seen before, eventually everywhere (Harvey 2007, p. 33). "A wave of innovations occurred in financial services to produce not only far more sophisticated global interconnections but also new kinds of financial markets based on securitization, derivatives, and all manner of future trading. Neoliberalization has meant, in short, the financialization of everything" (Harvey 2007).

Although social scientists have different definitions,[2] they generally agree that financialization refers to the growing dominance of capital market financial system that results in the explosion of financial trading with a myriad of new financial instruments (Ahn 2017, p. 40). As briefly mentioned above, one of the socio-economic impacts entailed by increasing financialization is the detrimental concentration of wealth among finance rentiers. In an article titled, "The richest 1 percent now owns more of the country's wealth than at any time in the past 50 years," Christopher Ingraham of *The Washington Post* reports, using economist Edward N. Wolff's data, that while from 2013, the share of wealth owned by the 1 percent shot up by nearly three percentage points, wealth owned by the bottom 90 percent fell over the same period (Ingraham 2017). Shockingly, the top 1 percent of households own more wealth than the bottom 90 percent combined (Ingraham 2017). Recently, *Forbes* also reports referring to UC Berkeley economist Gabriel Zucman that "U.S. wealth concentration seems to have returned to levels last seen during the Roaring Twenties" (Colombo 2019). According to Zucman, all the research on the issue also shows that this is a worldwide phenomenon that happened in China and Russia in recent decades. At a "more moderate rise," it also happened in France and the U.K. (Colombo 2019).

---

[2] For instance, Greta Krippner defines financialization as "pattern of accumulation in which profits accrue primarily through financial channels rather than through trade and commodity production." In a slightly different way, Gerald Epstein describes it as "the increasing role of financial motivates, financial markets, financial actors and financial institutions in the operation of the domestic and international economies" (Krippner 2005, pp. 174–75; Epstein 2005, p. 3).

Wealth, as such, may be morally neutral, but its concentration of such magnitude may not be neutral because it inevitably comes along with many serious socio-economic, political, and psychological consequences and implications. How is it so? Why is the excessive concentration of wealth problematic? I answer this question by critically appropriating the concept of "social capital." It is my contention that the excessive concentration of wealth is problematic because it inevitably tends to deplete and erode social capital in a radical way, engendering the proliferation of structural injustice in a deeply neoliberalized society. Indeed, an increasing number of social scientists and social philosophers are addressing this issue across the globe. Before exploring how neoliberal financialization and its results (excessive concentration of wealth) negatively impact on social capital, we first need to examine its concept and related issues. First off, what is the notion of social capital?

In the past three to four decades, many scholars in social science have researched the notion of social capital, and the ideas of Pierre Bourdieu, James Coleman, and Robert Putnam are especially widely recognized by social scientists. In his influential 1986 article, "The Forms of Capital," Bourdieu, for instance, defined social capital as follows: "Social capital is the aggregate of the actual or potential resources which are linked to possession of a durable network of more or less institutionalized relationships of mutual acquaintance and recognition—or in other words, to membership in a group—which provides each of its members with the backing of the collectivity-owned capital, a 'credential' which entitles them to credit, in the various senses of the word" (Bourdieu 1986, p. 251). Although he already adopted the term "social capital", in his 1984 *Distinction: A Social Critique of the Judgment of Taste*, Bourdieu's sociological interest related to it rather lies in uncovering the ways how society is reproduced, and particularly how the dominant classes retain their privileged potions. For this reason, David Gauntlett calls Bourdieu's definition of social capital "the most depressing of the models" (Gauntlett 2011, p. 132). Indeed, "where other writers see social capital as a fundamentally heartwarming network of social connections, however, Bourdieu uses it to explain the cold realities of social inequality." (Gauntlett 2011, p. 134).

American sociologist James Coleman also investigated the notion of social capital, but differing from Bourdieu, he develops a more comprehensive and broader view of social capital, which is not owned as stock by privileged or powerful groups. Social capital is reconceived to be available even to those who are powerless and marginalized within society. Coleman's notion is also distinguished from Bourdieu's because of its functional aspect. Coleman defines social capital as follows: "Social capital is defined by its function. It is not a single entity but a variety of different entities, with two elements in common: they all consist of some aspect of social structures, and they facilitate certain actions of actors—whether persons or corporate actors—within the structure. Like other forms of capital, social capital is productive, making possible the achievement of certain ends that in its absence would not be possible" (Coleman 1988, p. S98). He then adds that its function may not be necessarily useful or beneficial. "A given form of social capital that is valuable in facilitating certain actions may be useless or even harmful for others" (Coleman 1988, p. S100). Coleman differentiates social capital from other types such as human capital. According to him, while "human capital is created by changes in persons that bring about skills and capabilities," social capital "comes about through changes in the relations among persons that facilitate action" (Coleman 1988, p. S100). In this respect, social capital is less tangible because "it exists in the *relations*." (Coleman 1988).

American political scientist Robert Putnam made the term popular with his 1995 article, "Bowling Alone," published by the *Journal of Democracy* (later expanded into a book in 2000 with the same title). In this article, he defines social capital as follows: "By analogy with notions of physical capital and human capital—tools and training that enhance individual productivity—'social capital' refers to features of social organization such as networks, norms, and social trust that facilitate coordination and cooperation for mutual benefit" (Putnam 1995, p. 67). In his 2000 book *Bowling Alone*, Putnam distinguishes social capital into two forms: "bridging" and "bonding." While bridging social capital relates to relationship across diverse social cleavages encompassing people inclusively, bonding social capital tends to reinforce exclusive identities and homogeneous groups by looking inward (Putnam 2000, p. 22). Examples of bonding social capital include ethnic fraternal organizations, church-based women's reading groups, and fashionable country clubs, whereas examples of bridging social capital include the civil rights movement, many youth service groups, and ecumenical religious organizations (Putnam 2000). Putnam's key argumentation is that the healthy stock of America's social capital has been collapsing in the latter half of the twentieth century, and there are sociological reasons causing this phenomenon.

It is important to note here that the depletion and erosion of social capital is not merely a sociological phenomenon; it is an important moral and ethical issue as well. What does the diminution of social capital have to do with morals and ethics? In their article, "Social Cohesion, Social Capital and the Neighbourhood," sociologists Ray Forrest and Ade Kearns discover an important fact that there is a social scientific interaction between the erosion of social capital and the loss of social cohesion. The erosion of social capital leads neighborhood and community to the loss of social cohesion. Bartolini and Bonatti (2009) confirm this by stating that "the deterioration of this resource (social capital) can be interpreted as a decline in social cohesion and general trust that forces economic agents to raise their expenditure aimed at self-protecting from increased opportunism and defiant behavior" (p. 927). With regard to the perceived interaction between social capital and social cohesion, what we should particularly take note of is that social cohesion has intrinsically intertwined with moral ideals and values. According to Forrest and Kearns, there are five domains of social cohesion, and its three domains such as "common social values", "social order", and "social solidarity" reflect that the concept of social cohesion is deeply interconnected with moral ideals and principles.[3]

Above we have explored how the erosion of social capital is not merely a sociological problem. Interlinked with the loss of social cohesion, the depletion of social capital becomes a key moral and ethical issue, which social ethicists should especially address in an urgent manner. How, then, should Christian social ethicists engage in the neoliberal problem of the erosion of social capital? What is the specific role or task of Christian social ethicists in tackling the problem in an age of neoliberal financialization? In order to answer these questions, we need to firstly find out the root cause of the erosion of social capital. Why is social capital eroded and depleted in the U.S.? Putnam answers this question in *Bowling Alone*. He sums up his answer by formulating four factors as follows.

> First, pressures of time and money, including the special pressures on two-career families, contributed measurably to the diminution of our social and community involvement during these years. My best guess is that no more than 10 percent of the total decline is attributable to that set of factors.
>
> Second, suburbanization, commuting, and sprawl also played a supporting role. Again, a reasonable estimate is that these factors together might account for perhaps an additional 10 percent of the problem.
>
> Third, the effect of electronic entertainment—above all, television—in privatizing our leisure time has been substantial. My rough estimate is that this factor might account for perhaps 25 percent of the decline.
>
> Fourth, and the most important, generational change—the slow, steady, and ineluctable replacement of the long civic generation by their less involved children and grandchildren—has been a very powerful factor. (Putnam 2000, p. 283)

Besides these four factors, Putnam also acknowledges that globalization or "global economic transformation" has contributed to the erosion of social capital. He, for instance, writes, "the replacement of local banks, shops, and other locally based firms by far-flung multinational empires often means a

---

[3] Two other domains are social networks and place attachment (Forrest and Kearns 2001, p. 2129).

decline in civic commitment on the part of business leaders" (Putnam 2000, pp. 282–83) Putnam's sociological analysis of the erosion of social capital, however, is not complete because his list lacks a critical factor which has become a game-changer in an age of financialization—i.e., the global dominance of financial capital. It is my contention that social capital has been increasingly eroded as a result of its colonization by financial capital, and at the juncture of this colonization lies the pervasive neoliberal deployment of financial credit. What, then, does it mean by the "neoliberal deployment of financial credit?". What does this deployment have to with the erosion of social capital?

In his 2015 book, *The Business of America Is Lobbying*, Lee Drutman investigates the socio-political phenomenon of lobbying questioning "how and why for-profit corporations invest billions of dollars each year to influence political outcomes, and why that investment has been growing steadily for decades" (Drutman 2015, p. 1). Although Drutman defines lobbying broadly to mean "any activity oriented towards shaping public policy outcomes" (Drutman 2015, p. 15), he acknowledges that the key lobbying mechanism is money, which is basically credit given to lobbyists and policymakers. Lobbying is basically an act of claiming a credit on the money given for political purposes. Drutman discovers that there has been a progression of corporate lobbying in the U.S., which is interestingly coincided with the progression of neoliberalism. He outlines this progression in three stages:

The 1970s: the political awakening of corporate lobbying

The 1980s: the political entrenchment of corporate lobbying

The 1990s (and beyond): the political expansion of corporate lobbying. (Drutman 2015, p. 49)

The growth of lobbying is astounding during this period. According to Drutman, "between 1998 and 2010, the amount of money all corporations reported spending on their own lobbyists increased by 85 percent, going from $1.13 billion in 1998 to $2.09 billion in 2010 (in constant 2012 dollars)" (Drutman 2015, p. 12). According to *The Guardian*, "There are believed to be more than 30,000 lobbyists in Washington, outnumbering elected federal politicians by almost 60 to one" (Harris 2006)[4]. It continues to write, "The US constitution is often praised for its checks and balances between the president, Congress, and the Supreme Court. But where money equals power, no one predicted the unofficial fourth branch of US government: K Street" (Harris 2006).

Given that lobbyists are paid substantial amounts of money by special interest groups to sway the decisions of lawmakers to pass advantageous legislation,[5] lobbying is a key mechanism through which financial capital is translated into political power. This paid special interest money is none other than the financial credit. Based on their financial credit (paid special interest money), lobbyists are expected to buy political commodities—their clients' interested policies just as credit cardholders are entitled to buy goods, commodities, or services based on their credit. According to Drutman, an important consequence of the growth of lobbying is that "a harder-to-dislodge status quo tends to protect incumbent market players, thus limiting the capacity of the government to support policies would encourage innovation" (Drutman 2015, p. 42). In other words, the growth of lobbying tends to benefit those who have financial capital (the wealthy) disproportionately since they can access to the mechanism to keep their socio-economic privileges. This is the reason why Joseph Stiglitz argues in his 2013 book *Price of Inequality* that socio-economic inequality not only is bad for the U.S. economy but also has detrimental effects on its democracy (Ahn 2017, p. 45).

The 2008 financial crisis is an exemplary case which demonstrates how the neoliberal appropriation of financial credit could dramatically disrupt and even destroy social capital. It is a well-known fact that the rampant proliferation of subprime mortgage was one of the key factors that triggered the

---

[4] "K Street" refers to a line of sparking office blocks and fancy restaurants north of the White House. Available online: https://www.theguardian.com/world/2006/jan/08/usa.paulharris (accessed on 8 May 2012).

[5] https://www.investopedia.com/terms/l/lobby.asp.

financial crisis. This problematic proliferation was possible due to the repeal of the Glass-Steagall Act in 1999, which effectively separated regular banks from investment banks. As a result of this repeal, banks insured by the FDIC (Federal Deposit Insurance Corporation), whose deposits were guaranteed by the government, were motivated to engage in highly risky business for higher profits. The proliferation of subprime mortgages in the US housing market was indeed structurally interlinked with this repeal. Not many people, however, pay attention to the fact that the big-bank lobby pursued a long campaign to repeal the Glass-Stegall Act (Wilmarth 2017). Years of lobbying finally paid off, but it eventually resulted in dire and disastrous economic consequences radically disrupting the social capital across the globe.

Vijay Das and Arjun Singh Sethi of *USA Today* report that the financial crisis of 2008 "foreshadowed a global recession that cost the U.S. economy $22 trillion and devasted millions of American homeowners" (Das and Sethi 2016). They also emphasize that although no one was spared when the housing bubble collapsed, "communities of color and low-income neighborhoods were hit the hardest. ... They had long faced abusive financial practices like predatory lending, payday loans, and tax scams" (Das and Sethi 2016). In their paper titled "The Home Foreclosure Crisis and Rising Suicide Rates, 2005 to 2010," Jason Houle and Michael Light also uncover the social scientific data that during this period, the U.S. suicide rate increased nearly 13 percent from 11.0 to 12.4 per 100,000 people, but this rate particularly rose among the middle-aged, by nearly 30 percent from 13.7 in 1999 to 17.6 in 2010 (Houle and Light 2014, p. 1073). Without a doubt, the neoliberal appropriation of financial credit (e.g., lobbying) made it possible for banks to abuse financial credit system itself (subprime mortgages, mortgage-backed securities, etc.), and this eventually led to the sweeping destruction of social capital across the globe.

3. The Proliferation of Immoral Credit and the Quest for an Ethics of Credit

Above we have seen how social capital has been increasingly colonized by financial capital as neoliberalism has incrementally gained its control over economic and political system along with the rising financialization. According to social scientists Emanuele Ferragina and Alessandro Arrigoni, rising economic inequalities exacerbated by the 2008 financial crisis have demonstrated that "the neoliberal political agenda is incompatible with the aim to generate social capital" (Ferragina and Arrigoni 2017). By examining the critical case of Britain, they come to a conclusion that "social capital theory (at least Putnam's version) can no longer obscure the fact that the neoliberal political agenda has acted as a brake upon civic participation" (Ferragina and Arrigoni 2017, p. 363). For Ferragina and Arrigoni, rising economic inequality is an important reason why there is a growing incompatibility between the neoliberal agenda and the aim to create social capital. While neoliberalism tends to reduce socio-economic problems to a matter of individual choices (individualism), the erosion of social capital is more likely collective problems. "There is a tension between the individualization of social risks pursued by British political parties and the call to create social capital: it is becoming harder to blame the individual for collective problems" (Ferragina and Arrigoni 2017, p. 364). Ferragina and Arrigoni, however, stop short of explaining how rising economic inequality becomes a collective or structural problem that prevents a neoliberalized society from creating its own social capital.[6]

Many social scientists have engaged in exploring the relations between sociology (the realm of social capital) and economics (the realm of economic capital) by taking the rising impact of neoliberalism into account. These studies, however, are mainly focused on uncovering the role of social capital when there would be economic constraints in a society.[7] There seem to be hardly any

---

[6] Unlike Ferragina and Arrigoni, epidemiologists Richard Wilkinson and Kate Pickett examine in their 2011 book, *The Spirit Level: Why Greater Equality Makes Societies Stronger*, how rising economic inequality contributes to the erosion of social capital, among other social ills (Wilkinson and Pickett 2011).

[7] For example, following articles address the topic: Douglas and Browne (2011); Lindstrom and Giordano (2016); Frank et al. (2014); Pereira et al. (2017).

investigatory studies about how rising economic (financial) inequality becomes a structural factor in deteriorating and eroding social capital in an increasingly neoliberal society. Despite the lack of social scientific study of this relationship, we can develop a plausible hypothesis based on Putnam's notion of "reciprocity." According to Putnam, as one of the key components of social capital, "social networks" have intrinsically to do with "sturdy norms of reciprocity." He writes, "Even more valuable, however, is a norm of *generalized* reciprocity: I'll do this for you without expecting anything specific back from you, in the confident expectation that someone else will do something for me down the road. The Golden Rule is one formulation of generalized reciprocity" (Putnam 1995, pp. 20–21). It is not unreasonable to conjecture that rising economic inequality renders it increasingly difficult for the members of the society to be reciprocal among themselves. The lack of economic resources makes it unlikely for those who own wealth to be reciprocal with those who have no wealth. This lack of socio-economic reciprocity is even more so among those who have no wealth at all because they simply do not have anything to reciprocate with. From a bird's eye view, there seems to be an unfortunate dialectic established between social capital and economic capital (particularly financial capital). While social capital renders it possible for a society to build up its economic system and financial capital, the increasing economic inequality paradoxically destroys its own basis—social capital.

From a critical perspective, the rising economic inequality, especially excessive financial inequality, cannot but become an important social ethical issue in an age of neoliberal financialization. Why is it so? It is because the mass production of capital-less people interlinked with the excessive concentration of wealth would inevitably lead them to the dependence on the lending/borrowing system of the financial sector, and this dependence is based on the availability of credit and its deployment. Since credit becomes one of the most important socio-economic necessities, the way in which it is deployed becomes a key social justice issue. How, then, should we develop an ethics of credit in an age of neoliberal financialization? How is an ethics of credit possible? What does it mean that credit is *ethically* conceived and deployed? What is the moral criterion that renders any deployment of credit justifiable?

First off, we should admit that the idea of credit as we know it today may not be what it is originally meant to be. What does this mean? In an article titled "Exposing Mammon: Devotion to Money in a Market Society," Philip Goodchild points out that credit has been reduced to the mere "obverse of debt." He writes, "The recent financial crisis has exposed the extent to which the contemporary global economy is driven by credit. Yet credit is the obverse of debt" (Goodchild 2013, p. 47). A popular website focusing on investing and finance education seems to concur with Goodchild's view by outlining the idea of credit as follows: "Credit is a broad term that has many different meanings in the financial world. It is generally defined as a contractual agreement in which a borrower receives something of value now and agrees to repay the lender at a later date—generally with interest."[8] Although *Investopedia* acknowledges that "Credit also refers to the creditworthiness or credit history of an individual or company," since the notion of creditworthiness is defined by the borrower's abilities to pay back his/her debt, as Goodchild points out, credit seems to have become the mere obverse of debt. Credit is now exclusively interlocked with debt as if they are two sides of the same coin. It is my contention that in order to develop an ethics of debt, we should begin by dismantling the neoliberal notion of credit that it is nothing more than a mere obverse of debt.

Why, then, is the reduction of credit to the mere obverse of debt problematic? In his 2017 book, *Just Debt: Theology, Ethics, and Neoliberalism*, the author of this article develops an argument that debt has been reduced to an amoral economic tool in neoliberalized world, and its historical origin goes back to the late eighteenth century (particularly Jeremy Bentham's 1787 Defence of Usury). The argument is summarized as follows: "The reduction of debt to an amoral issue is enabled when the problem of debt is separated from its historical, cultural, political, or structural context. When debt is entirely decontextualized from its complex context... debt simply becomes a matter of individual responsibility

---

[8] https://www.investopedia.com/terms/c/credit.asp.

to repay" (Ahn 2017, p. 16). If credit is nothing more than the mere obverse of debt, credit would also become an amoral or non-moral financial entity as the mere obverse of debt. Indeed, the notion of credit has been largely reduced to a "credit score," and this number becomes an important indicator telling who we are in a neoliberal society. Reducing credit to the mere obverse of debt as an amoral contractual issue is deeply problematic because as a result of this reduction, the rich and deep social, historical, and moral meaning of credit is completely stripped off and thrown away by this reduction. In a world of amoralized credit, no one would be able to bring any moral or ethical judgment on any use of credit.

In their co-authored book, *Hidden Interests in Credit and Finance*, James Greenberg and Thomas Park uncover a largely forgotten historical fact that "credit played a key role in almost every aspect of the [Atlantic] slave trade."[9] How did credit play its role during the period of the Atlantic slave trade? According to Greenberg and Park, "At the highest levels of finance, a small circle of Italian bankers and merchants were heavily involved in financing the slave trade ... At lower levels of finance, many others were involved" (Park and Greenberg 2017, p. 126). Since the slave trade was a risky business, in order to spread their risk, merchants and ship owners were brought into trading expeditions—and each vessel formed a ship's company for the duration of the expedition. In doing so, they were involved in substantial use of credit (Park and Greenberg 2017, p. 126). For example, "sailors were commonly offered a mixture of incentives to sign on including some cash in advance, cargo space, rations, and a share of the profits at the end" (Park and Greenberg 2017). Since sailors' families needed money while awaiting their return, the payment of the crew was involved with substantial use of credit. Selling slaves in the New World also involved with the use of credit. In the colonies, little money was actually in circulation, and most businesses were conducted using credit. When slaves were sold at auctions, payment was made with a mixture of cash and credit (with the property as collateral). "When these merchants arrived home because planters had little cash, they usually had to sell on credit, and advanced slaves against the plantation's future harvests" (Park and Greenberg 2017, p. 134).

The case of the Atlantic slave trade demonstrates how the reduction of credit to the mere obverse of debt as an amoral or non-moral financial contract can be deeply problematic especially to those who are excluded from the privileged group. The Atlantic slave trade was possible because "credit was used not only to mobilize resources and launch enterprises [slave trade] even when coin was in short supply, but it helped to articulate modes of production, facilitating trade between economies without useful currency exchange rates" (Park and Greenberg 2017, p. 140). From a critical-moral perspective, denouncing the Atlantic slave trade without condemning the widespread use of credit is not holistic enough. The Atlantic slave trade must be denounced in the name of humanity. Its denounce, however, should be accompanied by the equal condemnation of the immoral use of credit during the Atlantic slave trade. Indeed, by reducing credit to the mere obverse of debt as an amoral or non-moral entity, Atlantic slave traders and their business cohorts (such as European banks, merchants, companies, buyers, etc.) committed one of the worst systemic and organized crimes against humanity in history.

We should note that the abusive and thus immoral deployment of credit as an amoral or non-moral entity was not terminated along with the dissolution of the Atlantic slave trade. Unfortunately, the deployment of immoral credit is still very much real today in different forms. The case of predatory payday loans exemplifies this. In an article, "Payday lenders preying on borrowers escape crackdown as rules rolled back," Jana Kasperkevic of *The Guardian* introduces a story of Asha Clark, who works full-time as a customer service representative ($8.25 an hour) in Las Vegas, Nevada. When her paycheck was not enough to cover all her bills, Clark would take out a payday loan. The trouble starts when borrowers like Clark get their check and spend most of it repaying the loan. If they end up short on cash again, they cannot but take out another payday loan. Next payday, the same thing would occur.

---

[9] In this book, Greenberg and Park argue that modern credit establishes a relationship of inequality between the powerful lender and the weak borrower, and we should not accept the economists' claim that the loans involve equality (the nominal contractual equality) (Park and Greenberg 2017, p. 140).

"The borrowers roll over that same $500 loan every two weeks, each time paying the fee. Over the span of the year, the fees [$75 for a $500 loan] alone can be as much as seven times the size of the original loan" (Kasperkevic 2019). According to Kasperkevic, "In some states, interest rates on payday loans [adjusted annual rate] reached nearly 700%. In Texas, borrowers paid on average 662%. In Nevada, that number was 652%, and in Kansas 391%" (Kasperkevic 2019).

What we cannot but witness in such cases as the Atlantic slave trade and predatory payday loans is the egregious distortion of the credit system that has been employed and justified by immoral creditors and their beneficiaries. How could we then rebuild and reconstruct an ethics of credit in an age of neoliberal financialization? How could we resuscitate the original moral ethos of credit that has been radically reduced and neutralized to a state of an amoral or non-moral entity? How is an ethics of credit possible?

The first step toward the reconstruction of an ethics of credit is to trace back the historical origin of credit. In another of their co-authored books, *The Roots of Western Finance*, Thomas Park and James Greenberg investigated the history of credit in early civilizations (such as Sumer, ancient Egypt, and classical Greece and Rome) to uncover the deep structures, processes, and inner cultural logics that made ancient institutions and social relations work, and they discovered that "investments in social capital were a key component of early finance just as they are today" (Greenberg and Park 2017, p. xvii). They conclude their study saying, "from an anthropological perspective, credit is not simply an economic transaction, it also depends on social relations" (Greenberg and Park 2017, p. xi). Echoing Park and Greenberg's anthropological discovery, Craig Muldrew also discovered that unlike the common perception, contemporaries of Adam Smith (early modern England) "did not, in fact, understand marketing through the use of a language which stressed self-interest, but rather one which stressed *credit relations*, trust, obligation and contracts" (Muldrew 1993, p. 183). For two reasons, Muldrew supports his argument: "The first is that, apart from wholesaling, most buying and selling was done on trust, or credit, without specific legally binding instruments, in which an individual's creditworthiness in their community was vital. Second, this network of credit was so extensive and intertwined that it introduced moral factors which provided strong reasons for stressing co-operation within the marketing structures of the period" (Muldrew 1993, p. 169).

Muldrew's study, as well as that of Park and Greenberg, offers us an important clue in developing an ethics of credit. We should be reminded that the original birthplace of credit is the social relation, not the neoliberal notion of amoralized financial contract. As Muldrew points out, in early modern England, market relations were interpreted in a way which stressed the consequences of actions on others and on the community, and "market relations were conceived of in explicitly moral terms, and not those of amoral self-interest" (Muldrew 1993, p. 177). Muldrew goes on further emphasizing that "the moral language of people's credit and honesty, of plain dealing and the keeping of promises, dominated the way in which market relations were conceived" (Muldrew 1993).

Based on Park and Greenberg's anthropological discovery and Muldrew's moral insight on the relation between moral credit and market economy, I would like to suggest two moral principles as a preparatory step toward the full reconstruction of an ethics of credit. The first principle, which I would call the "principle of inviolability," is established in a negative way. Although Muldrew does not specifically refer to the term "social capital", his work provides us with an important clue how the first principle should be established in relation to it. Succinctly put, the first principle of an ethics of credit is stipulated in such a way that the deployment of financial credit should not deplete or erode the existing social capital.[10] By the criterion of the principle of inviolability, then, the sub-prime mortgage frenzy during the 2000s is condemned to be an immoral deployment of financial credit.

---

[10] Although we do not investigate the case of Gramin Bank, a microfinance organization and community development bank, in this paper, it exemplifies what it would look like when credit respects existing social capital instead of depleting or eroding it.

While the first principle focuses on the inviolability of social capital in deploying financial credit, the second principle, which I would call the "principle of reciprocity," relates to the enhancement of the mutual and reciprocal relationship between social capital and financial capital. To be more specific, financial credit should be deployed in such a way not only to increase financial capital but also to enhance social capital. Any policies against the second principle are then morally unjustified. In his book, *The Great Transformation*, Karl Polanyi argues that neoliberal theorists' efforts to disembed the economy from society are doomed to fail (Polanyi 2001, p. xxvii). He attacks the idea of a self-regulating market system separated from social relations by stating that "the gearing of markets into a self-regulating system of tremendous power was not the result of any inherent tendency of markets toward excrescence, but rather the effect of highly artificial stimulants administered ... by the no less artificial phenomenon of the machine" (Polanyi 2001, p. 60). He goes even further, saying that "Robert Owen's was a true insight: market economy if left to evolve according to its own laws would create great and permanent evils" (Polanyi 2001, p. 136). The principle of reciprocity is developed to promote the mutual edification between social capital and financial capital by emphasizing the close relationship between the two. In summary, both principles are devised in such a way that the deployment of financial credit should meet the two-pronged ethical criteria: On the one hand, it should not disrupt social capital; on the other hand, it should promote and facilitate the reciprocal increase of both financial capital and social capital.

4. Laying the Groundwork for a Theological Reconstruction of Moral Credit

Above, although it is only an initial step, we have made a meaningful step toward the full-fledged establishment of an ethics of credit by formulating two principles for an ethical deployment of credit. How could Christian theology contribute to the development of a more holistic and substantive ethics of credit? What distinctive ethical insights could Christian theology offer to us as we develop a much-needed ethics of credit in an age of neoliberalism? Before we answer these questions, we should first investigate why Christian theology and the Christian church care about the neoliberal deployment of credit and its ethical establishment. Neoliberal deployment of credit is an important issue to Christian communities because, as seen above, it affects the formation and maintenance of social capital. In *Bowling Alone*, Putnam claims that "churches and other religious organizations have unique importance in American civil society" (Putnam 1995, p. 65). He then goes on further saying, "faith communities in which people worship together are arguably the single most important repository of social capital in America" (Putnam 1995, p. 66). Christopher Bunn and Matthew Wood particularly emphasize that between two dimensions of social capital ("bridging" and "bonding"), religious congregations and faith-based organizations are more specifically related to bridging social capital because they are oriented to "encompass people across diverse social cleavages such as the civil rights movement, many youth service groups, and ecumenical religious organizations" (Bunn and Wood 2012, p. 637). Other social scientists such as Kristin Stromsnes also hold that "religious involvement is positively associated with political engagement, social trust and tolerance" (Stromsnes 2008, p. 478; Casey 2014; Glatz-Schmallegger 2015). Theology and the church should care about the creation and preservation of social capital because church communities are one of the key storehouses and generators of social capital.

How, then, is a distinctive Christian perspective possible regarding the development of more holistic ethics of credit? The more holistic ethics of credit is possible because Christian theology views the problem of credit not merely as a sociological phenomenon, but also as a theological matter.[11] How

---

[11] For instance, a new Vatican document entitled "Oeconomicae et Pecuniariae Quaestiones" (Questions about the economy and money) emphasizes that financial considerations are not merely a matter of practical-economic policy because Catholic teachings also address them as an important matter of moral theology. From the lens of Catholic social teaching, the document calls for developing new forms of economy and of finance: "For this reason, the competent and responsible agents have the duty to develop new forms of economy and of finance, with rules and regulations

does this difference render a Christian perspective distinctive? The distinctive Christian perspective is possible because it raises a fundamental question about the phenomenon of credit: "What is credit?" In his book, *Neoliberalism's Demons*, Adam Kotsko formulates a critical insight on how neoliberalism has transformed the notion of the family by creating *its own* version, which would fit its political-economic agenda. He writes, "neoliberalism carries out its own 'great transformation' by reconfiguring the relationship between the political and the economic and reimaging the household precisely as a site of indefinite accumulation" (Kotsko 2018, p. 71). Kotsko is helpful because his theological critique can also be applicable to the economy of credit.

A Christian theological analysis of credit, then, begins with the following question: How has neoliberalism transformed the notion of credit by creating *its own* version that fits its political-economic agenda? Indeed, by successfully creating its own version of credit and deploying its mechanism (such as derivatives) in the name of financialization, neoliberalism has made the indefinite concentration of wealth possible. As a result of this, credit has been radically reduced to a mere obverse of debt, with its original historical, social, and religious significances nearly wiped out. This is the reason why we do not have any established form of an ethics of credit in today's neoliberal world. In order to reconstruct an ethics of credit, we should begin by dismantling the neoliberal ideology of credit itself. How could we deconstruct the depoliticized neoliberal notion of credit, and how is Christian ethics of credit possible? I argue that the deconstruction of the neoliberal notion of credit and reconstructive Christian ethics of credit are possible by discovering two critical-constructive ethical insights from Christian theology. What are these principles? How are they conceived?

Firstly, credit is supposed to be a form of a gift rather than a mere liability to be repaid. Since it is to be a form of a gift, credit should not be simply reduced to a contractual obligation to observe. Of course, it is constituted as a contractual matter with an obligation to repay. This, however, should not do away with the other key aspect that credit is given with the purpose of providing a service to its receivers. Secondly, the offering of credit should be available to all, especially to those who are excluded from eligible credits being socially marginalized, discriminated, and otherized. How, then, are these two principles conceived theologically? What does theology have to with the construction of these two principles? A more in-depth theological exploration of these two insights is in order.

First off, what does Christian theology have to do with the idea that credit is supposed to be a form of gift? Answering this question requires us to engage with the Christian tradition of apophatic theology largely known as negative theology. Why apophatic theology? As opposed to the types of ontotheology, which tends to reduce the Name of God to such invented ideas as "First Being, "Universal Sovereignty," or "prima causa" opening the door to their idolization, apophatic theology begins with negating any attempts to understand God in our images, thereby dismantling our theological and idolatries. According to apophatic theology, the negation of our attempt to understand God in our image is not the end of theology, but the beginning of theology because the mystery of God reveals itself to us in our ignorance. Apophatic theology, thus, offers us a more truthful and authentic knowledge of God. In his *On Learned Ignorance*, Nicholas of Cusa (1401–1464) captures the gist of apophatic theology as follows: "[t]he precise truth shines forth incomprehensibly in the darkness of our ignorance. This is the learned ignorance for which we have been searching, and, as we explained, by means of it alone we can draw near the maximum and triune God of infinite goodness" (Nicholas of Cusa 1997, p. 127).

Contemporary apophatic theologian Catherine Keller appropriates such classical apophatic images as "cloud" to refer to the unfolding epiphany of the mystery of God. She particularly emphasizes that this unfolding "cloud of our nonknowing" entangles "every register of our relations, every economy, every politics, every social or ecclesial movement, every ecology" (Keller 2015, p. 30). According to Keller, it is critical to see that the unfolding cloud of our nonknowing is known to us because

---

directed towards the enlargement of the common good and respect for human dignity along the lines indicated by the social teachings of the Church." The document was published on 17 May 2018, and it can be found at: http://press.vatican.va/content/salastampa/en/bollettino/pubblico/2018/05/17/180517a.html (Ladaria et al. 2018).

it has its own *generative* power. A French philosopher and Roman Catholic theologian Jean-Luc Marion illustrates this generative power of unfolding cloud of our nonknowing with an image of gift-giving love. As it may sound paradoxical, the knowledge of God is possible in its impossibility because God gives always. In other words, apophatic theology becomes possible despite its negativity because apophatic love is revealed and also exemplified through the apophatic practices of continual giving and forgiving. Marion writes, "the gift crosses Being/being ... the gift is not at all laid out according to Being/being, but Being/being is given according to the gift. *The gift delivers Being/being*" (Marion 1995, p. 101). He goes on further saying that "because God does not fall within the domain of Being, he comes to us in and as a gift ... for the gift does not have first to be, but to pour out in an abandon that, alone, causes it to be, God saves the gift in giving it before being" (Marion 1995, p. 3).

Despite its enigmatic aspect, Apophatic theology provides us a critical theological insight in developing an ethics of credit. According to this insight, credit should not be reduced to the mere obverse of debt. Instead, credit is to be reconceived as a form of a gift, which ultimately increases the overall sum of social capital. Since the generating power of the unfolding cloud of nonknowing encompasses "every register of our relations" including economic (financial) relation, this would mean that the relational act of offering and receiving credit between creditor and debtor is also to become an apophatic event, exemplifying God's original gift-giving love. Kathryn Tanner's notion of "economy of grace" is a further development of this apophatic theological insight (Tanner 2005). Although this new vision of economy grounded in God's original giftfulness is different from that of our everyday economic activities, reconceiving credit as a form of a gift can become an innovative project that brings a constructive sea change to this world.

The second critical-constructive insight which the apophatic theology offers to us is that the offering of credit as a form of gift should be all-inclusive and thus available to all, especially to those who are excluded from the networks of social capital being marginalized, discriminated, and otherized. Unfolding gift of God indeed encompasses all without any discriminations. Synoptic Gospels are full of stories which illustrate how Jesus intendedly visited and offered various gifts of healing to many people who were at the lowest rung of society. In his last sermons before his crucifixion, Jesus said to his followers: "truly I tell you, just as you did it to one of the least of these who are members of my family, you did it to me" (Mt. 25:40). In Luke 16, Jesus also illustrates how critical it is for those who have socio-economic capital to offer credit to the "least" of their social members in order to enter the kingdom of God. The story of "the Rich Man and Lazarus" begins with the description of a "rich man" who was dressed in purple and fine linen feasting sumptuously every day. The story, then, immediately introduces a new character named Lazarus. While the rich man and his cohorts were having a feast every day, he was lying at his gate longing to satisfy his hunger with what fell from the rich man's table. What is worse, Lazarus was covered with sores, and the dogs would come and lick his sores. Later both men died, and while Lazarus was carried away by the angels to be with Abraham, the rich man went to Hades and was being tormented there.

Why, then, is this story important to us, and what ethical insight should we discover from it in developing an ethics of credit? This story emphasizes that Lazarus was lying at the rich man's gate, which means that the rich man must have known that Lazarus was in need of his gift of mercy. The fact that the rich man and his cohorts were having a feast every day also indicates that he had enough economic sources to provide to his desperate neighbor. Why did not the rich man help the poor Lazarus? For the rich man, Lazarus was an invisible other whom he believed he did not have to take care of. Although the rich man apparently cared about his own family members (He begged to send Lazarus to his father's house so that his five brothers will not come into Hades), he did never extend the perimeter of his gift-giving love beyond the boundary of his family. The rich man's sin was not about doing something evil to others; his sin was rather about failing to do something good to rectify his neighbor's brokenness. In other words, his sin was not an action; his sin was rather an inaction.

One might raise a critical question: How did merchants and credit providers (banks) get involved in Atlantic slave trade during the early modern period, in which the use of a language that emphasizes credit relations, trust, obligation and contracts played a crucial role in marketing as Muldrew argues above? The answer lies in the point that the early modern European slave traders did not regard Africans as their equals who were worthy of their respects, but rather considered them as the "others" who were exempt from the community of giving and receiving credits due to their racial difference. The category of the "other" was then redefined as those who are devoid of any creditworthiness. As is evident, disconnection from credit renders anyone vulnerable to social and systemic violence.

Theologian Elizabeth O'Donnell Gandolfo recently explores the topic of human vulnerability in her book, *The Power and Vulnerability of Love*. According to her, vulnerability is an "inevitable dimension of the human condition" as a form of "givenness" (Gandolfo 2015, p. 4). She also defines vulnerability as "the universal, though diversely experienced and often exacerbated, risk of harm in human life" (Gandolfo 2015, p. 3). In reconstructing an ethics of credit, one of the key ethical insights of the apophatic theology is to extend the boundary of social capital in such a way to include all with no discrimination, especially those who are socio-economically poor and thus vulnerable. The availability of credit as a form of gift is indispensable for humanity to cope with the inevitable socio-economic vulnerability. Some might argue that the availability of payday loans to the poor and vulnerable proves that the market can really fulfill the theological insight that no one should be exempted from the availability of credit. This view is untenable because such a type of credit only erodes and dismantles social capital, rather than builds and strengthens it. The provision and availability of giftful credit to the socio-economic "others" is necessary for a society to continue to construct social capital, especially the type of "bridging (inclusive) social capital," which is increasingly called for as our society is getting more into neoliberalism, creating many different shapes of socio-economic "others" from all over the world.

5. Conclusions

Above, we have seen that an ethics of credit is possible only when the decontextualized and disembedded financial capital is re-anchored and re-embedded in social capital. It is right for Kotsko to argue that market mechanism "must be designed to serve social ends directly rather than creating a profit incentive and hoping the social end is served along the way" (Kotsko 2018, p. 142). In this paper, I develop an argument that the increasing erosion of social capital is one of the most significant theological issues of our time, and the church should respond to it. What, then, should the church do about it? First off, the church should realize that it is the church's key ecclesial responsibility in an age of neoliberalism not only to defend social capital from its erosion by financial capital, but also to rebuild and reconstruct it from its damage and devastation. Based on this realization, the church should particularly stand up for those who are most vulnerable to the colonizing power of neoliberalism at the margins of the social networks. We should be reminded that when Putnam distinguishes between "bonding social capital" from "bridging (or inclusive) social capital," he identifies the church as a key agency to represent "bridging social capital" (Putnam 2000, p. 22). As a key socio-religious institution, the church should be ready to engage in socio-religious political activism to protect and promote financial justice for all in an age of neoliberalism.

Funding: This research received no externalfunding.

Conflicts of Interest: The author has no conflict of interest.

References

Ahn, Ilsup. 2017. *Just Debt: Theology, Ethics, and Neoliberalism*. Waco: Baylor University Press.
Bartolini, Stefano, and Luigi Bonatti. 2009. Endogenous growth, decline in social capital and expansion of market activities. *Journal of Economic Behavior & Organization* 67: 917–26.
Bourdieu, Pierre. 1986. The Forms of Capital. In *Handbook of Theory of Research for the Sociology of Education*. Edited by John E. Richardson. West Port: Greenwood Press.

Bunn, Christopher, and Matthew Wood. 2012. Cultured responses: The production of social capital in faith based organizations. *Current Sociology* 60: 636–52. [CrossRef]

Casey, Coleen. 2014. Critical Connections: The importance of community-based organizations and social capital to credit access for low-wealth entrepreneurs. *Urban Affairs Review* 50: 366–90. [CrossRef]

Coleman, James S. 1988. Social Capital in the Creation of Human Capital. *American Journal of Sociology* 94: S95–S120. [CrossRef]

Colombo, Jesse. 2019. America's Wealth Inequality is at roaring twenties levels. *Forbes*, February 28.

Das, Vijay, and Arjun Singh Sethi. 2016. Tough Road for Great Recession Victims. *USA Today*. March 17. Available online: https://www.usatoday.com/story/opinion/2016/03/17/great-recession-housing-crisis-foreclosures-justice-column/81923182/ (accessed on 16 August 2019).

Desmond, Matthew. 2016. *Evicted: Poverty and Profit in the American City*. New York: Broadway Books.

Douglas, Daniel, and Anthony Browne. 2011. Surviving the Downturn: The Role of Social Capital in the Financial Crisis. *The Western Journal of Black Studies* 35: 128–38.

Drutman, Lee. 2015. *The Business of America is Lobbying: How Corporations Became Politicized and Politics Became More Corporate*. Oxford: Oxford University Press.

Epstein, Gerald. 2005. Introduction: Financialization and the World Economy. In *Financialization and the World Economy*. Edited by Gerald A. Epstein. Cheltenham: Edward Elgar.

Ferragina, Emanuele, and Alessandro Arrigoni. 2017. The Rise and Fall of Social Capital: Requiem for a Theory? *Political Studies Review* 15: 355–67. [CrossRef]

Forrest, Ray, and Ade Kearns. 2001. Social Cohesion, Social Capital and Neighbourhood. *Unban Studies* 38: 2125–43. [CrossRef]

Frank, Christine, Christopher G. Davis, and Frank J. Elgar. 2014. Financial strain, social capital, and perceived health during economic recession: A longitudinal survey in rural Canada. *Anxiety, Stress & Coping* 27: 422–38.

Gandolfo, Elizabeth O'Donnell. 2015. *The Power and Vulnerability of Love: A Theological Anthropology*. Minneapolis: Fortress Press.

Gauntlett, David. 2011. *Making is Connecting: The Social Meaning of Creativity, from Craft and Knitting to Digital Everything*. Cambridge: Polity Press.

Glatz-Schmallegger, Markus. 2015. Social Capital and Church-Based Social organizations. *Diaconia* 6: 167–82. [CrossRef]

Goodchild, Philip. 2013. Exposing Mammon: Devotion to Money in a Market Society. *Dialogue: A Journal of Theology* 52: 47–57. [CrossRef]

Greenberg, James B., and Thomas K. Park. 2017. *Hidden Interests in Credit and Finance: Power, Ethics, and Social Capital Across the Last Millennium*. Lanham: Lexington Books.

Gross, Terry. 2018. First-Ever Evictions Database Shows: We're in the Middle of a Housing Crisis. *NPR Fresh Air*. April 12. Available online: www.npr.org/2018/04/12/601783346/first-ever-evictions-database-shows-were-in-the-middle-of-a-housing-crisis (accessed on 16 August 2019).

Harris, Paul. 2006. Capitol Hill's dirty secrets laid bare in lobby scandal. *The Guardian*, January 7.

Harvey, David. 2007. *A Brief History of Neoliberalism*. Oxford: Oxford University Press.

Haugwout, Andrew, Donghoon Lee, Joelle Scally, and Wilbert van der Kalauw. 2015. Student Loan Borrowing and Repayment Trends, 2015. *Federal Reserve Bank of New York*, April 16.

Houle, Jason N., and Michael T. Light. 2014. The Home Foreclosure Crisis and Rising Suicide Rates, 2005 to 2010. *American Journal of Public Health* 104: 1073–79. [CrossRef] [PubMed]

Ingraham, Christopher. 2017. The richest 1 percent now owns more of the country's wealth than at any time in the past 50 years. *The Washington Post*. December 6. Available online: https://www.washingtonpost.com/news/wonk/wp/2017/12/06/the-richest-1-percent-now-owns-more-of-the-countrys-wealth-than-at-any-time-in-the-past-50-years/?utm_term=.27e8cafa4c88 (accessed on 16 August 2019).

Kasperkevic, Jana. 2019. Payday lenders preying on borrowers escape crackdown as rules rolled back. *The Guardian*. February 26. Available online: https://www.theguardian.com/money/2019/feb/26/payday-loan-protections-rolled-back-trump-administration (accessed on 16 August 2019).

Keller, Catherine. 2015. *Cloud of the Impossible: Negative Theology and Planetary Entanglement*. New York: Columbia University Press.

Kotsko, Adam. 2018. *Neoliberalism's Demons: On the Political Theology of Late Capital*. Stanford: Stanford University Press.

Krippner, Greta. 2005. The Financialization of the American Economy. *Socio-Economic Review* 3: 173–208. [CrossRef]

Ladaria, Luis, Peter Card Turkson, Giacomo Morandi, and Bruno Marie Duffe. 2018. Oeconomicae et Pecuniariae Quaestiones: Considerations for an Ethical Discernment Regarding Some Aspects of the Present Economic-Financial System. Available online: http://press.vatican.va/content/salastampa/en/bollettino/pubblico/2018/05/17/180517a.html (accessed on 16 August 2019).

Lazzarato, Maurizio. 2011. *The Making of the Indebted Man: An Essay on the Neoliberal Condition*. Translated by Joshua David Jordan. Los Angeles: Semiotext.

Lindstrom, Martin, and Giuseppe N. Giordano. 2016. The 2008 financial crisis: Changes in social capital and its association with psychological wellbeing in the United Kingdom—A panel study. *Social Science & Medicine* 153: 71–80.

Marion, Jean-Luc. 1995. *God without Being*. Translated by Thomas A. Carlson. Chicago: University of Chicago Press.

Muldrew, Craig. 1993. Interpreting the market: the ethics of credit and community relations in early modern England. *Social History* 18: 163–83. [CrossRef]

Nicholas of Cusa. 1997. *Selected Spiritual Writings*. Translated by H. Lawrence Bond, and Morimichi Watanabe. New York: Paulist Press.

Park, Thomas K., and James B. Greenberg. 2017. *The Roots of Western Finance: Power, Ethics, and Social Capital in the Ancient World*. Lanham: Lexington Books.

Pereira, Maria C., Filipe Coelho, and Oscar Lourenco. 2017. Who Feels Credit Constrained in Europe? The Role of Social Capital. *The Journal of Consumer Affairs* 51: 380–405. [CrossRef]

Piketty, Thomas. 2014. *Capital in the Twenty-First Century*. Translated by Arthur Goldhammer. Cambridge: Belknap Press of Harvard University Press.

Polanyi, Karl. 2001. *The Great Transformation: The Political and Economic Origins of Our Time*. Boston: Beacon Press.

Putnam, Robert. 1995. Bowling Alone: America's Declining Social Capital. *Journal of Democracy* 6: 65–78. [CrossRef]

Putnam, Robert. 2000. *Bowling Alone: The Collapse and Revival of American Community*. New York: Simon & Schuster.

Stromsnes, Kristin. 2008. The Importance of Church attendance and membership of religious voluntary organizations for the formation of social capital. *Social Compass* 55: 478–96. [CrossRef]

Tanner, Kathryn. 2005. *Economy of Grace*. Minneapolis: Fortress.

Wilkinson, Richard, and Kate Pickett. 2011. *The Spirit Level: Why Greater Equality Makes Societies Stronger*. New York: Bloomsbury Press.

Wilmarth, Arthur E., Jr. 2017. The Road to Repeal of the Glass-Steagall Act. *The Columbia Law School (CLS) Blue Sky Blog*. October 3. Available online: http://clsbluesky.law.columbia.edu/2017/10/03/the-road-to-repeal-of-the-glass-steagall-act/ (accessed on 16 August 2019).

© 2019 by the author. Licensee MDPI, Basel, Switzerland. This article is an open access article distributed under the terms and conditions of the Creative Commons Attribution (CC BY) license (http://creativecommons.org/licenses/by/4.0/).

Article

Liberating Discernment: Language, Concreteness, and Naming Divine Activity in History

Tyler B. Davis

Graduate Department of Religion, Baylor University, 1301 S University Parks Dr, Waco, TX 76706, USA; t_davis@baylor.edu

Received: 2 September 2019; Accepted: 27 September 2019; Published: 30 September 2019

Abstract: One of the revolutionary insights of early liberation theology was that theological discernment is, above all, a concrete undertaking. Yet this insight is accompanied by a persistent conundrum that arises from the way in which naming God's activity in history is perceived as collapsing God's objective distance into contingent affairs. This paper contends that this conundrum results from a constricting account of theological objectivity which is problematically conceived in opposition to concretization and so obstructs an account of liberating discernment. Locating this concern within the (de)colonial history of competing theological readings of the weather, and, in addition, prompted by Alice Crary's expansion of objectivity in ethical theory, I argue that theological objectivity must not only include but begin with theological languages of the oppressed as its essential point of departure. Recovering the insight of early liberation theologians, this paper contends that theology may speak of God objectively only as it concretely shares in the liberating life and words of the crucified peoples of history. The purpose of this argument is then to envision Christian ethics as language accountable to the apocalyptic activity of the God of the oppressed.

Keywords: liberation theology; ethics; language; the weather; praxis; apocalyptic; discernment; Alice Crary; James Cone; Beatriz Melano Couch

---

In Latin America, from the immersion in concrete struggle we question the scriptures and doctrine, trying to find direction for both thinking and action. The richer, more objective our knowledge of reality, the more relevant and profound will be our questioning of God's word in our search for faithfulness to God's will.

Beatriz Melano Couch[1]

In general, in a deep conflict, the eyes of the downtrodden are more acute about the reality of the present. For it is in their interest to perceive correctly in order to expose the hypocrisies of the rulers.

Immanuel Wallerstein[2]

What would theology look like if we were to take seriously the claim that Christian theology is poor people's speech about their hopes and dreams that one day "trouble will be no more"?

James H. Cone[3]

---

[1] (Melano Couch 1991, p. 443).
[2] (Wallerstein [1974] 2011, p. 4).
[3] (Cone 1985, p. 127).

1. Introduction

One of the revolutionary insights of liberation theology is that theological discernment is, above all, a concrete undertaking. Latin American liberation theologian Beatriz Melano Couch articulated this insight precisely in her insistence that the indispensable condition of theology is "immersion in concrete struggle" (Melano Couch 1991, p. 443). Theological discernment so formulated entails that language about divine activity must be baptized in people's struggles for freedom from enclosures of sin. Yet this insight is often displaced or covered over by a certain anxiety arising from the way in which naming God's activity in history seems to risk collapsing God's objective distance into contingent affairs. This anxiety is here explored as the *conundrum of concretization*. On the one hand, as God is discerned to be concretely involved in contingent creaturely affairs, theological language organically becomes intertwined with human action and praxis.[4] Theologically, to speak of signs of apocalyptic liberation or to name the Spirit of Christ's activity in the world presumes a relation to struggle. On the other hand, the same concretization also exposes theology to distortion, since the internal relation of language and action conflicts with prevailing conceptions of objective language with respect to God and the world. According to this anxiety, as divine activity is concretely related to human states of affairs, it risks transgressing objective thinking and speaking about God by conflating divine interests with subjective—or more perniciously—ideological investments.

This paper attends to this conundrum for the purpose of shedding light on the role of discernment in apocalyptic theologies of liberation.[5] My argument is that, despite the persistence of this conundrum, it is a misconception generated by a governing and constricting view of theological objectivity which is problematically conceived in opposition to concretization, and, precisely so, obstructs the recovery of liberating discernment articulated by Melano Couch and others. The consequences of this misconception include the idea that abstract and generalizable descriptions of divine activity are (most nearly) objective descriptions, in addition to a categorical resistance to concretization. In order to reimagine discernment apart from this view, this essay first attends to the entanglement of theology and readings of the weather in colonial modernity as a fraught yet generative history for considering the promise and perils of concrete, liberating discernment. The resistance to take seriously claims regarding divine activity in irruptive weather and meteorological conditions, which have been crucial to freedom dreams of oppressed people, evinces how prevailing ideas of objectivity restrict theologies of liberation. Second, to recast objectivity, I draw inspiration from Alice Crary's realignment of objective judgment in ethical theory. Crary's argument for a wider objectivity for ethics prompts a parallel clarification of concrete objectivity for theology, making possible a recovery and re-articulation of liberating discernment.

If Christian theology is, as James Cone piercingly writes, "language about the crucified and risen Christ ... language that is accountable to the God encountered in the oppressed community", then it has to unsettle conceptions of objectivity that resist the radical concretization necessary to make it so accountable (Cone 1985, pp. 122, 127). The purpose of this essay is to re-envision Christian ethics as language accountable to the God of the oppressed by setting forth divine discernment with the "terrifying and liberating concreteness" demanded by the gospel of liberation (Lehmann 1975, p. 37). Theology may speak of God objectively, I contend, only as it concretely shares in the liberating life and words of the crucified peoples of history.[6]

---

4 On the "organic" connection between concrete discernment and praxis, see (Dussel 1979, esp. pp. 57–58).
5 By this I mean accounts of liberation theology that begin with revelation (*apocalypsis*). For this formulation, see (Siggelkow 2018, p. 44).
6 On the theological concept of the "crucified peoples", see (Ellacuria [1978] 2013, esp. pp. 208–10).

2. Theological Meteorology and the Conundrum of Concretization

The hybrid history of theology's entanglement with meteorology provides an illuminating (if perhaps unexpected) case for considering the conundrum of concrete discernment. The birth of the modern science of meteorology was, as scholars in environmental and colonial history have argued, induced by the conquest culture and political directives of colonialism.[7] Like botany, cartography, astronomy, and other natural sciences, the application of scientific measurement and technological instruments (i.e., barometer, thermometer, and telegraphic networks) to collect, analyze, and transmit climate data, and ultimately to forecast the weather, served crucial colonial state building, economic, and administrative imperatives (Schwartz 2015, p. 80). Such imperatives included, for example, expediting transoceanic maritime trade, diminishing the risks posed by hazardous tempests, and coordinating planning and development across "plantation America".[8] Yet meteorological reflection also held a peculiar, hybrid relation to theology.[9] Environmental conditions were (and are) inseparable from theological discernments, and vice versa. In the context of modern colonialism, this was unmistakably evident in disaster discourses. These emergent discourses were not by any means limited to empirical observations about natural causation or Aristotelian speculations regarding elemental combinations and combustions.[10] Instead, like the plague narratives of Exodus, disasters were portents that spurred radically concrete claims of divine activity and culpability regarding regimes of human sin. Divided by the fault lines that colonialism created, disasters had the theological potential to reinforce and extend the violent conditions of colonial domination, but they also elicited emancipatory imaginations—those which, representing the dark side of freedom struggles, understood how unstable ecological conditions could catalyze liberation from plantation and racial regimes.[11]

Consider the following examples of theological discernment in meteorological disaster:

(1) Puerto Rico, 1868: The Lares rebellion. The anticolonial, people's movement for independence from Spain on the island successfully seizes the town of Lares, but fails to generate a general uprising and is suppressed. In the aftermath, colonial administrators and political leaders declare that discrete weather and seismic events were critical in undermining the political uprising. This, they further claim, is providential evidence of God's preservation of the Spanish regime (Schwartz 2015, pp. 175–78).

(2) Waco, Texas, 1953: A tornado rips through the downtown city center, devastating the mid-sized Texas city. Circulating among black residents in Waco, Texas, an oral tradition re-describes the tornado event by linking it to 1916 lynching of Jesse Washington, an event W.E.B. Du Bois termed "the Waco Horror". The tornado, according to this tradition, re-traced the very ground on which Washington's bodied was dragged, and becomes a sign of divine justice and reversal (Carrigan 2004, pp. 189–208).

---

[7] My narration of the colonial development of meteorology is informed by Schwartz (2015, pp. 79–80); see also (Williamson 2015). On the environmental and cultural history of meteorology, consult (Golinski 2007; Anderson 2005; Jankovic 2001).

[8] On the transnational notion of "plantation America", see the classic study by (Beckford [1972] 1999, esp. pp. 17–18).

[9] I invoke the term hybrid following Bruno Latour's influential distinction between purification and hybridization. Hybrids, according to this distinction, are those things that emerge from surprising and often concealed modern practices of mediation. They describe the unexpected entwinement of knowledges in modernity, despite its claims to separation and purification. See (Latour 1993).

[10] Contemporary disaster studies underscore the multifaceted social construction of disaster environments in contrast to reductive naturalist accounts. For a concise summary of this important emphasis, see (Luft 2009, p. 506). For a masterful example of "disaster before the disaster" analysis of Hurricane Katrina, see Clyde Woods's posthumous writings, (Woods 2017, esp. pp. 216–54), as well as the reflections by theologians, ethicists, and religious studies scholars gathered in (Kirk-Duggan 2006).

[11] On these strands of Christianity, see Joseph Winters' illuminative rendering of Vincent Harding's interpretation of Black Power: "If strands of Christianity emphasize the violence of divine judgment over the more idyllic images of lions lying with lambs, then Harding suggests that black power represents the darker side of black freedom struggles, the side that acknowledges how a better future requires some kind of violent interruption into the order of things. This is where things get difficult and interesting". See (Winters 2019, p. 165). On the notion of racial regimes, see (Robinson 2007, pp. xi–xvii).

(3) Rocksprings, Texas, 1928: A tornado devastates a small town in Edwards County in South Texas. In its aftermath, the tornado is described by local ethnic Mexicans as the retributive justice of God for the widespread anti-Mexican violence and vigilantism in the region, especially in the decade spanning 1910–1920. Furthermore, the tornado is tied to the specific racial terror lynching of Antonio Rodríguez in 1910, representing a discrete moment of divine justice in response to the failure of human justice in the aftermath of terror (Martinez 2018, pp. 67–69).

(4) Americas, 16th century: Jesuit theologian Bartolomé de Las Casas learns of an indigenous meteorological tradition observing that hurricanes increased in both frequency and severity in the Caribbean following colonial contact and conquest. Las Casas affirms the truthfulness of this tradition, arguing that increased hurricanes are the result of Spain's "new and many sins" (Las Casas 1968, p. 191).[12]

These examples represent moments in colonial modernity in which concrete theological discernments are braided with readings of the weather. It is important to acknowledge that they occur in different colonial contexts in the Americas and span over three centuries. Such differences are not immaterial and invite further investigation. Yet for the purposes of this essay, despite relative differences in history and geography, they display how theological accounts of the weather formed critical and extended modes of contestation within colonial relations of power. In all of them, ecological disaster events are more than mere natural occurrences; they are transformed into theological discourses wherein turbulent weather becomes, borrowing from Cone, "concrete signs of divine presence" (Cone 2013, p. 155). Moving beyond natural "disaster exceptionalism", they reframe the possibilities of creaturely life and arrangements by simultaneously saying something about the weather and something about God (Luft 2009, pp. 506–9). At the same time, they also exhibit significant theological variation in shape and substance. In terms of shape, the first three examples are apocalyptic: they relate irregular, catastrophic ecological events to the revelation of divine activity in the world. The fourth example is theodical: the theological connection between colonialism and hurricanes is not directly mediated by divine activity, but through an account of sin.

Moreover, the examples can be separated along colonial and decolonial or liberationist lines. The first example names divine activity in the weather as the justification of Spanish colonial suppression of a people's movement for freedom. Differentiated from the other three, it represents a form of colonial disaster apocalyptic. This way of reading disaster perniciously names ecological destruction as divine judgment upon victims of colonial violence and its rebels.[13] Examples two, three, and four contrastively reframe ecological disaster within the disaster of colonialism and so expose its injustice and illegitimacy. They thus take liberating shape, projecting theological discernments in disastrous weather conditions within a world wrecked by colonial violence and its afterlife. Examples two and three similarly discern apocalyptic divine activity in tornado events as the righteous judgment of God visited upon anti-Mexican and anti-black plantation lynching regimes in Central and South Texas. They recall the image found in the prophetic book of Amos, "Does disaster befall a city, unless the Lord has done it?" (Amos 3:6). Accordingly, these examples identify disruptive whirlwinds as apocalyptic signs of imminent divine deliverance. Example four, for its part, takes a similar decolonial shape. We may observe the distinction that where examples two and three recall a certain Amos pattern of apocalyptic discernment, example four approximates a Hosea pattern in that it follows the logic of disaster theodicy. As the prophetic book reads: "For they sow the wind, and they shall reap the whirlwind" (Hosea 8:7). The organizing idea of this mode of discernment is that sin is excessive, bearing a devastating momentum in the world. Hence, sinful colonial relations do not merely define

---

[12] Cf. (Schwartz 2015, p. 21).
[13] For more recent example, consult the reflections of Anathea Butler and others on a similarly pernicious mode of colonial disaster apocalyptic in the wake of the 2010 Haiti Earthquake in (Recla 2010). Apocalyptic theologies played a deep structural role in the colonial imagination. See the acute analysis in (Winn and Yong 2014).

the *effects* of climate catastrophe, they are its *causal* forces, the disaster before disaster. The sinful tide of Spanish colonialism generates destructive Caribbean hurricanes, as witnessed to by the indigenous tradition corroborated by Las Casas.

Showcasing theological meteorology's entanglements in modern/colonial fields of struggle, these disaster discourses disclose discernment's concretization. They exhibit claims about how God is actively involved in the world, claims which themselves presume a connection to ethical and political action—for example, action to suppress challenges to colonial terms of order (example one) and actions to overthrow that order (example two, three, and four). In so doing, they express the irreducibly concrete character of divine activity, its embeddedness within material ecologies, and that discernment concerns the languages people speak and the people who speak them. In revealing the concrete character of theological discernment, however, these examples may also evoke certain worries. For instance, can the examples of colonial and decolonial discernment be theologically differentiated? Or does speaking of God's involvement in weather catastrophes risk collapsing divine activity into political programs?

This line of questioning recalls the anxieties over what has sometimes been called political messianism, or the worry that concretely speaking of divine action as it bears on human states of affairs is a recipe for disaster. The specific notion of political messianism originated in the twentieth century with historian and theorist Jacob Talmon (Talmon 1960). In his view, binding theological claims about divine activity to political programs is fundamentally vicious and ideological, since it generates a dangerous desire for final deliverance in history. Michael Walzer influentially re-iterates this critique, arguing that such political messianism "is the great temptation of Western politics. Its source and spur is the apparent endlessness of the Exodus march" (Walzer 1985, p. 135, 138–39). Concrete discernment, according to this line of criticism, is the bad theology and bad politics that results from making differential judgments about divine activity within the confines of human states of affairs, resulting in political judgments that issue in bad faith. Lacking objectivity, it reduces theology to viciously circular and reality-obscuring ideology put in service of justifying political action. Returning to the weather examples, then, it is critical to recognize how, from this vantage, despite the differences between colonial disaster apocalyptic (example one) and the decolonial Amos (examples two and three) and Hosea (example four) discernments, all are reduced to manifestations of the same problem of concretization.[14]

This criticism expresses a paradigmatic anxiety regarding concrete discernment, and correctively implies a strategy of abstraction. If concrete discernment places theological language and speech at risk of becoming ideological, and, in equal measure, places politics at risk of becoming absolutist, then one prevailing response has been to moderate theology through abstraction and generalization. Found in various modern theological expressions, one instance of the preference for the moderating effects of abstraction may be found in Augustinian theologies that limit history after Christ of theological meaning through depleting the powers of discernment in the *saeculum*. Other examples can be seen in theological ontologies that normatively maintain that divine presence may only be generally related to the world, and therefore render unavailable gratuitous and differential identifications of divine action in history.[15] Such modes of abstraction, still, ought to be given their due: consider, in contrast to example one, wherein concrete discernment of divine activity functions as the justification of colonial repression through a providential construal of the weather, how the theological avoidance of concreteness has the benefit of undermining the grammar of violent, colonial discernments. That is to say, this mode of theology undermines all such concrete claims because of the nonobjective—which is to say, circular

---

[14] For a qualified re-iteration of the critique of political messianism in the context of black abolitionism, see (Glaude 2000, pp. 144–59).

[15] Consult (Tran 2018) for an assessment of how other established trends in contemporary theology similarly strand the task of concretization. For an example of such an ontology in the discourse of political theology, see the constructive account of divine presence without identity in (Smith 2014, esp. pp. 121–22).

and self-justifying—theological reasoning at work. Thus, this prevailing mode of abstraction addresses what it takes to be the basic problem and attendant risks of theological concretization.

Yet it is not only colonial discernment that is undermined. All four examples of theological meteorology present identical worries of ideology (lacking objectivity) on the basis of concretization. It follows that substantial distinctions between theological disaster discourses and imaginations (colonial and decolonial, apocalyptic and theodicy, Amos and Hosea) are inconsequential. All variety of material discernments about divine activity in relation to human affairs are problematically concrete and subjective in just the same way, betraying faulty theological reasoning, and, what is more, from the perspective of modern climatology, appear as so much mythology. The distinct content of discernment becomes immaterial to the overriding concern that speaking of God as intimately involved in the goings-on of the world will result in the distortion not the disclosure of reality.

At the most basic level, what philosophically determines the avoidance of concrete theological discernment is a dubious picture of how objectively speaking of God should work. The conundrum of concretization, this is to say, is predicated upon the view that discernment cannot meet the standard conditions of objectivity required by moral and political judgment. As I elaborate below, according to this view, the only permissible sorts of discernments are those that, in alignment with this narrow account of objectivity, exclude the connection between theological objectivity and human praxis. This version of objectivity is not only problematically limiting in regards to moral judgment, but it necessarily excludes concrete discernment altogether, since discernment is a language for speaking about God that is subjective, concrete, and praxis-oriented. If concrete discernment is to be recognized as more than the potential exposure of theology to the risks of political ideology and vicious circularity, it will have to be shown that this conundrum rests upon a misconstrual of the nature of judgment and objectivity. My interest, though, does not concern the nature of judgment in general; rather, I aim to articulate how an alternative picture of objectivity creates the theological conditions for discriminating between and giving preference to liberating discernments, particularly in keeping with the radical modes of naming God's apocalyptic action in history as exemplified by the Waco and Rocksprings traditions. In order to do that, what first needs to be shown is that the standard objection to concrete discernment, and the conundrum of concretization itself, depends upon a deficient view of objectivity. Turning to the work of Alice Crary, I explicate parallel resources from ethical theory for reimagining the nature and task of theological discernment.

3. Objectivity, Action, and Moral Judgment

Working in the intellectual tradition of Stanley Cavell, Cora Diamond, and Veena Das, Alice Crary's writings consider how ethical attention to language provides a distinct vantage for interrogating established views of knowledge and reimagining human life in the world.[16] Crary's specific challenge to established notions of objectivity brings into focus how theology might think differently about what it means to speak of God concretely. That challenge goes like this: *status quo* conceptions of moral judgment in contemporary ethical theory operate according to a stagnant and rigid metaphysical picture. According to this presumptive framework, no plausible account of ethics can simultaneously incorporate two basic features in our intuitive understanding of judgment. These features are, as Crary labels them, objectivity and internalism. By objectivity, Crary means how moral judgment is seen to be a matter of describing the way the world really is. Objective judgments are those that describe the world accurately and in keeping with a philosophically appropriate idea of disinterest. Adjacently, internalism names the practical connection or the internal relation between moral judgment and action (Crary 2009, p. 11). Internalist moral judgments are those which are closely related to motivation and praxis. According to this standard view that Crary means to challenge, what defines these two features of moral judgment is that they are mutually exclusive of each other. Moral judgments

---

[16] For a helpful introduction to Crary's work, see the interview by (LeNabat 2016).

cannot both be objective in assessment and oriented toward action. Modern moral philosophy is thus characterized by a certain either/or: proposals elect, in one way or another, for objectivity or internalism. Many contemporary moral realists, for example, opt for the former and abandon the latter altogether. The opposition between objectivity and internalism, Crary argues, is the governing metaphysical assumption in contemporary ethical theory. Crary writes:

> this assumption is generally taken to show that any ethical theory that tries straightforwardly to accommodate both of the above two features of our ordinary understanding of moral judgments—that is, any ethical theory that endeavors to be both *objectivist* in that it represents moral judgments as essentially in the business of answering to how things stand and also *internalist* in that it represents such judgments as internally related to action and choice—has to be rejected as untenable. (Crary 2009, p. 12)

Of particular interest is the concept of objectivity, for the idea that objectivity is opposed to praxis-oriented judgments is not limited to ethical theory but logically underwrites the conundrum of concrete discernment in theology described above. The reason that objectivity and internalism are held to be exclusive of one another has to do with how the traditional philosophical notion of objectivity is opposed to subjectivity. In this familiar scheme, a subjective property is a property for which no final or satisfactory conception can be formed beyond the perceptual or affective responses an object evokes. Additionally, what is subjective can, furthermore, be separated into two kinds, namely, the merely subjective and the problematically subjective. The former is straightforward enough: the merely subjective elicits an affective or perceptual response of any kind from a subject concerning an object, but yields nothing more, no relevant data apprehending objective reality. The latter then pertains to the kinds of properties or descriptions that an object evokes under certain circumstances—the kinds which may be situationally conducive to action. Both forms of subjectivity are excluded from objectivity. The idea here is that subjectivity tends to distort rather than disclose or display reality. Thus Crary: "if a given property stood in the sort of internal relation to sensibility or affective propensities that allowed it to be essentially practical, it would not count as properly objective. Conversely, if it had the sort of independence from human subjectivity that would distinguish it as fully objective, it would fail to be essentially practical. So here there can be no properties that are both objective and intrinsically motivational" (Crary 2009, p. 16).

Crary's contention is that the a priori exclusion of problematic subjectivity from objectivity is unwarranted and misconstrues—indeed *narrows*—the nature of ethical life. Instead, a more adequate, wider conception of objectivity should include problematic subjectivity, since, for Crary, what falls under the heading of problematic subjectivity is in reality the moral sensibilities and forms of life to which moral judgment cohesively belongs. In order to make room for this account of objectivity (and the implied parallel goods it provides for theological discernment), the standard notion of objectivity will need to be dislodged. Central to the standard, narrow notion of objectivity is a certain hostility to the idea that moral judgments themselves belong to moral sensibility. The hostility is due to the fact that this understanding is taken to "encod[e] a form of *circularity*" (Crary 2009, p. 32). By locating moral judgments within the context of moral sensibility, in other words, one becomes caught in a net of circular reasoning. And circularity assumes the problems of problematic subjectivity. According to the traditional philosophical notion of objectivity, then, moral judgment should be ideally construed in a non-circular fashion. Hence, the hostility to circularity, which impinges of the apparently ideal kind of moral judgment.

A significant way that this hostility to circularity gets worked out, according to Crary, is through an "abstraction requirement". This idea maintains that "the regularities constitutive of a sound conceptual practice must transcend the practice in the sense of being discernible independently of any subjective responses characteristic of us as participants in it" (Crary 2009, p. 21). The idea of an abstraction requirement, for certain ethical theorists, is that by defining objectivity exclusive of the subjective responses to conceptual practices, they embed a critical tool for breaking out of the circularity. Notice that, on this account, the objective meaning of a conceptual practice is peculiarly shifted to, and consequently defined by, the elements that exceed a practice, but not by the practice itself. This is the logic of abstraction, which it is hoped, provides a way to conceptualize moral judgment that is not reducible to circular reasoning. Hence, Crary:

> An ideally non-circular form of discourse would be suitably abstract insofar as, within it, applications of concepts would be beholden to standards that have content apart from the beliefs the pertinent mode of discourse embodies and that can accordingly be conceived as accessible independently of any practical sensitivities that we acquire in arriving at those beliefs. (Crary 2009, p. 33)

Yet the rigidity of the abstract requirement is a demand, Crary argues, that an ordinary account of moral judgment simply cannot resource, and for good reason. Here Crary points to an argument by Wittgenstein, namely, that concepts are not tools for picking out data independent of practice, but that concepts "are resources for thinking about aspects of the world to which our eyes are only open insofar as we develop certain practical sensitivities" (Crary 2009, p. 25). The import integrating concept and practice, for Crary, is that it conditions a reconsideration of objectivity, one in which we discover that, far from an obstructionist or distorting projection of unreality, subjectivity "figures in the best, objectively most accurate account of how things are and, further, that the person who lacks the subjective endowments that would allow her to recognize them is missing something" (Crary 2009, p. 28). The insight is that, instead of guaranteeing the most accurate representation of the world, the abstract requirement runs the risk of unnecessarily excluding essential features of what makes the world livable. In turn, if we reject the idea of an abstract requirement for certifying objectivity, we also reject the idea that non-circular discourse is the ideal or even preferable picture of what counts as philosophical objectivity. The upshot then is the expansion of objectivity inclusive of subjective responses (both mere and problematic subjectivity), an account capable of assessing the full context of moral judgment as belonging to moral sensibilities and forms of life, and one which figures moral judgments as internal to human action.

What does ethics look like if you drop the abstract requirement? As Crary elaborates in more recent work, it looks like a new way of imagining the ethical world, or more precisely, reimagining what counts as the ethical world, what states of affair ethically matter. A wider objectivity, one open to subjective responses, entails jettisoning "a picture of the world as somehow available to thought in an absolutely unmediated manner or, in other words, in a manner not informed by the sorts of subjective responses characteristic of us as participants in particular linguistic practices" (Crary 2016, p. 55). This means that what is objective must include what it has traditionally excluded, for the express reason that "our subjective responses contribute internally to our ability to grasp features of the world", and thus "bring the world into focus" (Crary 2016, p. 55). When it comes to assessing human action, we then ask different kinds of questions that focus on responses to the contextual circumstances. Crary writes, when "assessing an individual action ... [i]t is natural to interpret this as a question about appropriate responsiveness to—practical and hence moral—values encoded in relevant circumstance" (Crary 2016, p. 88). It follows, for Crary, that this kind of assessment is not something other than an assessment of objective moral values.

The allure of this picture of moral judgment is that, freed from the strictures of the abstract requirement of traditional philosophical accounts of objectivity, it contains an unanticipated element; or better, it entails that our moral imaginations of the world are defined by a irreducible *openness* that is as available to redefinition as subjective responses to worldly circumstances are diverse. Considering the moral lives of humans and other animals, Crary observes that "there can be no question of limiting the imaginative exercise that we accordingly face by specifying ahead of time which aspects of human beings' or animals' lives are of interest. For we cannot exclude the possibility that, once we have refined our conception of what matters in these lives, our understanding of them will shift, revealing that characteristics that once struck us as unimportant are in fact morally salient" (Crary 2016, p. 91). In short, this wider objectivity refashions ethics without the guarantees of abstraction, wherein evaluations of the world are not opposed to but imbricated with languages of praxis and commitment.

4. Concrete Objectivity and the Recovery of Liberating Discernment

Concretizations of divine activity naming God's liberating presence (for example, discernments of tornado disasters as signs of the divine interruption of ongoing racial regimes) threaten a certain notion of theological objectivity and so then risk reducing theology to political ideology. As described above, the critique of political messianism and correspondent move to abstraction charts one way to avoid this risk, since concrete discernment fails to render language regarding divine activity independent of the problematically circular reasoning of discerning subjects. The implicit criterion of this criticism is that the authentication of theological discernment, like moral judgment, involves its capacity to transcend the contextual locale of its genesis. This effectively amounts to the imposition of an analogous abstraction requirement on theological discernment. Ideal discernment, by this requirement, is certified to the extent that it is non-circular and abstracted from concrete situations where life and death and liberation are at stake. Returning to the theological meteorology examples, then, it is important to reiterate that they are similarly problematized as ideological precisely because they fail to meet the abstraction requirement for objectivity. Whether God's apocalyptic activity may be legitimately ascribed to the tempests and whirlwinds that aided in colonial domination or counteractively conjured freedom dreams of other worlds and new creation, or, moreover, whether the sources, languages, and sensibilities that inspired such competing discernments are worth theological attention are questions negated by design, in accordance with the abstraction requirement. Identifying the concrete with the ideological renders questions of source, language, and discernment inconsequential of concretization and ideology.

If, however, objectivity is not opposed to internalism, which is to say, if concretization does not violate but rather enables discerning the otherness of God, then the conundrum of concretization is suspended. The critical importance of Crary's argument lies in how her diagnosis and reframing of objectivity implies a parallel realignment of discernment. This is the insight that Crary foregrounds for theological purposes: far from being a threat to the integrity of God, the concretization of language is the very means of witnessing it. That concepts are not rigid epistemological credentials for purifying thought, but resources for thinking about the world "to which our eyes are only open", as Crary contends, unseats the worry over circularity which maintains objectivity is the exclusion of concretization. Following this insight, formal circularity, we are led to conclude, is not itself at issue in considering better and worse accounts of discernment. The fact that the examples of theological meteorology are circular is not necessarily problematic. No longer is the internal, organic relation of concrete discernment to praxis a reason to believe that discernment, of necessity, is any less objective. We can then say that the problem with the abstraction requirement is that it renders formal (circular versus non-circular) what is, in fact, a material—or better—*pneumatological* question, namely, the question of engaging in God's line of action through the Holy Spirit, who is the power of God in people's struggles for liberation (Melano Couch 1991, p. 448).

A material approach to interpreting the theological disaster discourses with which this essay began would be one that eschews the preoccupation with whether claims about God's revealed activity in the world are sufficiently abstract, as though an objective description of God is one that transcends the context in which God is encountered. Abstract objectivity disciplines a way of speaking of God that refuses to take seriously language that is not immediately generalizable beyond the situation in which God acts. This subverts languages that responsively speak of God as God is encountered within the world. By contrast, Crary's intervention in ethical theory aids in reconceptualizing theological objectivity as, necessarily, concrete objectivity. Concrete objectivity helps to reframe the conundrum of concretization not as a problem for discernment but as a misconception generated by a failed picture of theological reasoning that excuses theological language from commitment, praxis, and engagement in the world—so advancing abstract languages inattentive to the Spirit. We must ask why generalizing theological languages which transcend the life, strivings, and struggles of discerning subjects and communities should be given priority over idiomatic languages. This priority brackets the idea of what counts as theologically objective to the exclusion of language that, for theologies of liberation, centralizes the speech, prayers, *corridos*, blues, poems, and stories of the least and the last as the condition for truthfully and apocalyptically speaking of God. If God's righteousness is disclosed in the liberation of the poor, the eschatological reversal and undoing of racist and colonial regimes, and the justification of the oppressed, to be apart from the company of the poor and to fail to be accountable to their languages of God amounts to finding oneself "excluded from the possibility of hearing and obeying God's Word of liberation" (Cone 1985, p. 125).

Still, it is important to maintain the distinction between moral judgment and theological discernment at this juncture. We might say that this distinction amounts to different outcomes regarding the meaning of concretization: Crary's project concerning judgment is a constructive account of ethical life grounded in the natural world; discernment is alternately grounded in the apocalyptic disclosures of the Holy Spirit who graciously enlivens and emancipates but is not encoded within the natural world. This means, in part, that where Crary emphasizes that objective moral values are embedded within, and therefore perceptively available to, contingent circumstances, discernment is language accountable to the otherness of God, and may be thought of as speech responding to the objective irruption of values which occurs as God acts to liberate creaturely life within contingent enclosures of sin. To speak of the otherness of God here, however, is nothing other than the affirmation that theological objectivity is unavailable apart from a form of life shared with others similarly struggling for freedom. This shift then does not entail returning to an abstract objectivity or abstract revelation that takes leave of creaturely contingency. Rather, it insists that the distinction between God and world only truly obtains in concrete theological discernment, in recognition of the fact that discernment is an apocalyptic mode of speech defined by God's differential identification with the crucified peoples, those whom Gustavo Gutiérrez calls the "scourged Christs" of the earth (Gutiérrez [1995] 2003, pp. 45–66). Thus, as Melano Couch argues, it is only through joining in Christ's presence with crucified peoples that one can speak of God's salvation, since this is "where God's liberating action takes place" (Melano Couch 1991, p. 449).

This alternative availed by Crary is not a rejection of objectivity but a concrete conception accountable to the languages of discerning communities, in particular the languages of the oppressed. A parallel notion of discernment entails an attunement to subjective, contextual, and circumstantial realities as vitally relevant to objectively naming the revelation of God's action in history. It would include a range of considerations as theologically vital: theological accounts of ecological conditions (like, for example, the weather), invocations of scripture, the sensibilities and storytelling traditions of discerning communities, their structural location(s) in relation to colonial powers, and traditions of resistance.

However, concretization is not, on its own, sufficient for theologies of liberation. The discernment of the first example of theological meteorology in the wake of the Lares uprising relates how colonial and imperial discernment also take radically concrete shape. The concretization of theological discernment, accordingly, is simply the first task over and against theological abstraction. Having disarmed the abstraction requirement, concrete languages need to be differentiated according to the criterion of liberation, between, in this case, the colonial disaster apocalyptic of Spanish administrators according to the first example, and the decolonial Amos and Hosea modes of discernment embodied by the other three examples. It is for this reason that this essay has insisted, in keeping with the writings of liberation theologians like Beatriz Melano Couch and James Cone, that concretization must be essentially related to the struggle of crucified people for freedom. This christological criterion enables the recovery of naming God's activity in history with radical concreteness and additionally provokes visions of new creation for history's crucified and scourged Christs. Liberating discernment then must not merely include concrete language and descriptions regarding divine activity but must be disciplined through immersion in the life and words of the crucified. That liberating discernment prioritizes the emancipation of the least and last discloses its non-neutrality and one-sidedness. Yet this does not discount its objectivity. To the contrary, what Melano Couch called the "hermeneutics of engagement" is the precondition of objectivity, that is, the perspective that begins with reality as it is apprehended through the experience, suffering, and language of the oppressed is the essential standpoint for objectively bringing God's liberating activity into focus (Melano Couch 1976, pp. 305–6). Language committed to the liberation of the oppressed, accordingly, may not be *a priori* dismissed as problematically subjective or potentially ideological, for the express reason that objective language includes commitment. Moreover, liberating discernment's distinct christological commitment marks the essential position for objectively speaking about divine agency in the world.

One may worry that a consequence of this one-sided construal of discerning divine activity is that it tends toward absolutizing the theological claims, speech, and language expressed by and with crucified peoples. What may be said here, as a provisional response to this concern, is that the christological criterion of concrete discernment does not mean that such discernments of the crucified—like, for example, those apocalyptic articulations regarding catastrophic weather events in Rocksprings and Waco—issue in the final word on God's action in history. This idea would reduce the search for liberating concreteness to yet another search for certainty and finality. Rather, discernment always and everywhere bears the vulnerabilities proper to a "theology of restlessness", to borrow Manas Buthelezi's eloquent expression (Buthelezi 1978, p. 70). Far from conveying the end of discernment, the christological criterion locates the position or standpoint from which objective theological speech must begin. To return to Melano Couch's baptismal language from this essay's introduction, "immersion in concrete struggle" for the life and liberation of the scourged Christs of the earth does not guarantee the totality or finality of discernment; instead, as baptism, concrete struggle signals the indispensable point of departure for engaging in objective theological discernment.

The articulation of conditions that make for a recovery of concrete theological discernment and, in turn, *liberating* discernment has been the primary objectives of this essay. If objectivity with respect to speaking of divine activity in history is not opposed to but depends upon concretization, then theological discernment may be disarticulated from the conundrum of concretization and tied to the life and words of history's crucified people. Naming God's activity in history entails at once carefully discerning concrete signs of divine presence in the world and the correspondent militant action of faith. On the comparison to Crary's theory of moral judgment, theological discernment is both objective and praxis-directed, since it witnesses to divine activity and prompts engagement in it. What is critical about the discernments of God in the weather, as modeled in the decolonial Amos and Hosea patterns above, is the liberating activity of God to which these languages of the oppressed bear witness and the faithful action towards which they point. To speak of God concretely is not to speak of God with certainty or absoluteness. Discernment remains restless and unsettled, without guarantees. Yet it is language that seeks to reverse the present terms of order by first listening to the voices and languages of minoritized and oppressed peoples fighting for freedom for the purpose of naming how God is acting for liberation from enclosures and bonds of sin. It is thus a concrete language responsible to the God encountered in oppressed communities, belonging to what Melano Couch also describes as a "theology on the march", that is, to the ongoing labors of responding to God's liberating activity (Melano Couch 1976, p. 307). Liberating discernment so construed is accountable to the critical question Cone asks regarding all theological speech: "If God is the God of the poor who is liberating from bondage, how else can we speak correctly about this God unless our language arises out of the community where God's presence is found?" (Cone 1985, p. 124).

Funding: This research received no external funding.

Acknowledgments: The author would like to thank the direction of Jonathan Tran, critical responses from two reviewers, and commentary from Ry Siggelkow, Thomas Breedlove, and Matthew Harris.

Conflicts of Interest: The author declares no conflict of interest.

References

Anderson, Katharine. 2005. *Predicting the Weather: Victorians and the Science of Meteorology*. Chicago: University of Chicago Press.

Beckford, George L. 1999. *Persistent Poverty: Underdevelopment in Plantation Economies of the Third World*. Kingston: The University of the West Indies Press. First published 1972.
Buthelezi, Manas. 1978. Toward Indigenous Theology in South Africa. In *The Emergent Gospel: Theology from the Underside of History*. Edited by Sergio Torres and Virginia Fabella. Maryknoll: Orbis Books, pp. 56–75.
Carrigan, William D. 2004. *The Making of a Lynching Culture: Violence and Vigilantism in Central Texas, 1836–1916*. Urbana: University of Illinois Press.
Cone, James. 1985. Theology as the Expression of God's Liberating Activity. In *The Vocation of the Theologian*. Edited by Theodore W. Jennings Jr. Philadelphia: Fortress Press, pp. 120–34.
Cone, James. 2013. *The Cross and the Lynching Tree*. Maryknoll: Orbis Books.
Crary, Alice. 2009. *Beyond Moral Judgment*. Cambridge: Harvard University Press.
Crary, Alice. 2016. *Inside Ethics: On the Demands of Moral Thought*. Cambridge: Harvard University Press.
Dussel, Enrique. 1979. Discernment: A Question of Orthodoxy or Orthopraxis. In *Discernment of the Spirit and of Spirits (Concilium)*. Edited by Casiano Floristán and Christian Duquoc. Translated by Paul Burns. New York: Seabury Press, pp. 47–60.
Ellacuría, Ignacio. 2013. The Crucified People: An Essay in Historical Soteriology. In *Ignacio Ellacuría: Essays on History, Liberation, and Salvation*. Translated by Phillip Berryman and Robert R. Barr. Edited by Michael E. Lee. Maryknoll: Orbis Books, pp. 208–10. First published 1978.
Glaude, Eddie S., Jr. 2000. *Exodus! Religion, Race, and Nation in Early Nineteenth-Century Black America*. Chicago: University of Chicago Press.
Golinski, Jan. 2007. *British Weather and the Climate of Enlightenment*. Chicago: University of Chicago Press.
Gutiérrez, Gustavo. 2003. *Las Casas: In Search of the Poor of Jesus Christ*. Translated by Robert R. Barr. Eugene: Wipf and Stock. First published 1995.
Jankovic, Vladimir. 2001. *Reading the Skies: A Cultural History of English Weather, 1650–1820*. Chicago: University of Chicago Press.
Kirk-Duggan, Cheryl A., ed. 2006. *The Sky Is Crying: Race, Class, and Natural Disaster*. Nashville: Abingdon Press.
Las Casas, Bartolomé de. 1968. *Apologética Historia Sumaria*. Edited by Edmundo O'Gorman. Mexico City: Universidad Nacional Autónoma de México.
Latour, Bruno. 1993. *We Have Never Been Modern*. Translated by Catherine Porter. Cambridge: Harvard University Press.
Lehmann, Paul L. 1975. Black Theology and "Christian" Theology. *Union Seminary Quarterly Review* 31: 31–57.
LeNabat, Marianne. 2016. Alice Crary on Her Newest Book, Inside Ethics. *Social Research Matters*, September 7. Available online: http://socialresearchmatters.org/2071-2/ (accessed on 30 August 2019).
Luft, Rachel E. 2009. Beyond Disaster Exceptionalism: Social Movement Developments in New Orleans after Hurricane Katrina. *American Quarterly* 61: 499–527.
Martinez, Monica Muñoz. 2018. *The Injustice Never Leaves You: Anti-Mexican Violence in Texas*. Cambridge: Harvard University Press.
Melano Couch, Beatriz. 1976. Statement by Beatriz Melano Couch. In *Theology in the Americas*. Edited by Sergio Torres and John Eagleson. Maryknoll: Orbis Books, pp. 304–8.
Melano Couch, Beatriz. 1991. Theological Perspectives from the Point of View of the Oppressed. *Ecumenical Review* 43: 443–50. [CrossRef]
Recla, Matt. 2010. Biblical Disaster in Haiti: Pat Robertson and the Curse of Unyielding Ignorance. *Religion Dispatches*, January 17. Available online: http://religiondispatches.org/biblical-disaster-in-haiti-pat-robertson-and-the-curse-of-unyielding-ignorance/ (accessed on 23 August 2019).
Robinson, Cedric J. 2007. *Forgeries of Memory and Meaning: Blacks and the Regimes of Race in American Theater and Film before World War II*. Chapel Hill: University of North Carolina Press.
Schwartz, Stuart B. 2015. *Sea of Storms: A History of Hurricanes in the Greater Caribbean from Columbus to Katrina*. Princeton: Princeton University Press.
Siggelkow, Ry O. 2018. Ernst Käsemann and the Specter of Apocalyptic. *Theology Today* 75: 37–50. [CrossRef]
Smith, Ted A. 2014. *Weird John Brown: Divine Violence and the Limits of Ethics*. Stanford: Stanford University Press.
Talmon, Jacob L. 1960. *Political Messianism: The Romantic Phase*. London: Secker and Warburg.
Tran, Jonathan. 2018. Assessing Augustinian Democrats. *Journal of Religious Ethics* 46: 521–47. [CrossRef]
Wallerstein, Immanuel. 2011. *The Modern World-System I: Capitalist Agriculture and the Origins of the European World-Economy in the Sixteenth Century*. Berkley: University of California Press. First published 1974.

Walzer, Michael. 1985. *Exodus and Revolution*. New York: Basic Books.
Williamson, Fiona. 2015. Weathering the Empire: Meteorological Research in the Early British Straits Settlements. *British Journal for the History of Science* 48: 475–92. [CrossRef]
Winn, Christian T. Collins, and Amos Yong. 2014. The Apocalypse of Colonialism: Notes toward a Postcolonial Eschatology. In *Evangelical Postcolonial Conversations: Global Awakenings in Theology and Praxis*. Edited by Kay Higuera Smith, Jayachitra Lalith and L. Daniel Hawk. Downers Grove: InterVarsity Press, pp. 139–51.
Winters, Joseph R. 2019. The Religion of Black Power. *Religion and American Culture: A Journal of Interpretation* 29: 163–67.
Woods, Clyde A. 2017. *Development Drowned and Reborn: The Blues and Bourbon Restorations in Post-Katrina New Orleans*. Edited by Jordan T. Camp and Laura Pulido. Athens: University of Georgia Press.

© 2019 by the author. Licensee MDPI, Basel, Switzerland. This article is an open access article distributed under the terms and conditions of the Creative Commons Attribution (CC BY) license (http://creativecommons.org/licenses/by/4.0/).

Article

Challenge of Doing Catholic Ethics in a Pluralistic Context

Shaji George Kochuthara

Department of Moral Theology, Faculty of Theology, Dharmaram Vidya Kshetram, Bangalore 560029, India; kochuthshaji@gmail.com

Received: 24 October 2019; Accepted: 24 December 2019; Published: 29 December 2019

Abstract: The article discusses the possibility of doing Catholic ethics in a religiously and culturally pluralistic context. Beginning with the possibility of pluralistic approach in Catholic ethics, the article refers to the Indian context as an example for the discussion. Particularly it takes two issues—ecological ethics and sexual ethics—to reflect on the need and possibility of doing Catholic ethics in a pluralistic context. Although the arguments here may be applicable to other contexts of pluralism, the article mainly points out examples from the Indian contexts. The discussion here is basically from a Catholic perspective, namely, why Catholics should be open to different sources and approaches in ethics, and how they can work together with others in identifying common grounds for ethics. Although a few guidelines for constructing a pluralistic ethics are indicated, the attempt is not to propose a framework for such an ethics, but mainly to show the need and possibility of such an ethics.

Keywords: catholic ethics; hindu ethics; natural law; human rights; culture; inculturation; interculturation

---

1. Introduction: Plurality—A Reality of Life

Pluralism is a reality of life today. Pluralism "refers to "a situation in which a variety of viewpoints, explanations or perspectives are offered as accounting for the same reality" (Henn 1987, p. 770). Pluralism extends to various realms—religious, cultural, philosophical, social, ethnic, linguistic, and so on. In fact, pluralism existed always, but today we are more intensely aware of pluralism and its all-encompassing nature. Even a few decades back, the West was not considered basically pluralistic. Although various religions and cultures had their presence in the West, they were not predominant in the society as a whole; Christianity was considered the religion of the West. With globalization and drastic migration, this has changed very fast in recent decades. The number of people in the West belonging to other religions and cultures and ethnic groups is no more insignificant. Many of these religions have organized networks, places of worship, and organizations in many Western countries. Moreover, we acknowledge that pluralism will remain as a reality of life. An ever-increasing pluralism is inevitable and irreversible. "Today we are aware of the sources of pluralism: the mystery of God, the complexity of reality, infinite possibility and diversity of the human subject, limitations and historicity of human points of view and the differences in the objective world or context" (Pathil 2014, p. 326). The world today witnesses to diverse religious, theological, philosophical, ethical, ideological, and cultural systems and theories and their corresponding various practices (Pathil 2014, p. 327). However, our plural world is not contradictory, but complementary, mutually challenging, and enriching (Tracy 1975). At the same time, "Pluralism does not mean relativism or religious indifferentism or self-sufficiency, as pluralism has to go hand in hand with unity, the centripetal force of this universe" (Pathil 2014, p. 327). But, instead of an 'either-or' concept, pluralism stands for 'both-and'.

Beginning with the possibility of pluralistic approach in Catholic ethics, I shall refer to the Indian context as an example for our discussion. Although the arguments here may be applicable to other contexts of pluralism, I shall mainly point out examples from the Indian contexts. We shall particularly take two issues—ecological ethics and sexuality—to reflect on the need and possibility of doing Catholic ethics in a pluralistic context. Our discussion here is basically from a Catholic perspective, namely, why as Catholics we should be open to different sources and approaches in ethics, and how we can work together with others in identifying common grounds for ethics. Although we attempt to draw some conclusions and guiding principles for developing a pluralistic approach to ethics, within the limited scope of this article, we do not propose a new theory of pluralistic approach to ethics, but shall focus more on the possibility and need of developing such an approach.

2. Pluralistic Context of India

India is a land of religious pluralism. For example, according to 2011 census, in India, Christianity is a small minority with 2.3%; Hindus are 79.8%, Muslims are 14.23%, and Sikhs are 1.72%. Besides this, though small in number, Buddhism, Jainism, and many other religions continue to exert great influence in the Indian society (Census of India 2011a). Though in our discussions, we shall consider mainly religious pluralism in India, we cannot ignore other aspects of pluralism. In India there is a confluence of various cultures—Dravidic, Aryan, Subaltern, Tribal, etc. Moreover, each state or region can be said to have different culture or even cultures. There are various races—six main races with sub-races. There are also many languages—there are 22 official languages and thousands of dialects (Census of India 2011b). All these add to the complexity of the pluralistic nature of India. Besides this, there is a revival of Hinduism, which has also taken fundamentalist trends as well. Although prohibited by law, to a great extent the society continues to be hierarchical based on castes and sub-castes. In fact, with the prominence that right-wing groups have gained in Indian politics and society, there is an attempt to revive caste system, though not officially, as indicated by a sharp increase in the number of attacks on lower castes by higher castes. Furthermore, we have to consider the changing lifestyle influenced by globalization and neo-liberal economy. Economic condition also varies. Though India is already considered one of the economic powers of the world, even according to the most optimistic statistics, there are at least 350 million people living under the poverty line.

Developments in civil law highlight another aspect of the complexities in moral matters. Interventions by the court or legal system in ethical matters have been on the increase. This is based on the constitution of the country, irrespective of religious affiliation, considering all citizens equal, having equal rights and responsibilities. For example, on 22 August 2017, the Supreme Court of India declared unconstitutional the Islamic practice of Triple Talaq (Triple Talaq in India n.d.; The Guardian 2019). The Supreme Court verdict decriminalising homosexuality was also widely discussed. Similarly, the court verdict on LGBT/Transgender (Plathottam 2009), Pre-marital sex (Times of India 2010), extra-marital sex (Vaidyanathan 2018; Singh 2018), etc., raised mixed responses. In the past, such matters would be left to the discretion of the religions, as belonging to religious ethics. Or, take the case of court ruling permitting entry of young women into the Sabarimala temple (Economic Times 2018). The court is considering a case on Muslim women's entry into mosques, on the ground of equal rights of women. This is only one of the dilemmas that we face in ethical consideration today, namely, where the constitutional or legal morality and religious morality may come in conflict, or where they may differ. On the other hand, morality may differ according to religion and culture. This we have experienced always. However, this difference is sharply felt today, and sometimes they lead to conflicts. In such situations, how can we dialogue with others and live in harmony and peace?

3. Possibility of Pluralistic Approach in Ethics

The 20th century marked a greater awareness from the part of the Church of pluralism, the relative nature of the cultural and conceptual frames in which faith was expressed and, hence, a greater openness towards other cultures and philosophical traditions. This can be noticed in the Second Vatican Council documents, especially in *Nostra Aetate* and in the subsequent attitude of the Church towards other cultures and philosophical traditions, making interreligious dialogue and inculturation one of the major themes of theological discussions.

On the one hand, we say that Christianity from the beginning attempted to inculturate its message, to make the Gospel intelligible to the peoples imparting it through their languages and conceptual frameworks and dialoguing with their cultures and beliefs, accepting the presence of truth in them. On the other hand, attempts on the opposite direction also can be seen and in certain periods of history, for example, judging other cultures and religions as the work of the devil and considering Christianity as the sole depository of truth and salvation. Evidently, today we have come far from such negative and judgmental attitudes. However, hesitations, apprehensions, and precautions surround inculturation and, hence, in spite of positive efforts, determined and definite steps are yet to be taken. There is also resistance towards inculturation, not only from the Western Church, but also from the Asian and African Churches. Yet, others point out that even the term "inculturation" has an implication of superiority and domination and, hence, we should think in terms of inter-culturation (Chackalackal 2016, pp. 400–2). Similarly, many observe that together with the age-old traditional cultures, the new post-modern culture of globalization is also to be taken into account for inculturation; that is, inculturation cannot be limited to the cultural heritage of the past, but should be sensitive to the changed and changing cultural patterns (Painadath 2016, pp. 467–8). In spite of a variety of opinions, innumerable apprehensions, and lack of clarity of the precise steps to be taken, there is a growing awareness of the need of a more open, sincere, and profound dialogue with different religious and cultural traditions.

At the same time, we can also notice trends in the opposite direction, namely, strengthening of fundamentalist ideas within the Catholic Church itself. Such trends are visible in other religions as well. Furthermore, in spite of a greater openness to dialogue with various religious and cultural traditions, when it comes to ethics, the scenario looks different. Dialogue in ethics and openness to different ways of approaching ethics or ethical issues have not been much visible much in Christian ethics. Christian response to ethical matters/issues has been rather rigid and monolithic. Uniformity of thinking and practice in ethical matters have been the Christian response, based on the argument that they are clear to all people of good will, that they are proved by revelation and reason. That is, only Catholic understanding was considered correct, and it was taken for granted. Hence, the question is pertinent: Is pluralism possible in Catholic ethics? Can Catholic ethics accept pluralistic approaches? Can ethical norms different from the Catholic be considered salvific? Though much progress has not been made in pluralistic ethics, we can find that Catholic tradition offers various possibilities of developing pluralistic approaches in ethics.

3.1. Nostra Aetate and Subsequent Documents of the Church

As mentioned above, from *Nostra Aetate* we find a definite change in the Church's approach to other religions. Acknowledging that the Catholic Church "rejects nothing of what is true and holy in these religions" and that the Church has a "high regard for the manner of life and conduct" of these religions, the Council urges the members of the Church to enter into dialogue with other religions. Moreover, the Council urges Christians to "acknowledge, preserve and encourage the spiritual and *moral* truths found among non-Christians, also their social life and culture" (Vatican II 1965, para. 2). We cannot consider spiritual and moral life as two compartments. By acknowledging the spiritual value of other religions, the Council is also acknowledging the value of their moral wisdom and practice, though there can be differences. This openness in dialogue is continued in the subsequent documents of the Church. For example, John Paul II's *Fides et Ratio*, particularly article 72, explicitly speaks about the "new tasks of inculturation." The Pope speaks in detail of the "duty" of Christians in India "to draw from this rich heritage the elements compatible with their faith, in order to enrich Christian thought" (John Paul II 1998, para. 72). Though the Pope delineates certain criteria for the task of inculturation, the focus is not on precautions to be taken, but on the openness to other cultural and philosophical traditions. The Pope also clearly states that what is said about India is true regarding the great traditions of China, Japan, other Asian countries. and Africa (John Paul II 1998, para. 72).

Another example is the Synod of Bishops for Asia and particularly its final message: "We gladly acknowledge the spiritual values of the great religions of Asia such as Hinduism, Buddhism, Judaism, Islam ... We esteem the ethical values in the customs and practices found in the teachings of the great philosophers of Asia, which promote natural virtues and pious devotion to ancestors. We also respect the beliefs and religious practices of indigenous/tribal people, whose reverence for all creation manifests their closeness to the Creator" (UCA.News 1998).

For a long time, the Federation of Asian Bishops' Conferences (FABC) has focused on triple dialogue, considering the three main Asian realities of life: Dialogue with the vibrant religious traditions, ancient cultures, and teeming millions of Asian poor (Eilers 1997, p. 2).

3.2. Natural Law Tradition

Natural law tradition has been one of the major foundations of Catholic ethics. According to the concept of natural law, human beings can understand moral norms through the use of reason. This points to the God-given capacity that all human beings possess, irrespective of religious affiliation. That is, there is no contradiction between faith and reason, since reason itself is understood as the supreme gift of God. In the West, the origin of the natural law concept can be traced back to the Greek philosophical tradition. The Christian Fathers and theologians who made use of Greek philosophy to expound Christian faith, made use of the natural law concept as well. Thomas Aquinas developed this concept further, giving a solid foundation to the natural law concept in the Christian tradition (Thomas Aquinas 1947, pp. 90–108). In recent decades, there have been attempts to make use of the natural law concept to think about common foundations for ethics, and to promote interreligious and intercultural communication and consensus on ethical norms and issues. Following a series of interreligious and intercultural discussions on natural law in various continents, initiated by the Congregation for the Doctrine of the Faith, the International Theological Commission has published a document, *In Search of a Universal Ethic: A New Look at the Natural Law* (2009), which discusses in detail how the wisdom traditions and religions, though they may vary considerably, testify to the patrimony of moral values. At the very outset, the document shows the need for thinking together about common ethical standards:

"Are there objective moral values which can unite human beings and bring them peace and happiness? What are they? How are they discerned? How can they be put into action in the lives of persons and communities? These perennial questions concerning good and evil are today more urgent than ever, insofar as people have become more aware of forming one single world community. The great problems that arise for human beings today have an international, worldwide dimension, inasmuch as advances in communications technology have given rise to closer interaction among individuals, societies and cultures" (International Theological Commission 2009, para. 1).

The document acknowledges that in "diverse cultures, people have progressively elaborated and developed traditions of wisdom in which they express and transmit their vision of the world"; these wisdom traditions, which are often of a religious nature, convey an experience of what favors and what hinders the full blossoming of personal life and the smooth running of social life; they are "cultural capital" available "in the search for a common wisdom necessary for responding to contemporary ethical challenges." It is also acknowledged that these traditions reflect the divine wisdom (International Theological Commission 2009, para. 12).

In Search of a Global Ethic delineates the ethical traditions and contributions of various religions: In the Hindu traditions, the cosmos and human societies are regulated by *dharma*, an order or fundamental law, which one must respect in order not to cause serious imbalances. *Dharma* defines the socio-religious obligations of humans; good and bad actions and their consequences; the importance of disinterested action for the benefit of others; the importance of non-violence (*ahimsā*). It is also pertinent to note how *In Search of a Universal Ethic* cites an equivalent principle of the golden rule:

"I will tell you what is the essence of the greatest good of the human being. The man who practices the religion (*dharma*) of do no harm to anyone without exception (*ahimsā*) acquires the greatest good.

This man is the master of the three passions: cupidity, anger and avarice, and renouncing them in relation to all that exists, acquires success. ... This man who considers all creatures like 'himself' and treats them as his own 'self', laying down the punishing rod and dominating his anger completely, assures for himself the attainment of happiness. ... One will not do to another what one considers harmful to oneself. This, in brief, is the rule of virtue. ... In refusing and in giving, in abundance and in misery, in the agreeable and the disagreeable, one will judge all the consequences by considering one's own 'self'" (International Theological Commission 2009, para. 13).[1] "Several precepts of the Hindu tradition can be placed in parallel with the requirements of the Decalogue" (International Theological Commission 2009, para. 13).[2]

Following this, *In Search of a Universal Ethic* elaborates upon the noble truths in Buddhism and the five precepts and states: "The profound altruism of the Buddhist tradition, which is expressed in a resolute attitude of non-violence, amicable benevolence and compassion, thus agrees with the golden rule" (International Theological Commission 2009, para. 14). Islamic understanding also facilitates seeking common ground for ethics: "The Islamic ethic is, therefore, fundamentally a morality of obedience. To do good is to obey the commandments; to do evil is to disobey them" (International Theological Commission 2009, para. 17).

Here, our main concern is not to describe common teachings of various religions; rather, we shall point out the possibility of developing common ethical standards utilizing the natural law tradition, which has been so important in the Catholic tradition. Here, we have to also remember what many contemporary ethicists have often pointed out, namely, natural law is cultural, historical, experiential, proportional, and contextual (Gula 1989, pp. 242–6). This provides the possibility of variety and openness to different approaches. Moreover, *Amoris Laetitia*, Post-Synodal Apostolic Letter on the Joy of Love by Pope Francis, highlights an important aspect in the natural law theory of Thomas Aquinas:

"'Although there is necessity in the general principles, the more we descend to matters of detail, the more frequently we encounter defects ... In matters of action, truth or practical rectitude is not the same for all, as to matters of detail, but only as to the general principles; and where there is the same rectitude in matters of detail, it is not equally known to all ... The principle will be found to fail, according as we descend further into detail' (Thomas Aquinas 1947, q. 94, art. 4). It is true that general rules set forth a good which can never be disregarded or neglected, but in their formulation they cannot provide absolutely for all particular situations" (Francis 2016, para. 304). This again underlines the possibility of different approaches and variety of applications in ethical issues. In other words, based on the same natural law thinking, different religions and cultures may arrive at different conclusions, which are valid. This does not mean that all conclusions are equally correct. Everyone has the responsibility of reflecting on one's own conclusions through dialogue and to correct what is needed, and to seek possibilities of working together for a better ethical response.

3.3. Declaration of Human Rights

The Universal Declaration of Human Rights (UDHR) (Universal Declaration of Human Rights n.d.) in 1948 by the UN is yet another example of how we can work together for a common ground in a pluralistic context. Though it is not the first time that human rights are defined,[3] UDHR can be said to

---

[1] Referring to *Mahābhārata, Anusasana parva*, 113, 3–9 (ed. Ishwar Chundra Sharma and O.N. Bimali; translation according to M. N. Dutt [Parimal Publications, Delhi], vol. IX, p. 469), as cited in *In Search of a Universal Ethic*.

[2] See footnote 10 in the document: For example: "Let him say what is true, let him say what is pleasing, let him declare no disagreeable truth, and let him utter no lie to please someone; such is the eternal law" (*Mānava dharmaśāstra*, 4, 138, p. 101); "Let him always consider the action of striking a blow, reviling, and harming the good of one's neighbour, as the three most pernicious things in the string of vices produced by wrath" (*Mānava dharmaśāstra*, 7, 51, p. 156).

[3] Historical sources for bills of rights include the Magna Carta (1215), the English Bill of Rights (1689), the French Declaration of the Rights of Man and the Citizen (1789), and the Bill of Rights in the United States Constitution (1791). Early philosophical sources of the idea of human rights include Francisco Suarez (1548–1617), Hugo Grotius (1583–1645), Samuel Pufendorf (1632–1694), John Locke (1632–1704), and Immanuel Kant (1724–1804). Following UDHR, and based on it, there are many

be the most comprehensive and most widely accepted document on human rights. It is not easy to give a precise definition of human rights. Broadly, we can say that, "human rights are those claims that belong to the human person as a human person, based on what he/she is" (Kusumalayam 2008, p. 43). That is, all men and women, without any discrimination, irrespective of sex, age, race, nationality, wealth, religion, language, ideology, etc., have these rights. "Human rights are rights inherent to all human beings, regardless of race, sex, nationality, ethnicity, language, religion, or any other status" (Universal Declaration of Human Rights n.d.). Human rights include the right to life and liberty, freedom from slavery and torture, freedom of opinion and expression, the right to work and education, etc. The Preamble of UDHR says, "Whereas the peoples of the United Nations have in the Charter reaffirmed their faith in fundamental human rights, in the dignity and worth of the human person and in the equal rights of men and women and have determined to promote social progress and better standards of life in larger freedom . . . " (Universal Declaration of Human Rights n.d.). Though it may be considered as a secular document, without any direct reference to any religion, scholars have pointed out that religious traditions have contributed to the declaration of human rights (Christiansen 2018, pp. 244–45).

UDHR is an example of the achievement of dialogue in ethical matter in a pluralistic context. It shows that in spite of differences, there is the possibility of working together on ethical issues.[4]

3.4. Development/Change in Ethical Norms

Various authors have expounded the development in moral doctrine. In an article published in *Theological Studies* in 1993, John T. Noonan, Jr. highlighted some of the developments in moral doctrine (Noonan 1993), as against the popularly held (mis)conception that moral doctrines never change. Later, in his book, *A Church that can and cannot Change: The Development of Catholic Moral Teaching*, he has developed further his arguments (Noonan 2005). Some of the areas where we can notice development in moral doctrine are usury, marriage, slavery, religious freedom, etc. Analyzing these developments, Noonan concludes that "In each case one can see the displacement of a principle or principles that had been taken as dispositive." Besides, "these principles were replaced by principles already part of Christian teaching." He also points out that "In the course of this displacement of one set of principles, what was forbidden became lawful (the cases of usury and marriage); what was permissible became unlawful (the case of slavery); and what was required became forbidden (the persecution of heretics)" (Noonan 1993, p. 669). Another important work that discusses in detail the changes in official catholic moral teaching is the edited work by Charles E. Curran (Curran 2003).

Evidently, I do not intend to describe the developments in the moral doctrine or analyze them. I would like to point out that at no point of time can we claim an absolutely definite understanding of moral norms, at least on certain issues. This demands that we do not make absolute claims, and that we do not condemn different ethical positions as unethical; instead, we need to critically evaluate our own positions, being open to other positions, with humility and willingness to learn and to change.

3.5. Context

Theology, especially theological ethics, is contextual. Ethics develops in constant communication and dialogue with the context. The complexity of the context in ethics is not only that of different questions, different sources, different approaches, but also of different answers (Kochuthara 2011, p. 298).

---

human rights documents and treaties such as the United Nations, the Council of Europe, the Organization of American States, and the African Union.

[4] The concept of human rights and recognition of the equal rights of all (at least in on some basic matters) are incorporated into the constitutions of various nations. Yet, the concept of human rights may be different in a theocratic nation or a monarchy. Moreover, we cannot say that the concept of human rights is the same everywhere. For example, in some societies, human rights are understood more in terms of the rights of the tribe or community rather than the rights of the individual. Though we do not enter into a detailed discussion on this, it is good to remember that different understandings of human rights continue to exist. This also implies the possibility and need of continuing dialogue on this.

Instead of becoming exclusive or claiming superiority, what is needed is creative communication and self-critical dialogue among the different approaches in theological ethics. This is one of the tasks that moral theologians need to take up in future with renewed enthusiasm and openness. Here, the dialectical relationship between culture and morality, the growing awareness, and acceptance of religious pluralism as a given context that will continue to exist, and the dialectics between local and global concerns get more attention (Keenan 2007, pp. 101–45).

3.6. Culture and Inculturation in Ethics

"Culture concerns the totality of life" (O'Collins 2011, p. 339). Culture is a living reality in a continuous process of change. It is pertinent to see what *In Search of a Universal Ethic* says about culture and the role of culture in ethics: "Oriented by the persons who surround him [sic], permeated by the culture in which he [sic] is immersed, the person recognizes certain ways of behaving and of thinking as values to pursue, laws to observe, examples to imitate, visions of the world to accept. The social and cultural context thus exercises a decisive role in the education in moral values" (International Theological Commission 2009, para. 38). The importance of culture, the need for respecting its uniqueness, and its role in theologizing have been increasingly recognized in the recent decades. However, often, the role of culture in ethics or ethical formation has not received much attention, since ethical values and norms were considered universally valid. Considered against such a background, what Pope Francis says in *Amoris Laetitia* deserves our attention. The Pope says that though unity of teaching and practice is necessary in the Church, this does not preclude various ways of interpreting some aspects of that teaching or drawing certain consequences from it. "Each country or region, moreover, can seek solutions better suited to its culture and sensitive to its traditions and local needs. For 'cultures are in fact quite diverse and every general principle . . . needs to be inculturated, if it is to be respected and applied'" (Francis 2016, para 3). Evidently, it is a general principle, and the Pope does not give specific norms as to how this process of inculturation is to be undertaken. For example, there are elements that are positive, and that can be inculturated without any difficulty, but there can be also elements that cannot be easily accepted or that have to be rejected. However, though it is a general principle only, it is highly commendable as it is an affirmation of the values in other cultures and of the possibility of dialogue on ethical issues.

4. Initiatives for Doing Catholic Ethics in a Pluralistic Context

In the recent decades, as Amaladoss says, there is a deeper conviction that, "All religions can facilitate salvific divine-human encounter, so that people belonging to other religions are saved, not merely in spite of, but because of practicing those religions . . . " (Amaladoss 2011, p. 53). "Therefore, the only practical option before us is a third alternative: dialogue, positive relationship, collaboration and common pilgrimage and search for truth in view of the welfare, salvation and unity of the whole humanity . . . " (Pathil 2014, p. 329). Thus, there have been a renewed interest in dialogue with religions and cultures and various initiatives were taken for dialogue in ethics, and for doing ethics in a pluralistic context. It is pointed out that religions should be an active participant in developing an ethics in a pluralistic context. We find that there is a resurgence of religion in public life, though sometimes this is experienced negatively, for example, as in the case of fundamentalism and religiously motivated terrorism, etc. However, the society has not become 'secular' and attempts to construct a secular ethics without any reference to religion or religious ethics will be futile. One noteworthy contribution is that of Hans Küng, who has written extensively on a global ethics (Küng et al. 1986; Küng 1996, 1997, 1998). He has highlighted some of the areas of consensus and common interest: Human wellbeing; maxims of basic humanity; a reasonable middle way; the golden rule; horizon for meaning and identification of a goal; concept of virtues and vices, etc. (Küng 1996, pp. 55–64).

Though not at an extensive level, there have been many initiatives in recent years to dialogue with ethics of other cultures and religions. *In Search of a Universal Ethic* outlines several areas of convergence in ethics and collaboration. In his books and articles, Yiu Sing Lúcás Chan has elaborated upon building bridges between Christian and Confucian ethics based on the virtue concept in both religions (Chan 2008, 2009, 2011, 2013, 2015). Osamu Takeuchi has brought out the relationship between the Japanese concept of *Wa* and Christian ethics (Takeuchi 2010). In its various conferences and publications, Catholic Theological Ethics in the World Church (CTEWC) has been giving special attention to ethics in a pluralistic context (Chan et al. 2016).

5. Understanding Catholic and Hindu Approaches to Ecology and Sexuality

What I am attempting here is to briefly present two areas of ethical interest as examples of possible dialogue and communication—ecology and sexuality. With regard to ecology the possibility of convergence is more, whereas regarding sexuality, the differences may be more conspicuous.

5.1. Ecotheological Ethics

At least from the time of the publication of Lynn White's "The Historical Roots of Our Ecological Crisis" (White 1967), Christianity has been accused of having been responsible for the ecological crisis. Environmental activists and philosophers sharply criticize that Christianity, assigning to the humans the role of 'subduing the earth' and 'dominating' it, promoted unbridled exploitation of the nature leading to the present crisis. Any attempt to consider the nature as sacred would be labelled as pantheism and idolatry. Based mainly on the interpretations given to the creation narratives, the Christian tradition developed an anthropocentric perspective, which considered the natural world "a resource for human utility and not as a functioning community of mutually supporting life-systems within which the human must discover its proper role" (Chethimattam 1991, p. 54). In this worldview, the nature has only a secondary importance (Tucker and Grim 2002, p. xxi). Creation, redemption, incarnation, resurrection, and parousia were interpreted in an anthropocentric way, though other perspectives also are present in the bible. However, Christian theology of ecology has drastically changed in recent decades. Creation stories, and other biblical passages are (re-) interpreted in such a way that a more important place is given to the eco-system, the earth, and nature as a whole. The encyclical letter of Pope Francis, *Laudato Si', On the Care of Our Common Home* (Francis 2015), reflects this renewed understanding and the urgency of the issue.

Hinduism has been a strong proponent of the sacredness of the earth and everything created. One of the fundamental cosmological insights of the Indian tradition regarding this world is that it is indwelt by the Lord of the Universe and hence it is sacred:

"*Isavasyam idam sarvam yatkiṇça jagatyam jagat.*" (=This revolving world together with every minute particle in it is indwelt by the Lord) (*Isa Upaniṣd*, 1). As Nanditha Krishna, a noted Hindu expert on ecotheology in Hinduism, comments, "Hinduism believes that the earth and all life forms—human, animal and plant—are a part of Divinity. Man [sic] evolved out of these life forms and is a part of the creative process, neither separate nor superior." She further underscores that we should change our lifestyle and habits to simplify our material desires, without taking more than our reasonable share of resources (Krishna 2017, p. 223).

The same insight can be seen in the *Bhagavad Gita*: "*Sarvasya çāham hṛdi sanniviṣṭi.*" (=And I have inserted myself into the heart of everything) (*Bhagavad Gita*, 15:15). This is a basic Hindu conviction, and hence, nature is venerated by them, because they believe that "nature is a manifestation of the divine" (Krishna 2017, p. 11).

Bṛhadaranyaka Upaniṣd affirms this further, pointing out the simultaneous immanence and transcendence of the Divine:

He who is abiding in the earth, yet different from earth, ...

He who is abiding in the water, yet different from the water, ...

He who is abiding in the wind, yet different from the wind ... (*Bṛhadaranyaka Upaniṣd*, III, 7).

The Hindu vision affirms the sacredness not only of the human being, but everything in nature. The Hindu tradition reveres all life—human, non-human, plant, and animal. When humans imbibe this vision, they become servants of the Divine and all their actions, including those for protection of the world around them and all the beings therein, become acts of worship (Krishna 2017, p. 222). This calls for a new dimension in the human's relationship with nature: "Human life is sacred, as it is a sparkle of the Divine; so also is its environment. Since life and its setting are both sacred, we have to relate ourselves to humanity and nature on an equal footing" (Manickam 2008, p. 2).

Particularly of interest is the Hindu concept of the earth:

The Vedic attitude toward the earth springs from mankind's primordial experience of being on the one hand a guest, and on the other an offspring ... The earth is the foundation, the basis out of which emerges all that exists and on which everything rests. The earth is the basis of life and, when considered as divine being, she always occupies a special place among the Gods (Panikkar 1977, p. 120).

The worshipping of the earth is not adoration of a creature as an absolute, that is, it is not idolatry. In fact, it is the veneration of the highest value in the hierarchy of existence, for "undoubtedly this earth is the firstborn of being" (*Satapada Brahmana*, XIV, 1, 2, 10; Panikkar 1977, p. 121).

In the Hindu tradition, there is an underlying unity of all life, the world, and all that exists. The interconnectedness of all life and all creatures is affirmed by the scriptures (Bhattacharya 2006, p. 65).

Animals, in the Vedic vision, are not inferior creatures, but manifestations of gods on the lower scale of evolution compared to man. Animals like monkey, elephant, tiger, cow, bull, etc., occupy important places in the spectrum of gods. "Spiritually, there is no distinction between human beings and other forms of life. All forms, including plants and animals, are manifestations of god as limited beings (*jivas*). Even microorganisms are *jivas*, having souls of their own" (Cherian 2008, p. 191). The protection and worship of the cow symbolizes human responsibility to the sub-human world. This also stresses the reverence for all forms of life.

This attitude of reverence and gratitude to the earth and the whole cosmos in Hinduism shows us the possibility of working together to face the ecological crisis and to respond together to the spiritual inadequacy that many feel in the face of this crisis. There are differences in the basic faith vision and convictions, but a more critical re-evaluation of interpreting Hindu approach to nature as pantheistic and naturalistic will help us to understand better the richness of these traditions and to find common grounds to work together. Many have said the same regarding African religions, which have a reverential approach to the nature. Besides convincing us of the possibility of working together, this will also help us to re-discover our own eco-theology and eco-ethics, to reconsider the interpretations in the past, and to correct the imbalances.

The concept of nature and the approach of the two traditions may look different. However, we can notice that areas of convergence are identified today. Ecological ethics is an area where people belonging to different religions and cultures have begun to work together. There are publications in which scholars from various religions, including Christianity and Hinduism, have contributed. Some of the theological journals also have taken up the theme of ecotheology with the contribution of Hindu and Christian scholars. Recently, an inter-Asian workshop on the "Spirituality and Theology of Creation," under the leadership of Missio, Aachen, was conducted at Dharmaram Vidya Kshetram, Bangalore, India from 19–21 February 2019. This workshop was an attempt to look at the ecological issue from an intercultural, interreligious, and comparative perspective so as to promote the interreligious and intercultural dialogue on creation theology and environmental ethics. Scholars from Hinduism and Christianity presented papers and the papers will be published soon.[5] Scholars from Hinduism and Christianity find great possibilities for working together on ecological issues and for developing together an ecological ethics. However, not much has been achieved so far to concretize the possibility of developing an ecotheolgical ethics together. The rise of fundamentalist ideas, promoted by some

---

[5] The workshop brought together scholars from five religious traditions: Hinduism, Buddhism, Christianity, Islam, and Indigenous religions. For the announcement of the publication of the papers in German, please see Ibrahim, Isis, Shaji Kochuthara, and Klaus Vellguth, eds. forthcoming (Ibrahim et al. forthcoming). *Finding a Home in Creation: Asian Creation Spiritualities in Dialogue*. Ostfildern: Grünwald Verlag, (forthcoming), https://www.gruenewaldverlag.de/in-der-schoepfung-heimat-finden-p-1447.html. English version of this book will be also published soon.

groups including political parties, may be one of the main factors behind the reluctance to work together on such issues.

5.2. Sexuality

Christianity understands sexuality as good, willed by God, and as integral to the creative design of God. Based on the scripture, tradition, and theological developments, sexuality is understood to have basically three meanings or aspects: Love, procreation, and pleasure. Since most of the readers may be familiar with the Christian understanding of sexuality, I do not venture into a detailed discussion on this. Although these three are considered the basic aspects of sexuality, the understanding of the interrelationship among them has changed over time. For example, Augustine considered procreation as the primary good (of sexual relationship); for Aquinas, procreation was the primary end. From the time of Vatican II, the Catholic Church holds that procreation and love are the two inseparable purposes of marriage/marital sexuality. A theology of sexual pleasure is still in the phase of development.[6] Moreover, marriage is understood as the only legitimate context of sexual relationship and sexual enjoyment. With this brief consideration, let us turn to Hinduism to see how it visualizes the meaning of sexuality.

"Nowhere have close relationships of religion and sex been displayed more clearly than in India and, with divine and human models of sexual activity, sacramental views of sex were abundantly illustrated" (Parrinder 1980, p. 5). The Hindu conception of a full life consists in the harmony of Dharma (righteousness), *Artha* (wealth), and Kama (sexuality/sexual desire). Although Dharma has primacy, it is equally emphasized that neither *Artha* nor *Kāma* is to be neglected by a normally by a person.[7] Different approaches to sexuality can be identified in the Indian religious tradition. They may be perhaps broadly classified as follows:[8]

5.2.1. Mythical and Ritualistic Concept of Sexuality

In this approach, sexuality is considered godly. This is especially depicted in the creation stories, where the work of creation is presented as the result of the sexual desire and sexual act of god/gods. The Upaniṣads contain descriptions of ritual intercourse. The stories of creation as the result of the sexual intercourse of Prajapati are examples (*Brihadaranyaka Upaniṣad*, 1.4). Brihadaranyaka Upaniṣad describes sexual intercourse as a ceremony. The woman is considered the consecrated place where sacrifice is to be performed (*Brihadaranyaka Upaniṣad*, 6.4). Moreover, the godheads are always represented with their female consorts (Kapoor 2002, p. 3). The stories of gods engaging in love and sexual intercourse with goddesses or humans also have as their underlying principle this approach to sexuality. This is in general the basis of fertility cults and rites. Here, what is emphasized more is the procreative dimension of sexuality, although the recreational dimension also is not lacking. The whole

---

[6] Of the three aspects or meanings of sexuality, Catholic/Christian concept of sexual pleasure would be rather ambiguous. In the Catholic tradition, pleasure was not accepted as a good, end, or purpose [That is why I have presented it as one of the 'meanings' or 'aspects'. Rather, pleasure was often doubted as prone to lead humans to sin. At the maximum, pleasure would be recognised as a side-effect of the sexual act, which was basically oriented towards procreation. Greek philosophical concept, which did not accept pleasure as an end, was also influential in forming such an attitude towards pleasure in the Catholic tradition. However, we can see that the role of pleasure and its importance were acknowledged in negative terms, such as 'remedy for concupiscence', etc. In general, this can be said to be the Catholic concept of sexual pleasure until the mid-20th century. For the first time, positive value of conjugal sexual pleasure is accepted in an official document in 1951 (Pius XII 1951). A more positive view of sexual pleasure can be found in the works of contemporary theologians. For a detailed discussion, see Noonan (1986); Milhaven (1977, pp. 157–81); Census of India (2011a); Gudorf (1994); Brown (1998). My doctoral thesis was on the concept of sexual pleasure in the Catholic tradition: Kochuthara (2007).

[7] *Mahabharata*, 12.167: Cfr. Geoffrey Parrinder, *Sex in the World's Religions*, 14. However, here *kāma* is more as a precondition for all the other *puruṣārthas*. "Unless an individual has a desire to attain *artha*, to follow *dharma*, or to attain *mokṣa*, he cannot have *artha, dharma,* or *mokṣa*": Prasad (2008, p. 250).

[8] We have to remember, however, that we cannot make a watertight division of different approaches. The origin and foundation of different approaches can be seen in the same *puraṇas* and in the stories of the same gods and goddesses. Similarly, elements of different approaches can be found in the same approach. I have attempted this classification taking into consideration their major emphasis.

creation, fertility, and prosperity are considered to be the blessings of gods, who have engaged/engage in sexual activity. By worshipping the sexual powers of gods—which is often expressed by worshipping representation of the sexual organs of gods—and by engaging in ritual sexual intercourse, the devotees believe to attain fertility and prosperity.

5.2.2. Mystical Concept of Sexuality

The relationship and union between God and the human being/soul are symbolically presented in sensual and erotic language. The longing of the soul/human for God is described in vivid and explicit imageries of the sexual love and union of the devotee with the deity. Uninhibited description and narrative of the desire for the lover/deity, the pain of separation, and the joy in union are presented in sexual terms. Usually, the devotee is the female and the deity is the male. The *Kṛṣnaleela*, especially the love-play of Kṛṣna and Radha, in the *Bhagavata Purana*, is the best example for this. Other works in the *Bhakti* tradition also contain many such descriptions and stories.[9] Sexuality here is the symbol of the highest union and intimacy that is possible between the *bhakta* and the deity. Thus, sexuality is raised into the realm of spirituality and mysticism.

5.2.3. Tantric Concept of Sexuality

In the *Tantric* system, in which mainly the Mother Goddess is worshipped, sexuality occupies a central role. *Tantra*, instead of a withdrawal, encourages the fullest acceptance of human desires and feelings, since they are the via media between the physical world and the inner reality. The aim is not the discovery of the unknown, but the realization of the real: "What is here, is elsewhere; what is not here, is nowhere" (Pande and Dane 2001, p. 80). That is, *Tantra* is not a philosophy of the denial of the world or the physical, but of their affirmation. The world and the body are means of attaining spiritual realization. The body is not the enemy of the soul; the matter and spirit are not two opposing forces fighting with each other. The body is the means, through which alone the human can come to spiritual fulfilment. Spiritual powers are hidden in the body itself. Sex is a means of awakening the *kundalini*, of joining the female and male principles in the body, through which alone the spiritual powers of the body will be ultimately released and realized. Hence, sexual union becomes a ritual for spiritual realization.

5.2.4. Kāmaśāstra

This is the science of love and sex. This can be said to be the Indian sexology. Elements of Ayurveda and eugenics also can be seen in this. *Kāmaśāstra* is concerned merely to teach the means and manner through which man may enjoy *kāma* the best (Kapoor 2002, p. 35). *Kāma*, although often understood as sexual pleasure, "denotes the whole range of possible experience within the sphere of love, sex, sensual gratification and delight. *Kāma* is wish, desire, carnal gratification, lust, love, and affection" (Zimmer 1990, p. 145). *Kāmasūtra* by Vatsyayana is the most well-known work of *Kāmaśāstras*. *Kāmaśāstras* deal with the sex and man–woman relationship. Their chief concern is to help the human being attain pleasure. They also speak about family and the importance of the progeny, but what they underscore is the dimension of man–woman relationship and the attainment of pleasure in their union.

These different approaches to sexuality existed side by side in Hinduism, with some traditions or sects giving more importance to a particular approach or adopting only one. However, there was no attempt from a particular sect or tradition to condemn other approaches to sexuality. Different approaches were accepted as equally valid and as having their own value.

Comparing both the Catholic and Hindu concepts of sexuality, we can identify that the basic meanings are the sam; namely, love, procreation, and pleasure. However, the way they are understood

---

[9] Among love poetry based on the love of Kṛṣna and Radha, *Gita Govinda*, the works of Chandi Das, of Chaitanya (16th century), of the Ālvārs, etc. are among the most popular. Chaitanya used to dress himself as Kṛṣna and Radha.

and practiced, and the understanding of the interrelationship among them, are different. This does not mean that there is no possibility of dialogue or convergence. For example, especially for a better understanding of the positive value of sexual pleasure, Catholic theology can be helped by the Hindu approach to sexual pleasure. However, such initiatives need more profound dialogue. Moreover, it is also important to situate the values in sexual morality in the overall vision of values in human life.

6. Concluding Remarks and A Few Basic Considerations

1. Doing ethics in a pluralistic world is not about constructing new ethical system or principles or norms; that is, it is not about inventing a new ethic—that will become just an addition to different ethical systems already existing. Doing ethics in a pluralistic world is about understanding the ethics and approaches of each other; believing in the sincerity of each religion and culture in seeking the good; appreciating them; understanding areas of agreement; strengthening those areas of agreement; understanding the differences; and reflecting together on the differences without being judgmental.
2. Doing ethics in a pluralistic context is not succumbing to 'relativism'. It does not mean taking a position that there is no universally valid ethical norm or that any norm can be changed at any time. It is about understanding and appreciating the basic values behind the norms and understanding those values even when their expressions in the particular context through norms are different.
3. There can be areas on which agreement can be rather easy, whereas agreement on certain areas and issues may be difficult, which may demand more dialogue and critical evaluation together. What is important is how we are able to collaborate. If we wait until perfect consensus is arrived at before working together, we may never be able to collaborate. Instead, if we begin to collaborate on issues on which we agree, we may be able to understand each other better. However, in that process, we may learn to dialogue better even on areas of disagreement.
4. Attempts to develop a pluralistic ethics are founded on a basic trust in the goodness and good will of all, namely, all seek human wellbeing, all seek to do good, and avoid evil.[10] However, the concept of what is good and what is evil, especially in concrete issues, may differ. This difference also depends on the differences in the anthropological vision, world vision, and theological vision. This calls for an ongoing dialogue with each, not for mutual condemnation and fighting with each other. Uniformity cannot be set as the goal; relativism also cannot be a solution. Instead, a searching together for what is more humanizing for human beings individually and collectively can be undertaken.
5. Doing ethics in a pluralistic context demands a serious study, research, and search in the scriptures, traditions, and works by recognized scholars of each religion.
6. Each religion and culture may have various traditions and various opinions on a particular concept or ethical issue, sometimes conflicting and contradictory. There may be ethical norms that are not conducive to the wellbeing of the person and society. They need to be corrected. However, attempts to correct or change the ethical perspective, if at all they are needed, shall focus first of all inviting their attention to internal differences, or conflicts, and thus to understand the real value and ensuing ethical norm. If this possibility is not there, a critical evaluation of the proper perspective in light of the views of others may be requested, but without claiming any superiority.
7. Humility is one of the most fundamental virtues in dialogue. No one, including 'we', possesses the full truth and its understanding. God is beyond the full comprehension of everyone, including our own. We can help others in understanding and experiencing God better; similarly, others also

---

[10] This is the fundamental principle of natural law according to Thomas Aquinas. Cfr. Thomas Aquinas, *Summa Theologiae*, I–II, q. 94.

can help us. We do not possess the fullness of truth; perhaps others too do not possess it. We are seekers in the same path, seekers seeking together, learning from each other, helping each other to understand and experience the fullness of truth. This basic humility gives us the possibility of realizing our own limitations and incompleteness, and to understand the richness of others.

8. Plurality is a given-ness of life, and it is going to remain so. What matters is our approach to plurality, how we live together enriching each other and being enriched by others. Human existence is basically co-existence. We need to face together the ethical challenges of today: Violence, intolerance, injustice, poverty, suffering of the innocent, ecological crisis, terrorism, crisis of democracy and political leadership, etc. Any ethical issue anywhere in the world is or should be felt an issue in any other part of a globalized world, since humanity is interconnected, and since it must be approached as an issue about the basic dignity of the human person. What we need is a concerted effort to solve it in solidarity with others, in the spirit of dialogue, in humility and openness to others, and openness to the Spirit who is active in everyone, in every religion and culture.

9. Having said all these, we cannot claim that a clear theoretical framework is already there for a pluralistic ethics. For that, scholars from various traditions have to come together for dialogue. Only through such a dialogue even a framework for a pluralistic ethics can be developed.

Funding: This research received no funding.

Conflicts of Interest: The author declares no conflicts of interest.

References

Amaladoss, Michael. 2011. The FABC Theology of Religions. In *Harvesting from the Asian Soil: Towards an Asian Theology*. Edited by Vimal Tirimanna. Bangalore: Asian Trading Corporation, pp. 53–66.

Bhattacharya, Swasti. 2006. *Magical Progeny, Modern Technology. A Hindu Bioethics of Assisted Reproductive Technology*. New York: State University of New York Press.

Brown, Peter. 1998. *The Body and Society. Men, Women and Sexual Renunciation in Early Christianity*. New York: Columbia University Press.

Census of India. 2011a. Religion Census 2011. Available online: https://www.census2011.co.in/religion.php and https://pib.gov.in/newsite/printrelease.aspx?relid=126326. (accessed on 18 December 2019).

Census of India. 2011b. *Language*. According to This, There are 19569 Dialects. Available online: http://censusindia.gov.in/2011Census/C-16_25062018_NEW.pdf (accessed on 18 December 2019).

Chackalackal, Saju. 2016. Christianity's Encounter with the Spirit and Genius of India: An Unaccomplished Mission. In *Church on Pilgrimage: Trajectories of Intercultural Encounter*. Edited by Kuncheria Pathil. Bengaluru: Dharmaram Publications, pp. 398–429.

Chan, Yiu Sing Lúcás. 2008. Bridging Christian Ethics and Confucianism through Virtue. *Chinese Cross Currents* 5: 74–85.

Chan, Yiu Sing Lúcás. 2009. As West Meets East: Reading Zunzi's 'A Discussion of Rites'. In *'Ahme nach was du vollziehst.' Positionsbestimmungen zum Verhältnis von Liturgie und Ethik*. Edited by Martin Stuflesser and Stephan Winter. Regensburg: Friedrich Pustet KG, pp. 101–20.

Chan, Yiu Sing Lúcás. 2011. Bridging Christian and Confucian Ethics: Is the Bridge Adequately Catholic and Asian? *Asian Christian Review* 5: 49–73.

Chan, Yiu Sing Lúcás. 2013. Catholic Theological Ethics: Some Reflections on the Asian Scenario. In *Moral Theology in India Today*. Edited by Shaji George Kochuthara. Bangalore: Dharmaram Publications, pp. 101–21.

Chan, Yiu Sing Lúcás. 2015. *The Ten Commandments and Beatitudes: Biblical Studies and Ethics for Real Life*. Bengaluru: Dharmaram Publications. First Published from Rowman & Littlefield Publishers, 2012.

Chan, Yiu Sing Lúcás, James F. Keenan, and Shaji George Kochuthara, eds. 2016. *Doing Asian Theological Ethics in a Cross-Cultural and an Interreligious Context*. Bengaluru: Dharmaram Publications.

Cherian, Joby. 2008. Vedic Ethos and Environmental Concerns. *Journal of Dharma* 33: 185–96.

Chethimattam, John B. 1991. Ecology and Environment in Catholic Perspective. *Kristu Jyoti* 7: 46–59.

Christiansen, Drew. 2018. Commentary on *Pacem in Terris*. In *Modern Catholic Social Teaching: Commentaries and Interpretation*, 2nd ed. Edited by Kenneth R. Himes. Washington, DC: Georgetown University Press, pp. 226–52.

Curran, Charles E., ed. 2003. *Changes in Official Catholic Moral Teaching*. New York: Paulist Press.

Economic Times. 2018. Women of All Ages can Enter Sabarimala Temple, Rules Supreme Court. September 29. Available online: https://economictimes.indiatimes.com/news/politics-and-nation/supreme-court-allows-women-to-enter-sabarimala-temple/articleshow/65989807.cms (accessed on 10 October 2018).

Eilers, Franz-Josef, ed. 1997. *For All the Peoples of Asia: Vol. 2: Federation of Asian Bishops' Conferences Documents from 1992 to 1996*. Quezon City: Claretian Publications.

Francis. 2015. *Laudato Si'*. Available online: http://w2.vatican.va/content/francesco/en/encyclicals/documents/papa-francesco_20150524_enciclica-laudato-si.html (accessed on 18 December 2019).

Francis. 2016. *Amoris Laetitia*. Available online: https://w2.vatican.va/content/dam/francesco/pdf/apost_exhortations/documents/papa-francesco_esortazione-ap_20160319_amoris-laetitia_en.pdf (accessed on 18 December 2019).

Gudorf, Christine E. 1994. *Body, Sex and Pleasure*. Cleveland: The Pilgrim Press.

Gula, Richard M. 1989. *Reason Informed by Faith: Foundations of Catholic Morality*. New York: Paulist Press.

Henn, William. 1987. Pluralism. In *The New Dictionary of Theology*. Edited by Joseph A. Komonchak, Mary Collins and Dermot A. Lane. Dublin: Gill and Macmillan, pp. 770–72.

Ibrahim, Isis, Shaji Kochuthara, and Klaus Vellguth, eds. (forthcoming). *Finding a Home in Creation: Asian Creation Spiritualities in Dialogue*. Ostfildern: Grünwald Verlag, Available online: https://www.gruenewaldverlag.de/in-der-schoepfung-heimat-finden-p-1447.html (accessed on 18 December 2019).

International Theological Commission. 2009. *In Search of a Universal Ethic: A New Look at the Natural Law*. Available online: http://www.vatican.va/roman_curia/congregations/cfaith/cti_documents/rc_con_cfaith_doc_20090520_legge-naturale_en.html (accessed on 1 October 2019).

John Paul II. 1998. *Fides et Ratio*. Encyclical Letter on the Relationship between Faith and Reason (14 September 1998). Available online: http://w2.vatican.va/content/john-paul-ii/en/encyclicals/documents/hf_jp-ii_enc_14091998_fides-et-ratio.html (accessed on 12 December 2019).

Kapoor, Subodh. 2002. *Encyclopaedia of Indian Heritage, Vol. 45: Vatsyayana*. New Delhi: Cosmo Publications.

Keenan, James F. 2007. *Towards a Global Vision of Catholic Moral Theology. Reflections on the Twentieth Century*. Bangalore: Dharmaram Publications, pp. 101–45.

Kochuthara, Shaji George. 2007. *The Concept of Sexual Pleasure in the Catholic Tradition*. Roma: Editrice Pontificia Università Gregoriana.

Kochuthara, Shaji George. 2011. Context and the Future of Theological Ethics: The Task of Building Bridges. In *Catholic Theological Ethics: Past, Present, and Future: The Trento Conference*. Edited by James F. Keenan. Maryknoll, New York: Orbis Books, pp. 296–306.

Krishna, Nanditha. 2017. *Hinduism and Nature*. Gurgaon: Penguin Books.

Küng, Hans. 1996. *Global Responsibility: In Search of a New World Ethic*. New York: Continuum.

Küng, Hans. 1997. *A Global Ethic for Global Politics and Economics*. London: SCM Press.

Küng, Hans. 1998. *A Global Ethic for Global Politics and Economics*. New York: Oxford University Press.

Küng, Hans, Josef van Ess, Heinrich von Stietencron, and Heinz Bechert. 1986. *Christianity and World Religions: Paths to Dialogue*. Maryknoll, New York: Orbis Books.

Kusumalayam, John. 2008. *Human Rights: Individual or/and Group Rights*. Bandra, Mumbai: St. Pauls.

Manickam, Thomas. 2008. Holistic Ethics and Global Environmental Crises. *Journal of Dharma* 33: 111–32.

Milhaven, John Giles. 1977. Thomas Aquinas on Sexual Pleasure. *Journal of Religious Ethics* 5: 157–81.

Noonan, John T. 1986. *Contraception*. Cambridge and London: The Belknap Press of Harvard University Press.

Noonan, John T., Jr. 1993. Development in Moral Doctrine. *Theological Studies* 54: 662–77. [CrossRef]

Noonan, John T., Jr. 2005. *A Church that can and cannot Change: The Development of Catholic Moral Teaching*. Notre Dame: University of Notre Dame Press.

O'Collins, Gerald. 2011. *Rethinking Fundamental Theology*. Oxford: Oxford University Press.

Painadath, Sebastian. 2016. Christianity's Relationship with Other Religions: Emerging New Paradigms. In *Church on Pilgrimage: Trajectories of Intercultural Encounter*. Edited by Kuncheria Pathil. Bengaluru: Dharmaram Publications, pp. 467–84.

Pande, Alka, and Lance Dane. 2001. *Indian Erotica*. New Delhi: Roli Books.

Panikkar, Raimundo. 1977. *The Vedic Experience. Mantramañjari: An Anthology of the Vedas for Modern Man and Contemporary Celebration*. Delhi: Motilal Banarsidass Publishers, [Reprint 2001].

Parrinder, Geoffrey. 1980. *Sex in the World's Religions*. New York: Oxford University Press.

Pathil, Kuncheria. 2014. Pluralism, Dialogue and Communion. In *Revisiting Vatican II: 50 Years of Renewal, Vol. I: Keynote and Plenary Papers of the DVK International Conference on Vatican II*. Edited by Shaji George Kochuthara. Bangalore: Dharmaram Publications, pp. 322–34.

Pius XII. 1951. Address to Midwives (29 October 1951). *AAS* 43: 835–54.

Plathottam, George. 2009. Homosexuality: Faulty, Flawed Debates. *Indian Currents*, July 13–19, 32–33.

Prasad, Rajendra. 2008. A Conceptual-Analytic Study of Classical Indian Philosophy of Morals History of Science, Part I. In *Philosophy and Culture in Indian Civilization, Vol XII*. New Delhi: Concept Publishing Company.

Singh, Kuwar. 2018. India's Supreme Court Strikes Down a Colonial-era Adultery Law. *Quartz India*. September 27. Available online: https://qz.com/india/1404196/adultery-no-longer-crime-in-india-rules-supreme-court/ (accessed on 10 October 2018).

Takeuchi, Osamu. 2010. The Heart of *Wa* and Christian Ethics. *Asian Horizons* 4: 114–27.

The Guardian. 2019. 'Historic' Day as India Outlaws 'Triple Talaq' Islamic Instant Divorce. Available online: https://www.theguardian.com/world/2019/jul/31/triple-talaq-india-hails-historic-day-as-parliament-outlaws-islamic-instant-divorce (accessed on 12 December 2019).

Thomas Aquinas. 1947. *Summa Theologiae, I–II*. Translated by Dominican Fathers of the English Province. Notre Dame: Christian Classics.

Times of India. 2010. Live-in Relationship, Pre-marital Sex not an Offence: SC. Available online: http://timesofindia.indiatimes.com/india/Live-in-relationship-Pre-marital-sex-not-an-offence-SC/articleshow/5716545.cms (accessed on 23 March 2010).

Tracy, David. 1975. *Blessed Rage for Order: The New Pluralism in Theology*. New York: Seabury Press.

Triple Talaq in India. n.d. Available online: https://en.wikipedia.org/wiki/Triple_talaq_in_India (accessed on 12 October 2019).

Tucker, Mary Evelyn, and John Grim. 2002. Series Foreword. In *Jainism and Ecology: Non-violence in the Web of Life*. Edited by Christopher Key Chapple. Cambridge: Harvard University Press for the Centre for the Study of World Religions.

UCA.News. 1998. Message of Special Assembly of Synod of Bishops for Asia. May 14. Available online: post_name=/1998/05/14/message-of-special-assembly-of-synod-of-bishops-for-asia&post_id=1039 (accessed on 2 October 2019).

Universal Declaration of Human Rights. n.d. Available online: https://www.un.org/en/udhrbook/pdf/udhr_booklet_en_web.pdf (accessed on 12 December 2019).

Vaidyanathan, A. 2018. "Adultery Not a Crime, 'Husband Not Master of Wife,' Says Supreme Court". *NDTV*. September 27. Available online: https://www.ndtv.com/india-news/adultery-law-is-arbitrary-says-chief-justice-dents-the-individuality-of-women-1922922 (accessed on 10 October 2018).

Vatican II. 1965. *Nostra Aetate*. Available online: http://www.vatican.va/archive/hist_councils/ii_vatican_council/documents/vat-ii_decl_19651028_nostra-aetate_en.html (accessed on 18 December 2019).

White, Lynn, Jr. 1967. The Historical Roots of Our Ecological Crisis. *Science* 155: 1203–7. [CrossRef] [PubMed]

Zimmer, Heinrich. 1990. *Philosophies of India*. Edited by Joseph Campbell. Delhi: Motilal Banarsidass, reprint 2005.

 © 2019 by the author. Licensee MDPI, Basel, Switzerland. This article is an open access article distributed under the terms and conditions of the Creative Commons Attribution (CC BY) license (http://creativecommons.org/licenses/by/4.0/).

Article

Pursuing Ethics by Building Bridges beyond the Northern Paradigm

James Francis Keenan

Theology Department, Boston College, 140 Commonwealth Avenue, Chestnut Hill, MA 02467, USA; James.keenan.2@bc.edu

Received: 28 July 2019; Accepted: 16 August 2019; Published: 20 August 2019

Abstract: This essay narrates and explores the work of Catholic Theological Ethics in the World Church (CTEWC) in developing a network that connects roughly 1500 Catholic ethicists around the world. It highlights the impact that CTEWC has had in encouraging Christian ethics to become more inclusive, active, and mindful in advancing a network that builds bridges beyond the northern paradigm. In this narrative, we see how CTEWC planned and realized three major international conferences in Padua, Trento, and Sarajevo and six regional conferences in Manila, Nairobi, Berlin, Krakow, Bangalore, and Bogota. Together with its monthly newsletter, CTEWC has also sponsored a visiting scholars program in Bangalore, Manila, and Nairobi, a PhD scholarship program for eight women in Africa, and an international book series with eight volumes and over 200 contributors. Throughout, we respond to the challenge of pluralism by answering the call to dialogue from and beyond local culture. As it enters its second generation with new leadership, CTEWC pursues critical and emerging issues in theological ethics by engaging in cross-cultural, interdisciplinary conversations shaped by shared visions of hope, but always mindful that we must engage the Global South and go beyond the northern paradigm where most contemporary theological ethics occur.

Keywords: Network; conferencing; theological ethics; cross-cultural communications; bridge-building; northern paradigm; local culture; virtual tables

1. Introduction

This account about our network, Catholic Theological Ethics in the World Church (CTEWC), is not about how we imagine ethics in terms of new conceptual insights or new methods of investigation or of reporting, but rather about recognizing the need to expand our collegiality. This is a case for developing the field of Christian Ethics by enhancing the possibility of being more connected to more distant and isolated colleagues and their research so as to realize that our local investigations need to be connected to theirs.

Our understanding of global challenges like sustainability or migration, economic inequality, or gender identity is always developed by the resources and discussions that are accessible to us in our own localities. In the Global North, for instance, we have a plethora of pathways to research. However, often we do not hear or have access to research from those in the Global South because those ethicists are not as connected to the journals, forums, and universities of the Global North as we are and we do not often follow their journals or forums.

We in the Global North often cite our colleagues from the Global North because they are our interlocutors and therein we continue to work with unacknowledged biases in which the investigations remain in a privileged context and the questions asked, the agenda that is set, and the findings that are reported all concern the perspectives of those of us from the North. This is what we refer to in our mission statement below as "the northern paradigm"; it encases most of the presuppositions that assure that most of our research remains focused on colleagues from the Global North.

The metaphor of "bridge-building" is instructive here. Bridge-building suggests that two different locations can meet and when ethicists build bridges they are trying to create conversations beyond one's own locality so as to engage another's. Yet often enough, these bridges are built in the Global North, and somehow the encounters that they sponsor have those coming from the Global South as visitors. In a manner of speaking, often at these meetings, conferences, or intercultural dialogues, those from the Global North seem to presume that the dominant (nay, universal) way of understanding an ethical method, say regarding the virtues or human rights, is their way and that those from the Global South propose their "distinctively" different world views. In a critical essay, Lúcás Chan (Chan 2011) asked whether when bridge-building, we recognize the ways that we might water-down, reduce, or worse, assimilate the claims or proposals from the Global South into the northern paradigm. Is the bridge-building adequately conveying the distinctiveness of the world-views of each of the participants or are they filtered through the dominant, though regional language-games? Throughout this text, then, when we see bridge-building, we are proposing a form of meeting that tries not to compromise the world-view of others but rather acknowledges not only the congruities but the contrasts among the positions of the differing participants in the encounter.

The network that I describe here begins with the simple assumption that we ethicists need to be better connected.[1] We also realized during our years of work that we had to extend our network to those literally on the margins, to those whose voices have not been heard, and whose insights have not been recognized. That is, we began simply with the need to be connected with fellow ethicists but, in time, we realized we needed to extend ourselves in our connectedness geographically. Through our conferencing, our book series, our monthly newsletter, and our scholarship programs, we have tried to ask, is anyone missing, is there anyone we need to support or engage, is there anyone we have failed to recognize? Our network has become, then, a catalyst for re-envisioning how we investigate ethics and how we report our findings better by being better connected globally, through multitudinous localities, respecting the contributions of each. This is then a descriptive narrative of the somewhat organic developments of our discovery of the importance of our mission statement in trying to go beyond our contexts by encountering others long overlooked. Through a narrative of our expanding projects and decisions, I hope to convey the lessons we learned in our first generation of existence and to express our plans for the second generation.

Acting on the need for cross-cultural theological discourse began long before the international meetings of CTEWC theological ethicists at Padua in 2006 and Trento in 2010. This was, after all, the conciliar vision of the founders of the international Catholic journal *Concilium*, which has published for the past 54 years five issues a year in five different linguistic (English, German, Italian, Portuguese, and Spanish) editions.[2] Elsewhere, women especially have taken the lead in such discourse, making it almost always ecumenical in scope. In 1989, in Africa, the Methodist Mercy Amba Oduyoye established the "The Circle of Concerned African Women Theologians."[3] From the United States, Regina Wentzel Wolfe and Christine E. Gudorf (Wolfe and Gudorf 1999) edited cross-cultural case studies on ethics and world religions. In Asia, the *Ecclesia of Women in Asia* movement has hosted Pan-Asian conferences among women theologians since 2002, publishing two (Monteiro and Gutzler 2005; Brazal and Lizares 2007) collections of their conference papers.[4] Still, CTEWC, while like *Concilium* being almost exclusively Catholic in its participants, marks a significant development in the history of theological ethics and this essay hopes to capture its raison d'être and the course of its development.

---

[1] At the end of this essay, I return to this claim to highlight how it applies to all ethicists in religion or theology and how the narrative here helps to make that case.
[2] https://concilium.hymnsam.co.uk/.
[3] http://www.thecirclecawt.org/profile.html.
[4] http://ecclesiaofwomen.ning.com/.

2. Getting to Padua and Trento

In 2002, while teaching at the Gregorian University in Rome, I invited a visiting colleague from Boston College to a dinner with four ethicists from the two major faculties teaching Catholic theological ethics in Rome. Two were teaching at the Gregorian University, and the other two at the Alfonsianum University; each had taught for at least fifteen years in Rome and each had an internationally respected reputation; their universities were less than a kilometer apart. At the end of an exciting dinner, I asked, how often they gathered and discovered they had never met. I decided then to bring together Catholic theological ethicists from across the globe.[5]

I shared my idea with Paul Schotsmans at the Catholic University of Leuven, who helped me to present it to a major Catholic foundation. With Schotsmans and the foundation's support, I hosted an international Planning Committee of Catholic ethicists at Leuven in 2003 where we began imagining an international conference. At that time, we (Schotsmans 2019) articulated three reasons why Catholic ethicists needed to host such a conference. First, being on the practical side of theology, Catholic theological ethicists are often interlocutors with others from very different disciplines—medicine, public health, economics, political science, sociology, etc.; therefore, it would benefit our inquiries if we met once simply among ourselves. Second, before the twenty-first century, Catholic ethicists were for the most part trained at one of the Roman universities. In the 1950s, students of moral theology began attending other European universities as well. Since the 1970s, they began studying for doctorates at universities on their own continents. In the globalized world, the occasion for studying together became more and more rare and, we believed, that it would be good for those trained on the different continents to meet at least once together. Third, distinctive approaches to Catholic theological ethics subsequently arose on each continent. We needed to develop ways of communicating wherein the developments on one continent were known on the others. Our Catholicity was at stake.

Three fundamental decisions were made at Leuven. First, we developed a name: "Catholic Theological Ethics in the World Church" and articulated a mission statement:

> "Since moral theology is so diffuse today, since many Catholic theological ethicists are caught up in their own specific cultures, and since their interlocutors tend to be in other disciplines, there is the need for an international exchange of ideas among Catholic theological ethicists. Catholic theological ethicists recognize the need: to appreciate the challenge of pluralism; to dialogue from and beyond local culture; and, to interconnect within a world church, not dominated solely by a northern paradigm. In response to these recognized needs, Catholic theological ethicists will meet to refresh their memories, reclaim their heritage, and reinterpret their sources. Therefore, Catholic theological ethicists will pursue in this conference a way of proceeding that reflects their local cultures and engages in cross-cultural conversations motivated by mercy and care." [6]

Second, to be truly international, we would have to underwrite the travel and housing of most participants from the Global South. This would require major fundraising. Third, since some members of the planning committee had difficulty securing visas, we soon learned that Italy was the most hospitable Western European country in terms of granting visas. Deciding on Italy, we quickly selected Padua. The city of St. Anthony was a pilgrim's city but it was also the seat of one of Europe's oldest universities. The academy and the church were very present there.

To forge our catholicity at Padua, we had two different types of plenary presentations. First, we had continental panels from Africa, Asia, Europe, Latin America, and North America, wherein

---

[5] The term moral theologian has been used in the past to define Catholic theologians working in the field of personal ethics as opposed to those working in social ethics. In our network, we include both moral theologians and social ethicists as well as bioethicists and business ethicists under the title "theological ethicist." Throughout this essay, I will use the more inclusive term.

[6] http://www.catholicethics.com/padua/info/mission.php.

each panel had three presenters each from different parts of the continent but each responding to the same three questions: what are our moral challenges, how are we responding to them, what hope do we have for the future? We also hosted panels on four fundamental issues: the sources of our tradition, the question of pluralism, justice and globalization, and *sensus fidelium* and the magisterium. On these panels, we looked to achieve balance by having a truly diverse spectrum of presenters; a case in point, the notable debate between Paul Valadier (Valadier 2007) and Monsignor Giuseppe Angelini (Angelini 2007) over *sensus fidelium*, that is, the normative claim that the laity's faith has on the articulation of magisterial teachings.

On 8 July 2006, we hosted for the first time in history an international meeting of Catholic theological ethicists: 400 came from 63 countries to Padua. The major theme of the conference was listening, listening to voices beyond our own local culture. The meeting was a great success; the plenary papers were published by Continuum Press (Keenan 2007), though five other presses subsequently published them as well so as to assure international distribution. Linda Hogan (Hogan 2010), the co-chair of the CTEWC Planning Committee, edited a volume of the applied ethics papers.

From Padua, four developments emerged. First, more specific steps had to be taken to ensure the involvement of women in the field, especially out of Africa. For instance, after the three African speakers gave their continental addresses on African challenges, focusing on civil strife, colonialism, graft, and trade, each of the three African women participants challenged them on why not a word was mentioned on AIDS, healthcare, or, even, women. Their voices resonated throughout the conference and conference organizers responded with a pledge to secure funding for African women to begin graduate studies.

Second, cross-cultural initiatives began right at Padua. The forty African participants held their historic first meeting of African Moral Theologians at the conference. Days later, the Asians met as well. Immediately afterwards, Catholic ethicists (Chummar 2010) pursued other similar initiatives such as an "International Symposium on Natural Law" that was held eight months later at the Catholic University of Eastern Africa, Nairobi, Kenya. Similarly, Mary Jo Iozzio with Mary Doyle Roche and Elsie Miranda (Iozzio et al. 2008) engaged Paduan participants to contribute to a collection of essays by Catholic women theologians on the HIV/AIDS pandemic. Like the Padua conference, these global projects supported rather than diminished the concerns that were expressed locally: the local was *not* antithetical to the universal, but rather grounds for the possibility of the universal.

Third, eventually we began to receive comment on the papers from Padua. Only five months after the conference, *Rivista di Teologia Morale* published reports by several participants (Onyema 2006; Lourdusamy 2006; Fabri dos Anjos 2006; Cimperman 2006; Lorenzetti 2006) from across the world. From Padua itself, the senior theological ethicist Giuseppe Trentin (Trentin 2009) offered a critique concerning method, exhorting the plenary speakers to further more rigorous argumentation. Many other reports (see Steck 2011) on Padua would follow.

Fourth, the closing assembly unanimously called for a second international conference.

Four years later, the second international CTEWC conference was held in Trento, the site of the historical Council. The conference was even more successful than the first, with 600 participants from 72 countries. Inasmuch as at the sixteenth-century Council of Trent moral theology was established as a specific field of theological inquiry, the conference was designed to consider the past, the present, and the future of the field. It helped us establish a much stronger network because of five subsequent major developments. First, we built a website, www.catholicethics.com. Second, we launched a monthly newsletter, that contains regional news, updates, book launches, job openings and the now widely successful "Forum," a monthly op-ed section that posts essays by contributors from each of the five continents. Then, we also started a book series with Orbis Books. Keenan (Keenan 2011) edited the first volume, the plenary papers from Trento, that three other presses also published. We decided that each subsequent volume would have two editors from different continents and roughly 25 contributors from around the world. Each would be developed according to the specific themes. Then followed volumes on feminism (Hogan and Orobator 2014), environmental sustainability (Peppard and Vicini 2015), migrants and refugees (Brazal and Davila 2016), biblical ethics (Chan et al. 2018), and finally, the theological ethicist in the local church (Autiero and Magesa 2018).

With over 150 different contributors in these six volumes, the series has so affected theological and ethical research, that no one today addressing any ethical theme would publish a volume that was not international, and in particular, did not engage the Global South; the series has prompted all theological ethicists to think globally, to look beyond their localities and to try not to be dominated by the northern paradigm.

Fourth, we developed a visiting scholars program where ethicists would have the opportunity to teach at participating schools in Manila, Bangalore, and Nairobi. A scholar's services were pro bono, but the room, board, and hospitality were provided by the hosting institution, and the travel was supported through grants secured by CTEWC. Finally, reflecting on an initiative by the Filipina Agnes Brazal (Agnes Brazal et al. 2010) who invited ethicists across Southeast Asia to Manila in 2008, we decided to host continental conferences. We hosted the first pan-African meeting in Nairobi in 2012. Realizing the need to build bridges between Western and Eastern Europe, we met first in Berlin in 2013, and a year later in Krakow. These first four regional conferences hovered between 40 and 50 participants for each conference. For three years, one of our Planning Committee members, Lúcás Chan (Chan et al. 2016), began preparing with Shaji George Kochuthara a pan-Asian conference for more than 100 Asian theological ethicists; sadly Chan died of heart failure on its eve in summer 2015. Finally in 2016, we (Cuda 2017) hosted another large regional conference in Bogotá.

With our regional networks secured, it was time to call a third international conference. We decided on Sarajevo, a city that is neither the industrialized North nor the Global South, but instead a place in-between that tries to bridge both worlds. In the wake of its historic siege (1992–1995), Sarajevo offered three vital contexts: peace building in the aftermath of ethnic conflict; inter-religious and cross-cultural dialogue in a predominantly Muslim city (85%); and, economic struggle (40% unemployment).

Furthermore, we wanted to make our network more effective to address three compelling issues; the climate crisis; its impact on already marginalized populations; and, the tragic banality of contemporary political leadership that pretends to contradict the urgency of the first two issues. We went to Sarajevo, therefore, because as ethicists, we need to be further engaged. In a world where nationalistic populism tears apart any global cooperation, where the abandonment of the Paris accord mirrors the abandonment of migrants and refugees, where civility is sacrificed by the banality of self-interest and the common good is trampled underfoot, we need to be globally connected and active, abandoning the domination of the Global North and looking beyond local interests. In order to achieve these goals, we needed to rethink what a Catholic international theological conference should be.

3. Planning a New Form of Conferencing for Sarajevo

As we finished our conference in Bogotá, we began developing a whole different type of conference for our international gathering in Sarajevo. First, we needed younger leadership; we turned to Kristin Heyer, a noted ethicist from Santa Clara University, to join Hogan and me as co-chair of the Planning Committee and to take charge of the entire program design for Sarajevo. We also asked another committee member, Andrea Vicini, an Italian Jesuit teaching at Boston College, to oversee and accompany the recruitment of participants.

Second, we decided that we needed to go to Rome and to meet with church leaders to introduce them to our network. In March 2017, seven of the planning committee members met with Mons. José Rodriguez Carballo, ofm, and the Congregazione per i Religiosi; Cardinal Kevin Farrell and his Pontificio Consiglio per i Laici, la Famiglia, la Vita; Cardinal Fernando Filoni and the Congregazione per l'Evangelizzazione dei Popoli; Cardinal Gianfranco Ravasi and the Pontificio Consiglio della Cultura, Cardinal Peter Turkson and the Pontificio Consiglio della Giustizia e della Pace, and Cardinal Giuseppe Versaldi and the Congregazione per l'educazione cattolica. At each meeting, we were welcomed warmly. Our delegation also presented our work at three major Roman universities: the Alfonsianum, the Gregorian, and the Urbanianum. We met too with the newly elected Father General of the Society of Jesus, Arturo Sosa. And, finally, we met for nearly an hour with Pope Francis on 17 March.

These meetings helped us to realize that we needed to think of the conference not as connecting ideas first, but instead as connecting actual persons. We needed to meet one another as we are, not primarily as we write. Moreover, we needed to appreciate the diversity we had developed in our network. Just as we developed in Europe a bridge between Western and Eastern Europe, we needed to connect our theological ethicists worldwide with one another. Instead of attending to political diversity, we wanted to make sure that we had voices of the church from everywhere we could find an ethicist, so as to understand what their actual challenges and hopes were. Thus, we needed a conference that would train us for global partnership in a challenging and troubled world further compromised by poor political leadership.

At Sarajevo, we (Heyer 2019) decided that we would start the conference in July 2018 by going through five stages. First, there was a word of welcome. While we invited Sarajevo's Cardinal Vinko Pujlic to welcome us, we also wrote Pope Francis if he would send us a word of welcome. He sent us a detailed three-page letter expressing how well he understood our work of building bridges, not walls.[7] His letter gave us immediate international recognition.[8] Finally, on behalf of the planning committee, Keenan offered a word of welcome, concluding that after sixteen years of developing a network, CTEWC had now arrived at a second generation and that it was time for him and Hogan to step down and make room for new leadership, announcing that Heyer, Vicini, and Kochuthara had agreed to assume the new responsibilities. The conference started then with enormous support, hope, and vitality.

Then, we attended to our immediate context, the church and people of Sarajevo. We invited Fr. Darko Tomasevic, the dean of theology at the University of Sarajevo, and Zilka Siljak, a Muslim feminist theologian. Each spoke about struggles of Sarajevo during and after the siege. We concluded the opening session with a film about the early days of the siege when the national library at city hall was fire-bombed and burned for four days, and then in one of our first of many religious acts, we held a procession through the old city, from our conference site, the major Catholic high school of Sarajevo to the newly restored city hall where we hosted our opening reception. Here we saw tangibly the fruits of reconciliation, solidarity, and restoration.

We began the next morning with listening to the voices of seven of our world-wide members, not talking about their projects, but rather talking about being connected. After we heard two senior voices, we heard from young, emerging voices; the first woman theologian from India, a lay woman from Uganda, and a dynamic lecturer from Hungary. In each case, though they were new to the field, they shared with us the vocation of the theological ethicist and the importance of their being connected to us as they worked as newcomers to the field. Finally, we concluded with voices from isolated contexts: the singular woman ethicist from Bosnia and the first woman ethicist from Vietnam. Here, we were meeting those on our margins who were defining us by being connected.

Next, we held a memorial service for all those who died since Trento. This call to prayer through remembrance and mindfulness of our friends and colleagues brought us great consolation as thirty-two people described their colleagues and lit candles of witness to our late colleagues and friends. We stayed, again, connected with one another, including those in glory.

Finally, we hosted a large poster session. Here a word of explanation is needed. Scientific conferences have poster sessions where scholars post their findings and others read their work.

---

[7] http://w2.vatican.va/content/francesco/en/messages/pont-messages/2018/documents/papa-francesco_20180711_messaggio-etica-teologica.html.

[8] https://www.vaticannews.va/en/pope/news/2018-07/pope-francis-message-conference-theological-ethics-ctewc-sarajev.html; http://www.lastampa.it/2018/08/04/vaticaninsider/a-sarajevo-abbiamo-cercato-di-offrire-risposte-positive-alle-sfide-del-mondo-ftUIj3It56UP1yB9WUl0DN/pagina.html; https://www.ncronline.org/news/theology/francis-tells-500-theologians-world-needs-renewed-leadership; https://www.google.fr/amp/s/www.la-croix.com/amp/1200956548.

Theologians do not normally present posters, but prefer to give papers. At Trento, for instance, we sponsored a poster session but only 24 posters were submitted. Instead, we ceded to others' requests for presentations and hosted three concurrent sessions with twenty-five panels of three presenters each. This meant that 225 ethicists presented their papers. However, in every session, a person had the opportunity to attend only one panel and not the other 24! This meant that, though everyone heard nine presenters during the three sessions, we missed the other 216!

In preparation for Sarajevo, Heyer continuously encouraged participants to present posters. She limited the program to only two concurrent sessions of 25 panels, with two presenters, leaving only 100 slots for papers. Heyer argued that presenters would have more and better encounters if they did posters. The posters, moreover, were not about one small focused project as one finds at most conferences. Rather, for CTEWC, one's poster was to serve as an introduction to the trajectory of one's work, thus furthering our goal of connecting us to one another.

Then, 136 participants brought their posters to Sarajevo and, by the end of the conference, they were glad they did. Heyer hosted two extended poster sessions during which participants could meet all 136 presenters. The results were extended conversations about one's work. Of the many, many responses that we received, praise for the poster sessions was the greatest. Assuredly, posters will be at more and more theological conferences in the future.

Finally, Heyer hosted later in the day a second extended plenary panel, this time inviting two junior scholars from each of the five regions to explore how the method of theological ethics in each continent developed from Padua to Trento to Sarajevo. This was a remarkable session that helped us to appreciate the wide array of methodological advances that had occurred throughout the past twenty years. For instance, the Africans presented how their contextual/liberation theology let them deepen their appreciation of their original historical cultural context while still being critical of those cultural biases that might hinder the flourishing of persons and communities. The Asians spoke of inter-religious dialogue and North Americans described how virtue ethics has taken a distinctively social turn in examining social structures of virtue and vice. Europeans highlighted how the earlier language and agenda of autonomy was now being replaced by the more relational, social claims and responsibilities of human rights. Finally, Latin Americas described how the advocacy of liberation theology had morphed into a closer-to-the-ground encounter with poor through the so-called "theology of the people." Here, showcasing young theologians who knew their own emerging methodological issues well, we built bridges inter-generationally within each of the regions while highlighting how extensive of a turn to the social was embedded in local developments in moral methodology.

At the end of the day, we returned to prayer, this time for peace. First, we invited from Sarajevo, *Youth for Peace*, an inter-religious fellowship that works for reconciliation across the generations of Bosnia and Herzegovina. They witnessed how their own solidarity brought them healing and peace. Then, our liturgy committee brought us a call for peace from each of the five regions.

On the third day, we heard in the third plenary four presentations on the triple theme of the conference: climate change, its impact on migration and the marginalized, and the disenfranchising leadership of nationalist politicians. These papers mirrored the work of the 100 panel presentations and 136 posters. Indeed, throughout the conference, these three themes were the stuff of our concern.

However, the plenaries were designed less for hearing about these issues and more toward taking us through a social training ground that would form us as a network into greater solidarity as well as greater freedom and competency for social action. In a way, the conference was designed to be transformative, whence the importance of a variety of spiritual and ethical practices. Thus, right after the panel on climate and political crises, we invited each of the five regions to meet with their respective colleagues and reflect on how well they have networked regionally during the first generation of CTEWC. The first of two such "Continental Discussions" was specifically labeled as a collective examination of conscience. After these discussions, Charles Curran (Curran 2019) gave a powerful presentation on how theological ethics has become more conscious of its social orientation as it calls persons and societies to work more inclusively together toward greater justice and mercy in the world.

Later, we broke for the first of the two extended concurrent sessions. Again, these sessions were designed to bridge-build on each panel. For instance, one panel on global climate action had someone from Kenya speaking with someone working in Switzerland; at a panel on the far-reaching consequences of climate change, an Indian moralist working with local farmers presented alongside someone from Zimbabwe. The entire session reflected the three topics cast through the vision of bridge-building. Then, our fourth plenary engaged us in a session on ethics and public discourse, led by a journalist who coached all the participants into understanding how to connect with the media so that their research would not simply be for academics but for the greater public square and the entire church. Other ethicists (from Brazil, the Philippines, and Spain) complemented the journalist's counsel with their own testimonies of bringing ethics out of the academy and into the public sphere.

We moved to the cathedral for the Eucharistic liturgy on Saturday evening. Cardinals Vinko Pujlic of Sarajevo and Peter Turkson of Ghana presided, while Cardinal Blase Cupich of Chicago, reflecting on John 6 and the feeding of the hungry listeners, invited us to enter into history to effect long-standing social change. Reminding us that the call to respond to the work of God not only belongs to the past and the future, but more immediately to the present, Cupich urged us to hear the immediate summons to serve and act collectively.

The final day began with a plenary on three networks that aim through dialogue for peace and reconciliation, exemplifying the call we each shared. Then, the regions gathered for the second continental discussions, this time working for strategies for action in hope. A second concurrent session followed, structured much like the earlier, one allowing us to descend into the particular challenges of climate change, migration, and poor political leadership by bridge-building.

The final afternoon turned to three events. First, speakers presented other organizations that network for social change. Then, we moved to prophetic calls from Pablo Blanco (Blanco 2019) of Argentina, Emmanuel Katongole (Katongole 2019) of Uganda, and Linda Hogan (Hogan 2019) of Ireland, who called us to a new vulnerability and a new solidarity to consider and accompany the marginalized as the Gospels summon us. Finally, at the closing banquet, Cardinal Turkson called us to attend to human development.

Throughout the conference, but most especially in the poster sessions, there was a hermeneutics of generosity among the participants. Besides this basic disposition, there was something deeply liturgical about our programmatic call for social transformation. Besides celebrating the Eucharist each day, we processed, remembered the dead, examined our consciences, heard the call to reconciliation, prayed for peace, and dismissed the assembly with a prophetic missioning. Certainly not everyone may have found it as Heyer and the rest of us planned it and certainly some of the participants may have wanted more political diversity than the diversity that was easily in evidence. Others, too, remarked how the coffee breaks, dinners, and other opportunities for conversation were extraordinarily rich and wished for more colloquies. However, these wishes and admonitions were within the strong bond of solidarity for sharing the same vocation as a theological ethicist, working locally and globally.

4. A New Form of Conferencing for Whom?

Hosting the conference in Sarajevo meant many more challenges than Trento. In Trento we were the beneficiary of many gifts from the province, the city, the University of Trento, and the archdiocese. Sarajevo had no such local beneficiaries, though they assisted us every step of the way. We knew that we would have to provide all our own resources.

Moreover, logistics were limited; Trento provided facilities that accommodated more than 600 and thus we could welcome whoever would come; Sarajevo, on the other hand, had its limits that would force us to think otherwise. Because the high school auditorium could only accommodate 450 people, and because we had over thirty other participants who were not theological ethicists (translators, technicians, local speakers like Youth for Peace), we could only host the conference with any respect for global diversity by invitation only. Sarajevo's challenges became ours and, in truth, we learned a lot from them as they accompanied us throughout.

Furthermore, the government of Bosnia and Herzegovina had very few consulates outside of Europe and securing required visas, especially for those from Asia and Africa, would prove extraordinary. For this reason, after we asked Heyer to construct the program, we realized how challenging Vicini's work would be in accompanying our registrants.

At the opening, Vicini (Vicini 2019) gave a rich account of our participants; 422 theological ethicists participated: 140 women and 282 men. For the first time in any of our conferences, one third of the participants were women. The participants were young too: 71 were new faculty; 29 of them were women, and of those, 19 were from the Global South. Another 48 were doctoral students. Together, these young people nominated by senior scholars made up nearly a third of our participants. Of the 140 women present, 118 were lay women and the rest religious sisters. Among the 282 men, 147 were lay men and 135 ordained and 97 of these belonged to religious congregations.

Of note, 78 countries were represented. From the Global North (Australia, Israel, Japan, Western Europe, Canada, and the USA), there were 169 participants; from the Global South, there were 253 participants. As Vicini (Vicini 2019, p. 13) announced: "We are very pleased that, for the first time, the countries and the colleagues from the Global South are the majority of the participants."

This sea change took us years of bridge-building. For instance, because of interventions made at Padua by the three African women ethicists, CTEWC pursued funding for doctorates in theological ethics for women in Africa. Under the leadership of Agbonkhianmeghe Orobator, S.J., as well as Hogan and Keenan, we developed a doctoral program for eight women in Africa. At Sarajevo were five of these women. This program served as a catalyst for others to support and sustain African women's voices. Thus, at Sarajevo, there were 15 of the now 24 women Catholic ethicists in Africa. Similarly, when we met in Trento, the Europeans were overwhelmingly from the West, but in Sarajevo, 46 of the 116 Europeans came from Central and Eastern Europe.

Getting people to Sarajevo was another challenge. Vicini secured the help of an ethicist in Sarajevo and the collaboration of the Bosnian Foreign Ministry and processed over 100 Bosnian visas. All but one were secured.

We supported many, though not all, from the Global South to come. We covered the flights for 238 participants and contributed part of the traveling expenses of a few doctoral students. Vicini also brilliantly secured housing for 260 colleagues. In short, the mission statement we developed a generation ago continues to guide us as we build bridges for networking in Catholic theological ethics.

At the end of the conference, Heyer, Vicini, and Keenan edited the plenary papers for our seventh international volume *Building Bridges in Sarajevo: The Plenary Papers from CTEWC 2018*, which will appear in October 2019. At the same time, the new leadership asked Autiero and me to remain on the new CTEWC Planning Committee and invited three others to join the new Planning Committee: Michelle Becka from Germany, Alexandre Martins from Brazil, and Toussaint Kafarhire from the Democratic Republic of Congo. Along with the CTEWC administrator, Toni Ross, the nine members meet virtually monthly to continue directing the network.

5. Plans for the Future

Immediately after the conference, Mark McGreevy, the founding director of the Institute for Global Homelessness, hosted a conference in November 2018 for ethicists and advocates to work together for greater responsiveness to the challenge. McGreevy engaged us in CTEWC and nearly half of the participants at the conference were members of our network. Learning that no ethicist had ever published as much as an article on the topic, Keenan and McGreevy (Keenan and McGreevy 2019) decided to edit a volume on *Street Homelessness and Catholic Theological Ethics*, which became the eighth volume in our series. This marks the first time CTEWC is partnering with another global network and is publishing a collection by authors who are either housing experts or ethicists. The volume is due out this November. In a similar way, The Centre for the Protection of Children, an initiative that follows the sexual abuse scandal in the Catholic church and that is stationed at Rome's Gregorian University, began plans, again with the assistance of CTEWC, to host an international conference called, "Doing Theology in the Faces of the Sexual Abuse Scandal." In March 2020, 100 theologians and ethicists will gather in Rome from across the globe to reflect on the crisis.

At this juncture, we have entered our second generation and the public effectiveness of our network is more and more in evidence. For this reason, our new leadership has called for a meeting in Munich in October 2019 of roughly 50 of the most active members to consider further developments within our network. At the same time, they commissioned from the Center for the Applied Research in the Apostolate an extensive survey of the membership to estimate the effectiveness of our structures and to generate new ideas and programs for the second generation. The survey has been completed and the results will be shared at the Munich meeting.

Through our Planning Committee we have earmarked a number of projects for greater consideration. Among these, Heyer has already begun to redesign our website, to become a more accessible archive for the work of our members and to develop our site's capacity for greater on-line engagement of the "Forum" contributions. Second, we hope to develop our book series to continue to take on concrete issues irrupting locally, but known globally, that need to be given a Catholic ethical hearing, like sexual abuse, the collapse of democracies, religious intolerance, and sexual minorities. Third, we want to expand our visiting scholars program. Fourth, in a similar way, we want to see institutions, particularly universities and major seminaries, participating more clearly in our network. For instance, already the Ateneo de Manila and St. Vincent's University in Manila, Dharmarham in Bangalore, Catholic University of East Africa, and Hekima College became hosting institutions for the visiting scholars program. Similarly, Boston College began awarding post-doctoral fellows to the eight African women PhDs and then visiting fellowships to other faculty from the Global South. New York's St. John's University dovetails by hosting some of BC's fellows at their institution, while Trinity College Dublin offered a scholarship to an African woman for PhD studies.

Finally, we are considering two other major projects. First, just as the Europeans decided to bridge-build from Western to Eastern Europe, several leaders from the United States are planning on building border initiatives of solidarity with those in Mexico to respond to the on-going crisis generated by President Donald Trump's own border initiatives in that region. Second, we want to meet more often and effectively to address increasingly urgent issues and we are planning on developing virtual tables that will host continued discussions with committed leaders and members. This might become our most ambitious project, which first emerged at Sarajevo, when younger members proposed that colleagues offer set themes at different tables during our Saturday luncheon. More than 27 different thematic tables were sponsored then on that day. At Munich, we will decide how to sponsor virtually six or seven such tables on major themes like sustainability, economic inequity, global migration, peace-building, and sexual abuse. These tables will meet with some regularity (every six weeks?) with a set chair and members who will decide how they will discuss the issues and what actions they may need to take in light of their meetings. Together with our newsletter and newly revamped website, this final initiative might provide us with a way of deepening our network without having to meet internationally again. We will not know how successful the virtual tables project will be until we try them.

6. Assessing Our Work for This Volume

At the beginning of this essay, I claimed that ethicists need to be better connected and then presented a Catholic instance of nearly twenty years developing on multi-levels a network of connectedness. In a moment, I shall try to highlight the specific lessons we learned in CTEWC, but first I want to return to my general claim in light of having presented the narrative with the many apparent goods that such connectedness yielded.

Our claim that ethicists need to be better connected stands as a witness and as a challenge to how we need to re-envision Christian ethics today. At first sight, this might seem easily valid, but as a matter of fact, the academy and its allies do not readily promote or recognize the merit of such connectedness. Certainly we know ethicists who believe in the sufficiency of their own ideas, who believe that they do not need to be connected beyond their usual bibliography, their usual academic cohort, or their own locality. Academic publishers support that stance in as much as they show greater interest in publishing and marketing singular authors and their contributions rather than edited collections, and effectively undermine the efforts of connectedness. Similarly, they argue that collections require subventions, while single authored works generally do not. If one asks them why, the response is "sales." University administrators, too, in their assessments of faculty members' academic performance, often underestimate the significance of editing collected works; therein again dissuading such work of connecting. The single authorship of a manuscript is incomparable in institutional merit to the work of a faculty member who plans and realizes a conference and then sets about editing in a sophisticated way the subsequent papers for a publication that offers a multi-perspectival read on a singular, but diversely realized, global problematic.

These institutional strategies to promote the individual as individual belong in a very particular way to the humanities faculty member. As Keenan (Keenan 2015) argues at length in *University Ethics: How Colleges Can Build and Benefit from a Culture of Ethics*, the humanities professoriate differs remarkably in its isolated individualism from almost any other type of contemporary professional. While police officers, physicians, nurses, lawyers, financial consultants, and political advisors all work in teams, the humanities professor works alone, writes alone, teaches alone, and holds their own singular office hours. The dissertation as the capstone entry into the professoriate is marked usually by two to three years of extraordinarily solitary labor and is unlike any other professional entry qualification. Not all university faculty work this way. Today, in university labs, faculty members in the sciences research together with their students and other colleagues and publish collectively authored papers routinely. While being connected is self-evident to most other professionals and even other faculty like scientists and social scientists, only the humanities faculty and their administrators and publishers need an argument for being connected. It was therefore not surprising that, at that Roman dinner with which I began this narrative, none of the four faculty teaching at institutions within a kilometer of each other had ever met during their more than 15 years of work there.

For nearly one hundred years, we have known from sociologists like Karl Mannheim, that research needs to be multi-perspectival. Today, in the field of ethics, we know that the two most challenging global tasks, climate change and migration, have no real singular privileged viewpoint. We cannot credibly address climate change without the research coming from the varied populations affected by climate change locally. Similarly, we cannot appreciate the overwhelming challenges of migration without understanding the multitudinous reasons for why more than 60 million people are now on the move.

Just as we need to be connected in order to understand the issues, we need to be connected to act responsively to these issues, for the end of all ethical investigations is to act. In his terrifying introduction to the *Future of Ethics*, Willis Jenkins (Jenkins 2013, p. 1) writes "Ethics seems imperiled by unprecedented problems. The accelerating expansion of human power generates problems that exceed the competency of our laws, our institutions, and even our concepts. What does justice mean for climate change, a problem in which humans from many nations, traditions, and generations find themselves collectively responsible for how a planetary system will function over centuries?" Indeed, now more than ever, we realize the inevitable importance of connection. And so, this essay is an invitation to hear the urgent summons to connect as the very first step to re-envisioning Christian ethics.

Yet, now let me conclude with what we learned from hearing that summons in 2003. From our first meeting until today, as we prepare for our strategy meeting in Munich in October 2019, we have grown consistently as a network of Catholic theological ethicists, influencing theological inquiry across the world and throughout the local churches. More than anything, we grew organically, trying always to expand our connectedness throughout the world and, in particular, throughout the extensive Global South. We have, through it all, avoided any formal memberships, while rotating frequently regional directors, forum writers, planning committee members. We have always attended to newly emerging junior scholars and remote or isolated colleagues, while deeply committed to the global struggles to provide platforms, especially for women to express their own voices and have them heard. Though fundraising has been essential, what guarantees our success is that we have worked and deliberated collectively.

We have re-envisioned Christian ethics interpersonally in praxis. We have created contexts for encounter and engagement, whether through our international or regional conferences, our forum and newsletter, our visiting professors program, or our book series. In each context, we have sought to expand and deepen the connectedness of our network while sharing insights, methods, and challenges. Our first volume on feminism, for instance, was edited by Hogan from Ireland and Orobator from Nigeria and the contributors whom they invited into the project represented a diversity that most discussions on even feminism have not been able to realize. Similarly, our work on sustainability and resource extraction took us from islands in the Pacific to the heart of Africa. Those contributors, in turn, became involved in our conferencing.

Yet we wonder whether we should continue with large-scale conferencing or whether we should construct more frequent encounters in virtual reality. After three major international conferences, we wonder whether we can transition into these virtual connections. Yet, what other choice do we have when, as ethicists, we find it hard to validate a conference that has 600 international flights? We know we have to connect and we hope that, after 16 years of building the network, we might be able to try more ecologically ethical strategies to meet and work together. That is why we are going with a small group to Munich.

Now, we find ourselves connecting with other networks, while becoming more virtual in our praxis. We still continue to connect as Catholic ethicists, though each of us is connected to regional guilds and networks that are ecumenical or even inter-religious, whether through the Society of Christian Ethics, *Societas Ethica*, the Circle of Women in Africa, or the Ecclesia of Women in Asia. This Catholicism is what we try to embody, a Vatican II Catholicism that appreciates the global or universal, but realizes that it is only understood and alive in the local. And in that, our network has quite an affinity to the on-going reforms of Pope Francis, who raises up continuously the local church so as to understand its universal Catholicism.

Still, we ethicists are not solely mindful of our church. We realize that, in a world like ours where political powers and movements are avowedly anti-bridge-building, particularly in considering the Global South, we believe that we are on the right path of envisioning Christian Ethics for these troubled times. And while we might not have a fixed vision or a set method of what our world should become, we at least know that our interlocutors are now available in nearly every corner of the world precisely so that in these trying times we can together teach, publish and act effectively, collectively, and ethically. And perhaps in that solidarity, we can offer a model and a vision that is not often seen.

Funding: This research received no external funding.

Conflicts of Interest: The author declares no conflict of interest.

References

Agnes Brazal, Aloysius Casrtagenas, Eric Genilo, and James F. Keenan, eds. 2010. *Transformative Theological Ethics: East Asian Contexts*. Quezon City: Ateneo de Manila University Press.

Angelini, Giuseppe. 2007. The *Sensus Fidelium* and Moral Discernment. In *Catholic Theological Ethics in the World Church: The Plenary Papers from the First Cross-cultural Conference on Catholic Theological Ethics*. Edited by James F. Keenan. New York: Continuum, pp. 202–9.

Autiero, Antonio, and Laurenti Magesa, eds. 2018. *The Catholic Ethicist in the Local Church*. Maryknoll: Orbis Books.

Blanco, Pablo A. 2019. A "Bridge-building" Theological Ethics: A Brand New Theological Approach. In *Building Bridges in Sarajevo: The Plenary Papers from CTEWC 2018*. Edited by Kristin E. Heyer, James F. Keenan and Andrea Vicini. Maryknoll: Orbis Books, pp. 219–24.

Brazal, Agnes, and Maria Theresa Davila, eds. 2016. *Living with(out) Borders: Catholic Theological Ethics on the Migrations of Peoples*. Maryknoll: Orbis Books.

Brazal, Agnes, and Andrea Si Lizares, eds. 2007. *Body and Sexuality*. Manila: Ateneo de Manila Press.

Chan, Lúcás. 2011. Bridging Christian and Confucian Ethics: Is the Bridge Adequately Christian and East Asian? *Asian Christian Review* 5: 49–73.

Chan, Yiu Sing Lúcás, James F. Keenan, and Shaji George Kochuthara, eds. 2016. *Doing Catholic Theological Ethics in a Cross Cultural and Interreligious Asian Context*. Bangalore: Dharmaram Press.

Chan, Yiu Sing Lúcás, James F. Keenan, and Ronaldo Zacharias, eds. 2018. *The Bible and Catholic Theological Ethics*. Maryknoll: Orbis Books.

Chummar, Paul, ed. 2010. *Natural Law ... in Search of a Common Denominator*. Nairobi: Catholic University of East Africa.

Cimperman, Maria. 2006. America settrionale: Dare voce all'etica sociale Cristiana. *Rivista di Teologia Morale* 152: 501–6.

Cuda, Emilce, ed. 2017. *Hacia una Etica de Participacion y Esperanza: Congreso Latino Americano de Etica Teologica*. Bogotá: Javeriana University.

Curran, Charles. 2019. Responding to Contemporary Crises: Resources from the Tradition. In *Building Bridges in Sarajevo: The Plenary Papers from CTEWC 2018*. Edited by Kristin E. Heyer, James F. Keenan and Andrea Vicini. Maryknoll: Orbis Books, pp. 149–60.

Fabri dos Anjos, Marcio. 2006. America Latina: Un continente di speranze. *Rivista di Teologia Morale* 152: 483–92.

Heyer, Kristin E. 2019. Introducing the Program. In *Building Bridges in Sarajevo: The Plenary Papers from CTEWC 2018*. Edited by Kristin E. Heyer, James F. Keenan and Andrea Vicini. Maryknoll: Orbis Books, pp. 9–12.

Hogan, Linda, ed. 2010. *Applied Ethics in a World Church: The Padua Conference*. Maryknoll: Orbis Books.

Hogan, Linda. 2019. Vulnerability: An Ethic for a Divided World. In *Building Bridges in Sarajevo: The Plenary Papers from CTEWC 2018*. Edited by Kristin E. Heyer, James F. Keenan and Andrea Vicini. Maryknoll: Orbis Books, pp. 231–37.

Hogan, Linda, and Agbonkhianmeghe Orobator, eds. 2014. *Feminist Catholic Theological Ethics: Conversations in the World Church*. Maryknoll: Orbis Books.

Iozzio, Mary Jo, Mary Doyle Roche, and Elsie Miranda, eds. 2008. *Calling for Justice Throughout the World: Catholic Women Theologians on the HIV/AIDS Pandemic*. New York: Continuum.

Jenkins, Willis. 2013. *The Future of Ethics: Sustainability, Social Justice, and Religious Creativity*. Washington, DC: Georgetown University Press.

Katongole, Emmanuel. 2019. Seven Convictions of an Emerging Prophetic Theological Ethics in Our Time: A Call to Action. In *Building Bridges in Sarajevo: The Plenary Papers from CTEWC 2018*. Edited by Kristin E. Heyer, James F. Keenan and Andrea Vicini. Maryknoll: Orbis Books, pp. 225–30.

Keenan, James, ed. 2007. *Catholic Theological Ethics in the World Church: The Plenary Papers from the First Cross-cultural Conference on Catholic Theological Ethics*. New York: Continuum.

Keenan, James, ed. 2011. *Catholic Theological Ethics, Past, Present, and Future: The Trento Conference*. Maryknoll: Orbis Books.

Keenan, James F. 2015. *University Ethics: How Colleges Can Build and Benefit from a Culture of Ethics*. Lanham: Rowman and Littlefield.

Keenan, James, and Mark McGreevy. 2019. *Street Homelessness and Catholic Theological Ethics*. Maryknoll: Orbis Books.

Lorenzetti, Luigi. 2006. Europa: Le nuove sfide dell'etica teologica. *Rivista di Teologia Morale* 152: 507–17.

Lourdusamy, Paul. 2006. Asia: Le ingiustizie della globalizzazione. *Rivista di Teologia Morale* 152: 475–82.

Monteiro, Evelyn, and M. M. Antoinette Gutzler, eds. 2005. *Ecclesia of Women in Asia: Gathering the Voices of the Silenced*. Delhi: ISPCK.

Onyema, Anozie. 2006. Africa: Una via africana all' etica teologica. *Rivista di Teologia Morale* 152: 467–74.

Peppard, Christiana, and Andrea Vicini, eds. 2015. *Just Sustainability: Technology, Ecology and Resource Extraction*. Maryknoll: Orbis Books.

Schotsmans, Paul. 2019. Senior Voices. In *Building Bridges in Sarajevo: The Plenary Papers from CTEWC 2018*. Edited by Kristin E. Heyer, James F. Keenan and Andrea Vicini. Maryknoll: Orbis Books, pp. 24–27.

Steck, Christopher. 2011. Catholic Ethics as Seen from Padua. *Journal of Religious Ethics* 39: 365–90. [CrossRef]

Trentin, Giuseppe. 2009. Situazione e problemi della teologia morale cattolica. *Studia Patavina* 56: 471–90.

Valadier, Paul. 2007. Has the Concept of *Sensus Fidelium* Fallen into Desuetude? In *Catholic Theological Ethics in the World Church: The Plenary Papers from the First Cross-cultural Conference on Catholic Theological Ethics*. Edited by James F. Keenan. New York: Continuum, pp. 187–92.

Vicini, Andrea. 2019. Who Are We, Where Do We Come From, and How Did We Get to Sarajevo? In *Building Bridges in Sarajevo: The Plenary Papers from CTEWC 2018*. Edited by Kristin E. Heyer, James F. Keenan and Andrea Vicini. Maryknoll: Orbis Books, pp. 12–15.

Wolfe, Regina Wentzel, and Christine E. Gudorf, eds. 1999. *Ethics and World Religions: Cross Cultural Case Studies*. Marknoll: Orbis Press.

© 2019 by the author. Licensee MDPI, Basel, Switzerland. This article is an open access article distributed under the terms and conditions of the Creative Commons Attribution (CC BY) license (http://creativecommons.org/licenses/by/4.0/).

Article
Christian Ethics and Ecologies of Violence

Luke Beck Kreider

Religious Studies, University of Virginia, Charlottesville, VA 22903, USA; lbk3vx@virginia.edu

Received: 13 August 2019; Accepted: 30 August 2019; Published: 31 August 2019

Abstract: This essay introduces "ecologies of violence" as a problem for Christian ethics. Understanding the links between violence and the natural environment will be critical to the pursuit of justice, peace, and sustainability in the twenty-first century. Yet these links often evade political action and escape moral attention because they do not fit comfortably within any of the fields requisite to address them. In most cases, the available resources for confronting these issues—"environmental issues" and "peace and conflict issues"—exist in separate toolkits, and no single discourse has developed resources to address their progressively merging spheres of concern. The essay outlines four types of ecological violence, examines recent work in Christian ethics relevant to them, and then argues for a dialogical method of ethics to confront them. Doing Christian ethics at the intersections of violence and environmental issues will require careful attention to environmental ethics as well as to the ethics of violence. More than that, it will require judicious efforts to navigate between them within case-based and place-based ethical analyses. Ecologies of violence invite Christian ethics to develop possibilities of ethical discernment and reparative action that do justice to the deep entanglement of ecological and sociopolitical systems.

Keywords: Christian ethics; environment; ecology; war; violence; environmental ethics; ethics of war and peace; ecological theology; political theology

1. Introduction

The interconnections between violence and the natural environment are attracting attention, and for good reason. When the United States Department of Defense urged Congress to consider climate change an "urgent and growing threat to our national security" in 2015, they echoed a widening corpus of scholarly literature suggesting that human-caused environmental changes compound the conditions for violent conflict.[1] At the same time, researchers have drawn attention to the enormous ecological significance of contemporary warfare, as modern weaponry and military-industrial production exert both immediate and long-term impacts on non-human species and ecological systems.[2] Understanding the links between violence and the environment will be critical to the pursuit of justice, peace, and sustainability in the twenty-first century. How Christian ethics engage ecologies of violence will help determine how the field conceives its purposes and executes its methods, and will play a major role in shaping what the Christian tradition comes to mean in an era of entangled social and environmental systems.

Ecologies of violence often evade political action and escape moral attention because they do not fit comfortably within any of the fields requisite to address them. The causes and consequences of violence exceed the purview of ecological ethics, environmental policy, or resource management;

---

[1] (United States Department of Defense 2015; Homer-Dixon 1999; Diehl and Gleditsch 2001; Burke et al. 2015).
[2] (Stockholm International Peace Research Institute 1975; Westing 1990; Grunawalt et al. 1996; Austin and Bruch 2000; Hupy 2008).

frameworks responsive to political violence do not account for the conveyance of harm and hostility through ecological systems. Especially within North Atlantic Christianities, the available resources for confronting these issues—"environmental issues" and "peace and conflict issues"—exist in two separate toolkits. The field of Christian ethics in particular has neglected to develop discourses or practices addressing their progressively merging spheres of concern.

This essay introduces ecologies of violence as a problem for Christian ethics. It distinguishes four broad types of connection between violence and natural environment, all prominent and morally urgent in diverse places across the globe today. It offers an explanation for why these issues have rarely been treated as matters of Christian concern despite clearly falling within the scope of the tradition's ethical interests, before turning to a few recent works in the field that take initial steps toward Christian ethics attuned to the links between climate change and violence. The essay builds from critical engagements with these pioneering works toward a constructive argument for how to do Christian ethics for ecologies of violence. Doing Christian ethics at the intersections of violence and environmental change will require careful attention to environmental ethics as well as to the ethics of violence. More than that, it will require judicious efforts to navigate between them, to develop possibilities of ethical discernment and reparative action that do justice to the deep entanglements of ecological and sociopolitical systems.

With rare exceptions, the gap in moral discourses and practices connecting ecology and violence spans the entire range of Christian denominations and theological schools in the North Atlantic. Focused efforts to critique and expand Christian capacities to engage violent ecologies will no doubt take diverse paths, drawing from distinctive theological, cultural, and sociological sources. But the conceptual and functional rift at the intersection of sociopolitical and ecological systems is a remarkable point of confluence among the tradition's many streams. That rift is this essay's point of departure.

2. Ecologies of Violence

Violence can be propelled by, committed against, and conveyed through ecological systems. This has always been the case, but a number of factors converged in the late twentieth century to make the environmental dimensions of violence more visible and more pressing.[3] Several media-saturated military campaigns—notably the Vietnam War and the Persian Gulf War—perpetrated catastrophic environmental damages, raising alarms about the ecological consequences of armed conflict. In the United States in the late 1970s, grassroots groups organized in opposition to public and corporate land use practices that disproportionately exposed working class minority communities to harmful toxins, ultimately spawning a national movement and a moral paradigm ("environmental justice") focused on how discriminatory patterns of land management diminished the lives of people of color by contaminating their environments and thereby poisoning their bodies; they thus drew attention to how ecological systems may become channels of racialized violence.[4] Most prominently, ever-increasing concerns about climate change have forced attention to the intimate relations of human society, political economy and earth, as planetary forces (shaped at least in part by human forces) threaten to generate or intensify social and political turbulence at multiple scales.

In short, there has been a general trend toward seeing the natural environment entangled with various forms of violence. But seeing this as a trend requires gathering together distinct and disparate strands of contemporary discourse on conflict, violence, and ecological stress. For the most part, these issues emerged independently and have been treated under separate cover. A rare effort to engage several in tandem is made in Nicole Detraz's book *Environmental Security and Gender*, which distinguishes but also interlinks three now-prominent fields at the intersections of security and environment: (1) *environmental conflict*, which considers armed conflict over natural resources,

---

[3] See (Stone 2000).
[4] See (Bullard 1990).

(2) *environmental security*, which engages environmental degradation as a problem for human health and well-being, and (3) *ecological security*, which treats environmental degradation as a problem in itself, assessing strategies to protect non-human creatures and ecological systems from the negative effects of human behavior.[5] In addition to providing one of the most lucid and comprehensive overviews available, Detraz shows how each of these intersections is further entangled with gender, and so develops a compelling argument for a feminist environmental security discourse.[6] In the fields of Christian theology and ethics, the idea that despoliation of the environment is intimately linked to the oppression of women has been well-established by eco-feminists and ecowomanists since the mid-1970s,[7] and the gendered dimensions of warfare were famously raised by Jean Bethke Elshtain and more recently by Susan Brooks Thistlethwaite.[8] Conceptual parallels and historical alliances between white supremacist violence and colonialist patterns of environmental exploitation have been highlighted by James Cone, George Tinker, and Dianne Glave, among others,[9] while Martin Luther King, Jr. is only the most celebrated name to have preached about the interlocked dynamics of racism and militarism in the United States.[10] But rarely have Christian thinkers followed Detraz in closing the triangle, engaging identity-based oppressions where environmental issues and political violence converge. Still fewer consider these intersections together in light of the religious practices and frameworks through which they are often experienced, constructed, reinforced or resisted.

To treat links between violence and environment as a problem for Christian ethics means to ask questions about Christian moral life amidst this tangled web of relations. It means struggling to orient ecclesial responses to complex systems of suffering that traverse conceptual boundaries and bind together spheres of life that Christians (of the North Atlantic) have traditionally considered separate. The term *ecologies of violence* attempts to capture this complexity. The field of ecology engendered a paradigm shift in the life sciences in the early twentieth century, as the new discipline endeavored to understand organisms in terms of their relationships with others and with their environments, examining how the cycling of energy and nutrients through the biotic and abiotic elements of a community shape the patterns, quality, abundance, distribution and diversity of life in a place. Natural scientists do not typically use the term "ecology" as a plural noun—the dynamic systems they study are not "ecologies" but rather "ecosystems"—but humanists and social scientists speak of "ecologies" to describe the systemic interrelations that shape the conditions and the experiences of human communities, especially in light of the environmental channels—transformations of land, extractions and distributions of water and minerals, energy regimes, emissions of particulates into the air, alterations to global atmosphere, and so on—through which humans interact with each other and with other creatures. In this modified usage, *ecologies* entail the many ways human individuals and communities continuously shape and are shaped by their social and natural habitats. The term *ecologies of violence* directs attention to how ecological systems and environmental conditions affect, integrate, and convey relationships of harm, domination, and diminishment among human beings and between human communities and the rest of nature.

Understood in this light, the connections between violence and the environment are not narrow concerns or niche interests reserved for specialists. They encompass the intersectional dynamics of violence in exceptionally wide scope. For Christian ethics, attention to ecologies of violence invites thinkers to reconnect political theology to creation and theological anthropology to place; it attunes social and environmental ethics to systemic and intersectional problems, raising questions about how to conceive and orient Christian life where the orders of creation bear the wounds of human sin;

---

[5] (Detraz 2015, pp. 25–57).
[6] (Detraz 2015, pp. 58–86).
[7] See (Ruether 1975; McFague 1993; Warren 1997; Williams 1993; Baker-Fletcher 1998; Harris 2017).
[8] (Elshtain 1987; Thistlethwaite 2015).
[9] (Cone 2001; Tinker 2008; Glave 2006).
[10] (King 1991).

it keeps the field responsive to lived reality, and elicits virtues of dialogue now crucial to the discipline and basic to moral engagement in pluralist environments.

2.1. Ecologies of Violence: Four Types

One possible reason that the ecology of violence has not been treated as a subject for Christian ethics is that the links between violence and environment are so many and so varied that they confound integrated analysis. An important first step is to map the relations at a legible scale. Although a fair bit of reductionism is involved in any such effort, Christian ethics could begin to engage ecologies of violence with attention to four basic types.

2.1.1. The Ecological Drivers of Conflict and Peace

The first type tracks the various ways that environmental changes, ecological forces, and natural resources factor into the onset, objectives, and resolutions of violent conflict. This encompasses what Detraz and others refer to as "environmental conflict," meaning conflict over scarce natural resources. Knowing that heightened climatic variability is likely to create severe stresses—and in many places critical scarcities—for the basic necessities of human life (e.g., water and food), many now predict a marked rise in "resource wars." The logic is straightforward: if environmental change leads to resource scarcity, and if people groups compete and often fight over scarce resources, then environmental change is likely to occasion inter-group competition and probably violent conflict.

But competition over resources like water and arable land is just one way ecological forces bear on conflict. Another is that planetary changes—e.g., sea-level rise and ocean warming—and related extreme weather events contribute to human migration, which in turn seem to affect the entrenchment of national identities and to deepen ethno-religious resentments, uprooting vulnerable populations and often driving them into other ecologically marginal and/or politically hostile lands. Another is that changing land- and seascapes factor into the transformation and renegotiation of regional and global political economy, threatening to unsettle already unstable civil and international relations.

The prevalence, probability and relative causal force of all these (and more) ecology-violence connections are debated; what is no longer questionable is that they merit urgent attention. The oft-cited potential for global climate change to displace peoples, catalyze resource conflicts, and aggravate social hostilities[11] is only the most sensational aspect of a growing body of scholarship tracing the relationships between environmental conditions and the prevalence of violence. Political scientists attempt to measure the impact of environmental factors on the outbreak of armed conflict, and debate the causal mechanisms at play.[12] Scholars in the adjacent fields of international relations and strategic peacebuilding discuss the significance of resource management and sustainability for violence prevention and conflict resolution.[13] "Environmental peacemaking" is now an active field of research and practice,[14] and climate change is arguably "the hottest issue in security studies."[15]

The issues have attracted so much attention, in fact, that many now worry about the "securitization" of ecological discourse and environmental politics.[16] Hans Günther Brauch argues that national security and defense now constitute the main reasons offered in public for combating climate change, at least in the Global North. He tracks a marked increase in global climate policy discussions framing Anthropocene challenges in terms of existential threats and national security concerns. Interpreting climate change as a national security risk (rather than an environmental problem or a justice issue) has been instrumental in mobilizing the climate change mitigation and adaptation regimes of North

---

[11] (Klare 2001; Parenti 2011; Alvarez 2017).
[12] (Diehl and Gleditsch 2001; Hsiang et al. 2011; Buhaug et al. 2014).
[13] (Jensen and Lonergan 2012; United Nations Environment Programme 2009).
[14] (Conca and Dabelko 2002). **See also** https://environmentalpeacebuilding.org.
[15] (Parsons 2010).
[16] (Graeger 1996; Buzan et al. 1998. Barnett and Dovers 2001).

Atlantic countries, he claims.[17] It is therefore no surprise to notice that the Department of Defense and the armed forces are arguably the sectors of the U.S. federal government that have engaged most seriously with climate change. Timothy Doyle and Sanjay Chaturvedi point to the recent "securitization and often militarization" of state responses to human migration as a key reason to be cautious about embedding climate politics within a security framework.[18] Daniel Deudney and Mark Zeitoun worry that security frameworks inject parochial assumptions, antagonistic norms, and militarized institutions into environmental politics, replacing important values like justice, participation, and human rights.[19]

Securitized environmental discourses also tend to view the significance of climate change and ecological degradation in an entirely anthropocentric frame. They risk foreclosing moral considerations or political strategies that include the interests of non-human creatures or the earth itself, or that honor the intimacies of human communities with their ecological relations. Relatedly, they often reinforce what Pope Francis calls the "technocratic paradigm," which treats creation as an inert object awaiting rational management by human experts and elites. The field's dominant disciplinary frameworks sheer the issues of key religious and moral valences. This poses both a problem and an opportunity for Christian analyses of environmental conflict. These same challenges will attend Christian reflection on ecologies of violence across all four types.

2.1.2. The Environmental Consequences of War

The second type concerns the impacts of warfare and military industrial production on natural environment. Armed combat endangers human and non-human inhabitants in and around warzones as it destroys or intoxicates the ecosystems in which they live. Used as a weapon, threatened as a target, and imperiled as collateral of military aims, the environment has never been immune to the violence of war. War's environmental impacts are especially pernicious in the advent of modern weaponry, the production and deployment of which releases chemical and biological particulates that cycle through water, air, and soil, and often into human and non-human bodies. For this reason, environmental scientists now attempt to track the impacts of modern warfare on war-zone ecologies, biodiversity and the human environment,[20] and military ethicists and international lawyers seek frameworks to evaluate and regulate the environmental effects of war-making.[21]

Much of this scientific, legal, and moral attention to wartime environmental destruction was catalyzed by the international scrutiny that followed the Vietnam War, during which the United States used herbicides and high-explosive munitions, systematically cleared land and bombed dams, and tinkered with the possibilities of strategic climate modification, endeavoring to turn the weather into a weapon of war.[22] The Persian Gulf War prompted another wave of consternation, when Iraqi troops set oil wells ablaze and caused the world's worst-ever oil spill, while coalition forces used cluster bombs and depleted uranium shells to destroy Iraq's water and sanitation works. The fallout from these conflicts illustrated how the environment broadens and magnifies war's destructive power, lengthening its temporal horizon, widening its spatial reach, carrying its sting across the borders of species and into the guts of the earth.[23]

The environmental impacts of war are distinct for the ways they spread the hazards of battle through ecological ripple effects—violence relayed through ecosystemic relations.[24] The effects of a discrete, carefully calibrated combat action may fan out through food chains and energy cycles, or leave its toxic legacy blowing in the wind or flowing through rivers, aquifers and pipes. When the

---

[17] (Brauch 2009).
[18] (Doyle and Chaturvedi 2012).
[19] (Deudney 1990, 1999; Zeitoun 2013).
[20] (Stockholm International Peace Research Institute 1975; Westing 1990; Hupy 2008).
[21] (Grunawalt et al. 1996; Austin and Bruch 2000; United Nations Environmental Program 2009; Rayfuse 2014).
[22] See (Diederich 1992).
[23] (Stockholm International Peace Research Institute 1976).
[24] (Schmitt 1997, p. 96).

environment is a victim of war, it also becomes a medium of political violence toward creatures great and small. When wars degrade the natural conditions necessary for life and well-being, they perpetrate arbitrary harms on civilians and other noncombatants. In the traditional language of military ethics, environmental destruction in war is *indiscriminate* violence—it extends the brutality of combat into the dwellings of innocents, human and non-human alike.

In fact, some ethicists have begun to consider how the Just War Tradition (JWT) could be adapted to interpret and address war's environmental impacts. Gregory Reichberg and Henrik Syse attempt "to show how the rich soil from which the just war tradition has grown includes elements relevant to the contemporary debate on the environmental consequences of war."[25] They draw on the theology of Thomas Aquinas to suggest how the tradition's philosophical foundations could also ground the moral value of nature, and so bring environment under the protections of the JWT's *in bello* principles. Mark Woods argues that careful considerations of potential environmental impacts should be part of just war deliberations *ad bellum*.[26] More recently, Matthew Shadle and Laurie Johnston have engaged Catholic Social Teaching on war in light of environmental degradation.[27] These efforts indicate the potential for Christian ethicists to deploy classical concepts in new ways to confront the challenge of ecological violence.

Yet the standard frameworks for morally assessing violence as well as the established ways of doing environmental ethics are vexed by the environmental consequences of war. Christian ethics of war and peace have not developed conceptual resources to grasp what is at stake—ethically or theologically—in the destruction of nature, and they have limited practical tools to orient lived responses to ecological violence. For environmental ethics, the complex couplings of ecological and human systems always create complications, but war is typically understood as a unique moral sphere, "a zone of radical coercion, in which justice is always under a cloud."[28] There are few precedents for interpreting and applying ecological values under the fog of war.

2.1.3. Land Conflict

Conflicts over land—including disputes over how to value, use or inhabit particular lands, and clashes over who land belongs to (or who belongs to the land)—entail a third kind of connection between violence and environment. Land conflict in the sense meant here is related to but distinct from what is typically called "environmental" or "resource" conflict. Environmental/resource conflicts are typically defined by competition over scarce resources, and are characterized by the ways ecological forces—especially environmental stresses and changes—stimulate those struggles. But conflicts over land use are not necessarily motivated by resource competition or driven by climatic or other environmental changes. Although they may sometimes feature disputes about the economic value of land, they are ultimately about the moral value and cultural meaning of contested places. Land conflicts share features of religious conflicts, in that they are often clashes of identities organized around group-defining lifeways and emplaced worldviews.

In *After Nature*, Jedediah Purdy argues convincingly that the embattled history of American land settlement and management is in part a story of rival "environmental imaginations." Environmental imagination refers to a people's way of thinking about and acting in relation to their natural environments. It is a group's distinct "way of seeing" the natural world, their "pattern of supposing how things must be." Carried by myths, narratives, lifeways, land policies, and so on, environmental imagination encompasses the significance of a group's ecological thought and practice to their

---

[25] (Reichberg and Syse 2000, p. 451).
[26] (Woods 2007).
[27] (Shadle 2011; Johnston 2015). Shadle also addresses environmental degradation as a "cause" of war.
[28] (Walzer 2004, p. x).

constructions of identity and meaning. "It is an implicit, everyday metaphysics, the bold speculations buried in our ordinary lives," writes Purdy.[29]

> From the beginning—unmistakably from the time of the first indigenous settlement, and overwhelmingly from the time of European colonization—the human presence in North America has been ecologically revolutionary, wiping out species, changing soils and plant mixes, and reshaping the surface of the earth. At least since Europeans conquered the continent, that ecological revolution has been deeply involved in contests over imagination, over the meaning of the world and the right way to live in it.[30]

After Nature shows how the bloody struggles over the possession and character of American soil transformed landscapes across the continent according to opposing conceptions of nature—ecological worldviews embodied in communities, enshrined in law, and religious in depth. America's originary history of ethno-religious land conflicts helped mold the nation's cultural and political identities as it fashioned a country speckled with sacred places disputed by many, protected and preserved for some, pillaged, desecrated and displaced for others.

Some of America's most celebrated sacred places—e.g., Yellowstone National Park—remain theaters of conflict between rival cultures and their competing land policies. In *The Battle for Yellowstone: Morality and the Sacred Roots of Environmental Conflict*, Justin Farrell argues that conflicts over the Greater Yellowstone Ecosystem remain embittered and intractable because dominant frameworks for understanding environmental policy disputes fail to grasp the "deeper cultural mechanisms" at play. The long-simmering hostilities at America's favorite secular sanctuary are part of "an underlying struggle over deeply held 'faith' commitments, feelings, and desires that define what people find sacred, good, and meaningful in life at a most basic level."[31]

Purdy's history of U.S. environmental policy and culture, and Farrell's sociological analysis of conflict at Yellowstone both reflect a pattern visible in diverse political and geographical contexts across the world: Land use disputes are more than inter-group conflicts over competing interests; they are cultural, ideological, and religious clashes. This is true even where parties are avowedly "secular" actors. At stake are the intertwined histories of nature and culture, of environment and identity—the pairs bound together by the embodied environmental imaginations hosted within a place, by their everyday ecological politics and their engagements with the sacred.

There is no field of study or body of research dedicated to land conflict so defined. Here is an opportunity for scholars of religion to lend their field knowledge and disciplinary tools to the critical study of ecologies of violence. For Christian ethicists to contribute to this work, however, the field will have to develop strategies for historically-informed and place-based inquiry into conflicted ecological faiths. Christian communities have lived such faiths in many times and places, with monumental implications for the formation of the tradition, for the moral lives of its practitioners, for their neighbors, and for the lands they passed through and in which they dwell.

2.1.4. Structural Violence Conveyed through Environmental Systems

Many climate justice advocates argue that the injustices associated with climate change reflect and even mediate deep-seated patterns of violence. Climate change is a symptom and a vehicle of *structural violence*, they argue.[32] Johan Galtung, a pioneer of peace and conflict studies, famously defined structural violence as "violence [that] is built into the structure and shows up as unequal power and consequently as unequal life chances."[33] For Cynthia Moe-Lobeda, structural violence names

---

[29] (Purdy 2015, pp. 9, 22).
[30] (Purdy 2015, p. 7).
[31] (Farrell 2015, p. 3).
[32] (Moe-Lobeda 2013; O'Brien 2017; Goldtooth 2017; Agarwal and Narain 1991; Nixon 2011).
[33] (Galtung 1969, p. 171).

systemic, interlocking processes which operate through human agency but function independently of any individual humans to "degrade, dehumanize, damage, and kill people by limiting or preventing their access to the necessities for life or for its flourishing." It is "harm that certain groups of people experience as a result of unequal distribution of power and privilege," and it includes the "complicity or silent acquiescence of those who fail to take responsibility for it and challenge it."[34]

Calling climate change structural violence focuses moral attention on the conditions of persistent inequality that follow climate change from its origins in the developed world's disproportionate uses of environmental resources and atmospheric space, through its political negotiation in global arenas marked by radical imbalances of power, to its projected consequences, which will be most severe for the poor and other vulnerable groups. A close look at climate change attunes us to the strange possibility that violence may flow through ecological and atmospheric systems. This sort of violence, despite its structural scope, environmental medium, and accidental infliction, is no less real: it still strikes, still harms, still coerces and deprives.

The idea of ecologically-mediated violence need not seem strange, suggests Willis Jenkins, because ecology itself is political.[35] Nothing reveals that more clearly than persistently unequal distributions of environmental hazards. In the U.S., for example, toxic exposures, ecological degradations, and severe resource deficiencies are distributed along lines of class and especially race. The color of your skin is the best sociological predictor of how many unwanted chemicals have penetrated your body through your water, air, and soil.[36] Globally, the environments of the poor and the indigenous are degraded and destroyed through long-term dynamics of "resource capture" and "unequal ecological exchange."[37] Those historical relations are also implicated in the global poor's special vulnerabilities to climate-shaped threats like sea-level rise, severe drought and flooding. In short, the wounds wrought by climate change and other forms of environmental change highlight how harms flow gradually across time and space, finding vulnerable victims through the politically forged channels of ecological systems. Rob Nixon calls this "slow violence"—ecologically-transmitted violence that occurs "out of sight, a violence of delayed destruction . . . an attritional violence that is typically not viewed as violence at all." Slow violence is "incremental and accretive," with "calamitous repercussions playing out across a range of temporal scales."[38]

The concept of slow violence makes visible processes and relations that degrade and destroy through hidden channels. It thereby aims to subject environmental injustice to the strict moral censure reserved for acts of violence, and elicits moral and political responses that take seriously the suffering of its victims and the malice, negligence, or complicity of its perpetrators. Similarly, when advocates of climate justice place the causes and effects of climate change under the category of violence, they present a more dire account of the problem, and arguably appeal to a more demanding and holistic set of responsibilities. The category also guards against seemingly effective, efficient solutions that would nevertheless reinforce underlying patterns of inequality and exploitation.[39]

Typically, the field of climate justice is concerned with how to allocate fairly the costs of mitigating and adapting to climate change.[40] It argues over what factors should matter most when assessing those allocations, and how to measure and weigh harms and risks that are inequitably distributed across the globe's already uneven geographies of vulnerability, wealth, and power. Movements for environmental justice likewise take systemic inequalities and structural oppressions into account when meting out justice, but typically remain within a proceduralist and distributivist paradigm. Acknowledging climate change, racist ecologies, and resource capture as forms of ecologically-mediated structural

---

[34] (Moe-Lobeda 2013, pp. 72–78).
[35] (Jenkins 2013).
[36] (Bullard et al. 2007).
[37] (Martinez-Alier 2002; Roberts and Parks 2006, 2009).
[38] (Nixon 2011, p. 2).
[39] See (Goldtooth 2017; Francis 2015).
[40] e.g., (Martin-Schramm 2010; Broome 2012; Shue 2016).

violence implies that justice requires more than fair cost allocation and burden sharing, more than due process and equitable distributions of benefits and burdens. At minimum, interpreting such relations within the moral and political jurisdiction of violence seems to call forth practices of rebuke, accountability, and repair.

A full picture of the requirements of justice will depend on which moral frameworks and political precedents for responding to violence are brought to bear on cases of ecological violence. Here is another opportunity for Christian ethics to take up the challenge of addressing crucial contemporary connections between violence and the environment. But the challenge here is considerable. While structural violence seems an apt description of many of the evils of climate change, determining just responses to climate violence is difficult because responsibility and culpability is hard to track across all the confounding spatial and temporal scales through which climate change contributes to human suffering. Another important question is whether the paradigm of structural violence can make moral sense of humanity's relations to the non-human world, or whether the typically anthropocentric category of violence obscures the pain and silences the cries of "Sister, Mother earth."[41]

It is worth noting that the typology of ecological violence above is not the only possible way to map this material, nor is it necessarily comprehensive. As the fourth type makes clear, the question of how violence relates to the environment is partly an interpretive question, and always a discursive strategy, an attempt to frame pressing moral issues in terms of their social-ecological intersections. As all four types indicate, interpreting these issues at their intersections is a strategy with both promise and peril, risking, among other things, anthropocentering and securitizing environmental discourses, overextending and thus weakening the moral scope of violence, and overwhelming ethical competencies. Yet ethical reflection at these junctions holds considerable promise, not only for helping Christian moral life to catch up to Anthropocene challenges, but also for restoring Christian faith to an integral understanding of human personhood in the context of creation, and so to help Christian communities remain responsive to God's self-disclosive activity in the world.

Other possible maps might chart anthropogenic environmental degradation as a form of direct violence against non-human creatures or against the earth. Perhaps high-intensity agriculture does violence to the soil, or deforestation commits violence against forest creatures, and this should be treated as a distinct form of ecological violence. While plausible, this interpretation is not explored here. Not including it signals an impulse to set limits on the interpretive frame of violence for Christian environmental thought. As a concept describing acts and relationships, "violence" illumines some qualities of relations and obscures others. Applying it in so direct a way to human treatments of nature may crowd out ecocentric ways of understanding our ecological connections, even as it attempts to de-anthropocentralize the concept of violence. A strong argument could be made for adding a type to encompass the use of armed force to protect the environment[42] and the militarization of ecological conservation.[43] If these dynamics continue to grow in prominence, they may come to warrant separate treatment, but for now can be treated as distinctive forms of land conflict. Still other possible maps would create special places for the ecological dimensions of race-, class- or gender-based violence. But these intersections permeate the entire range of violent ecologies, so they are not treated as distinct types here. Instead they should be understood as pervasive features of the sociology of ecological violence. All four types should be investigated with attention to these penetrating and constitutive dynamics.

What the four types have in common are the embedded inter-relations of human societies within ecological systems, and thus the ways environments bear the forces of human enmity and strife.

---

[41] (Francis 2015). Willis Jenkins raised questions like these in (Jenkins 2017).
[42] See (Eckersley 2007). Eckersley proposes "ecological intervention" as an ecocentric corollary to humanitarian intervention, probing the ethical implications of the "responsibility to protect" in light of imminent threats to nature.
[43] (Duffy 2014).

Despite their differences, they all demand integrated moral analyses that cross environmental, political, and religious thresholds. Can Christian ethics do such work?

3. Perennial Gaps, Unprecedented Problems, and Some Recent Christian Ethics

Long-standing efforts to call attention to the ecology of violence—notably on land use conflicts and climate change, and mostly from thinkers from the Global South, indigenous communities, and liberationist traditions—struggle to influence the dominant Christian ethical discourses in the North Atlantic, where a violently won sense of environmental security combines with a deeply rooted conceptual poverty, making claims of ecological violence from the margins appear morally unimportant, if not theologically unintelligible. One way of accounting for the incapacity of North Atlantic Christian ethics to grasp the nature and significance of ecologies of violence can be found in Willie J. Jennings's extraordinary book *The Christian Imagination*, in which he argues that modern Euro-American Christianity was born in the severance of peoplehood from land. Recall Jedediah Purdy's notion of *imagination* as a "way of seeing, a pattern of supposing how things must be" and an "implicit, everyday metaphysic." Jennings argues that the dominant North Atlantic Christian imagination has seen human beings in terms of race instead of place, portable bodies enfleshed in color rather than integral peoples in kinship to earth. With the colonial construction of race as a category of human identity—forged in processes of frontier settlement through land seizure that displaced millions, and patterns of land and property ownership that objectified places into resources and people into slaves—Christianity "rendered unintelligible and unpersuasive any narratives of the collective self that bound identity to geography, to earth, to water, to trees."[44]

If these colonial histories seem remote—they are not—the underlying religious imaginations still readily appear. The Native American theologian George "Tink" Tinker writes of native peoples' continual frustrations in the struggle to have their collective identities "recognized and respected as distinct political entities based on specific land territories." Instead, well-meaning liberals bundle native concerns under the placeless logics of race- or class-based politics.[45] "The earth has been taken from us and given back to us changed," laments Jennings. "Thus our lives, even if one day freed from racial calculations, suffer right now from a less helpful freedom, freedom from the ground, the dirt, landscapes, and animals, from life collaborative with the rhythms of God's other creatures."[46] Perhaps this is one reason Christian ethics has struggled to grasp ecologies of violence as problems for Christian life: the Christian imagination, even in its progressive forms, will not conceive social or political life as enmeshed in ecological relations.[47] Ethicists have inherited practical and epistemic incapacities to do politics with nature, symptoms of a still deeper split between collective identity and place.

Further evidence for such a divorce is reflected in the near total separation between environmental and political theology, between the tradition's ecological ethics and its moral reflections on violence, conflict and peace. Christian environmental thought has developed quite a large library since the 1970s, but has almost never treated the problem of inter-human violence as part of its domain. Christian ethics hosts rich streams of reflection and practice on the ethics of violence, justice, and peacemaking, but these seldom encompass relations with non-human nature or the slow flow of harms through ecosystemic processes and atmospheric space.

The tradition's moral and practical frameworks for confronting environmental issues and political violence rarely overlap. Environmental ethics and the ethics of violence and peace remain discrete domains, even as their spheres of concern entwine in increasingly visible ways. Both want to promote flourishing in a world where it is no longer possible to think about justice and peace apart from ecological systems and environmental conditions, but both face questions foreign to their fields.

---

[44] (Jennings 2010, p. 59).
[45] (Tinker 2008, p. 23).
[46] (Tinker 2008, p. 290).
[47] Cf. (Jenkins 2018).

How should environmental ethicists respond to resource conflicts spawned by both environmental change and social divisions? How do peacebuilders assess and redress the ways environments mediate structural violence? For now, each field works with tools adapted for its own parochial environs, and a lack of dialogue threatens to leave both disciplines lagging behind the demands of their subject matter.

Yet growing concerns about climate change are just beginning to spark efforts to do ethics across some of these boundaries and to tackle the intersectional issues of climate violence. Perhaps that is because some in the field are beginning to see that the tradition's typical moral patterns are "imperiled by unprecedented problems," as Willis Jenkins has put it. The complexities and uncertainties of climate change occasion ethical innovation "when reform projects take their incompetence as a demand to create new possibilities from their inherited traditions."[48] Four Christian ethicists have recently tackled connections of violence and climate change, offering clues to how the field could proceed.

Michael Northcott diagnoses a problem similar to the one discussed above, but instead of implicating the Christian imagination Northcott blames the "modern West" and its secular analysts with their Enlightenment roots. "The foundational Enlightenment separation between nature and culture, and hence between natural history and the history of the earth, is the core conundrum of climate change," he writes in *A Political Theology of Climate Change*.[49] Northcott argues that Western political scientists miss the connections between climate and conflict because they tend to "decontextualise politics from geography, and culture from nature." To make sense of the fractious politics of a warming world, contemporary conflict "needs to be presented in ways that make the connections between climate and culture."[50] He claims that the "Enlightenment distinction between nature and culture, facts and values," has left moderns with an objectified vision of nature, rendering the moral and political significance of climate change conceptually opaque.[51] For Northcott, the modern West's continual resistance to the reality of climate change is rooted in an ingrained Kantian folly—namely, the decoupling of scientific and practical reason, and the segregation of rational human activity from the sacramental vitality of the natural world.[52] Climate science takes on theological significance as it "reveals that the cosmos is again, as it was for the Ancients, a source of value and revelation, a living being with which humans are in a living relations, involving exchange and negotiation."[53] Christians learn the same in church (or they should), where eco-structural sins are repented and worshippers "rediscover the primordial unity of all persons and creatures."[54]

Northcott takes pains to argue that Christian leaders and organizations were among the very first to address climate change as a genuine moral and political challenge.[55] But while he claims that Christian political theology has the necessary resources to confront environmental conflict, he offers no explanation for why the field has overwhelmingly failed to do so. Even Northcott's own work, which acknowledges climate conflict as a problem worthy of theological reflection, does not attend to the particular relations between environmental change and human violence from a Christian perspective. Still, if the conceptual alienations of nature and culture, place and identity, underlie the practical incompetence of Christian ethics before ecologies of violence, then Northcott's project represents one plausible way forward, focused on theological repair of public imagination. On the other hand, when his self-assured, even triumphalist account of Christianity attempts to evade complicity in the entangled legacies of colonialism, white supremacy, and the anti-ecological imaginations he agrees are at the root of climate change, Northcott abdicates responsibility for his own tribe's history of

---

[48] (Jenkins 2013, pp. 1, 6).
[49] (Northcott 2013, p. 188).
[50] (Northcott 2013, pp. 7–12).
[51] (Northcott 2017, p. 291). See also (Northcott 2007).
[52] (Northcott 2013, pp. 161–200).
[53] (Northcott 2017, p. 291).
[54] (Northcott 2007, p. 184).
[55] (Northcott 2017, p. 287).

violence, and so replicates the very kinds of politics that insulate from scrutiny the structural violence of climate change.

Mark Douglas's important new book *Christian Pacifism for an Environmental Age* takes a much more critical approach to Christian history and theology. He argues that Christian pacifism formed around a mythologized narrative of immaculate origins, and that early pacifist pretensions to ecclesial purity were implicated in the formation of an imperial church that pursued political power by recourse to coercion and exclusion.[56] The early church's pacifism was furthermore bound up with anti-Semitism, developing supersessionist hermeneutics and "schismatic tendencies" that have endured in pacifist theological politics, tendencies too often "rooted in judgments against and condemnation of other politically weak, marginalized, and/or oppressed communities."[57]

But Douglas's criticisms are part of an effort to reconstruct the Christian ethics of nonviolence in light of natural history and especially "climate-shaped conflict." "We are entering a new social imaginary shaped by environmental concerns," he writes. Living in the Anthropocene—Douglas calls it "the Environmental Age"—humans now understand the world and their place within it "through environmental lenses." Christian pacifists need to reform their ideas and practices for this emerging epoch, when conflict and violence are increasingly "environmentally shaped."[58]

Reconstructing Christian pacifism begins by "understanding our place in *time*."[59] By this he means primarily three things. First, it means understanding something about the particular moral challenges of the Environmental Age, including environmental conflict. Second, it means better understanding the history of Christian pacifism. And finally, it means interpreting both of the above within a theological understanding of God's action in history.

The vast majority of the book is devoted to the second task, which for Douglas is an effort to use historical method to complicate and destabilize the mythic narratives pacifists have rallied around. "In demythologizing pacifism, I hope to temporalize—and thereby humanize—it," he explains.[60] It is by humanizing pacifist history that he hopes to help today's pacifists acclimatize to the Environmental Age. When pacifists realize that the early church was never uniformly pacifist and that the tradition's founding theologians were anti-Semites complicit in the theological formation of empire, perhaps they will stop closing ranks, stop turning their noses up at the rest of the world, and instead learn to accept responsibility for their contributions to global environmental problems and to "pursue common cause with disparate others in dealing with climate-shaped conflict."[61]

One of the most illuminating features of the book is that Douglas attempts to narrate the rolls played by weather, climate, and geological events in the formation of pacifist tradition. As climatic changes shaped conflicts in late medieval Europe, "they also shaped the movements of pacifist thought."[62] Climatic changes have shaped the Christian ethics of violence and nonviolence—this is a momentous insight, especially for an environmental age, when ecological changes are predicted to be unsettling at unprecedented scales.[63] By arguing that traditions of Christian moral thought developed within communities' theo-ethical responses to environment, Douglas takes a step toward relocating religious history in its ecological setting, and so opens space for Christian ethics to grasp ecological violence within the orbit of lived faith.

Where Northcott rehabilitates a premodern doctrine of Creation to re-stitch culture and politics to earth, Douglas turns to recent work in environmental history to show how natural forces usher traditions through time. Both are efforts to link Christian political imagination to ecology in order

---

[56] (Douglas 2019, pp. 65–111).
[57] (Douglas 2019, p. 60).
[58] (Douglas 2019, pp. 2–3).
[59] (Douglas 2019, p. 3). My emphasis.
[60] (Douglas 2019, p. 9).
[61] (Douglas 2019, pp. 60–63, 79–81, 103–111, 125, 226).
[62] (Douglas 2019, p. 236).
[63] Cf. (Jenkins et al. 2018, pp. 97–99).

to prepare Environmental Age communities to address problems fundamentally linked to planetary change. But the most forceful conclusion drawn from *Christian Pacifism for an Environmental Age* is not about the natural world but about the nature of history. "When we ignore the impact of climate on history, we unnecessarily and unduly truncate the range of forces that shape history."[64] The theological significance of climate change seems primarily to reinforce certain best practices for religious historians: It is one reason among many to adopt a more subtle hermeneutic of tradition, so that those who look to history for moral inheritances can supply more complex and ambiguous readings of the past. Complex and ambiguous religious histories are, in turn, useful in the Environmental Age—more useful than essentialized, mythologized histories—because the moral postures they support are unburdened of perfectionism, purity, and divisiveness, and more open to irony, bricolage, and collaboration. Irony, bricolage, and collaboration will be virtues in the environmental age because climate change reveals moral conditions of universal complicity, ambiguity, and interconnectedness, and because meaningful solutions require working together. These are important points, if a bit simplistic, and the overall achievements of the book are a tremendous contribution to the history and historiography of Christian pacifism and an insightful effort to renew the tradition for a new era.

But what that renewed tradition can offer in terms of orienting practical pacifist moral engagement with climate-shaped conflict remains under-developed in the book. What can pacifist ethics do for climate violence? In the Afterward, Douglas envisions another book, one "that picks up where this one leaves off. How will Christian pacifism respond to violence caused by the movements of climate refugees, the competitions over increasingly scarce basic resources like grains and water, the political destabilizations of new pandemics, and other politico-ecological crises?" He says he hopes to write this book soon.[65]

Writing that book well will likely require some engagement with environmental ethics and Christian environmental thought. For a project aiming to renew traditions of Christian morality in light of environmental concern, Douglas's book has surprisingly little to say about the moral or theological significance of natural environment. How, where, and why does the non-human world have moral and/or theological value? Of what import is ecology to Christian faith? How does creation make claims on Christian lives? These questions matter for how Christian ethics engage ecologies of violence, and any practical approach to issues like climate-shaped conflict will answer them implicitly if not reflectively. Douglas's account seems to frame environment primarily as a set of external conditions creating social pressures. Mainly, it is the weather, which over time or through extreme events can be "disordering" to established ways of thinking and living. Climate change is a theological problem just because all serious shifts—"whether technological, political, or economic"—to the objective conditions of social life prompt people to ask questions, some of them theological, typically about God's presence in history.[66]

"In Euro-American (and European) philosophical and theological history it is more common to see intellectual reflections on the meaning of time; it is far less common to see intellectual reflections on space," observes Tinker. Most Native American worldviews and lifeways centered on space, he says. This has been reflected in their deep attachments to particular places, where peoplehood is conceived in responsible kinship to earth, to land and its diverse inhabitants. The genocidal displacement of native peoples in North America was the triumph of *time*—the conquest of land and people within providential history, interpreted as progress, sustained still in liberal narratives of development and in the banishment of earth from political imagination.[67] "The most destructive value that the European invaders imposed is the quantification and objectification of the natural world," writes Tom Goldtooth (Executive Director of the Indigenous Environmental Network) in a paper about the moral dangers of

---

[64] (Douglas 2019, p. 239).
[65] (Douglas 2019, p. 248).
[66] (Douglas 2019, p. 235).
[67] (Tinker 1997, pp. 96–99).

many seemingly reasonable responses to climate change.[68] Where history replaced creation as the primary domain of God's presence, environment was desacralized, and promptly desecrated.

These are of course fairly sweeping narratives, and perhaps they are just the kinds of monochrome histories Douglas works so strenuously to unsettle in his book. But stories about the erasure of place and the expulsion of earth from modern North Atlantic theological imagination proliferate in environmental theological literature. They are important in the context of arguments about how to respond to climate violence because they show what is at stake ethically and theologically in how climate change is interpreted as a problem and, relatedly, how human communities decide to address it. For Goldtooth, responses to climate problems that replicate the objectification of earth also tend to "entrench and magnify social inequalities," and worse, they "promote violation of the sacred, plain and simple."[69] Pope Francis argued much the same thing in *Laudato Si*.[70] Understanding why indigenous peoples, religious leaders from the Global South, many theologians of color in North America, and many others see things this way requires, in part, an effort to understand the social and theological significances of place, natural environment, and ecological relationships. An effort to see ecology in its social and theological depth is requisite to the capacity to engage issues like climate displacement, land conflict, and "resource" scarcity in full moral scope. By focusing on the Anthropocene's recalibration of *time*, Douglas misses an opportunity to consider how climate change and other ecological stressors illumine the ethical import of *place*. Dialogue with some meaningful segment of the now voluminous moral and theological literature on the environment seems a necessary next step for Christian ethics aiming to approach ecologies of violence.

Two other books—Cynthia Moe-Lobeda's *Resisting Structural Evil* and Kevin O'Brien's *The Violence of Climate Change*—show how attention to religious environmental thought can help inform responses to climate violence. Both present compelling arguments that climate change should be understood as structural violence. Climate change is a keystone example of how economic and ecological exploitation interlock in complex, hidden, systemic patterns, argues Moe-Lobeda.[71] "To see climate change as violence is to see it as the product of a destructive system that degrades human lives, other species, and the world upon which all living beings depend," writes O'Brien.[72]

Writing to over-consuming, mostly North Atlantic Christians, Moe-Lobeda attempts to help readers see structural violence, recognize their complicity without lapsing into "moral oblivion" or overwhelmed paralysis, and develop theological resources for individual and collective resistance and reform. A central task is to develop the "ecological dimensions of love." Interpreting neighbor-love in the context of creation ties acts of justice and compassion toward non-human creatures to the fundamental vocation of Christian life. It binds human practices of minding "voices of earth" to the person of Jesus and the mystery of God—"an incarnate God, a God embodied in life's extravagant complexity and variation."[73] It also raises complicated questions about how moral norms forged for human individuals and societies apply to non-human species and biotic communities. Christian environmentalists too often ignore disjunctions between values of Christian morality and the principles of biology and especially Darwinian evolution, argues Lisa Sideris. Where this is the case, Christian ethics actually fails to attend to nature in its own integrity, and so pursues practical strategies unsettling to ecological systems.[74] Moe-Lobeda acknowledges these complexities, but does not attempt to resolve them. "The challenge of retheorizing love as an ecological vocation" remains "a weighty and morally compelling challenge for religion of the early twenty-first century."[75] Still, Moe-Lobeda

---

[68] (Goldtooth 2017, p. 464).
[69] (Goldtooth 2017, p. 462).
[70] (Francis 2015, §84–92, 106–11, 115–18, 170–72).
[71] (Moe-Lobeda 2013).
[72] (O'Brien 2017, p. 4).
[73] (Moe-Lobeda 2013, pp. 169, 200).
[74] (Sideris 2003).
[75] (Moe-Lobeda 2013, pp. 200–2).

claims a theologically grounded and ethically articulated praxis of love can transform moral agency for meaningful confrontation with ecological violence.

Kevin O'Brien draws on religious environmental thought to help interpret the multi-dimensional and multi-scalar problems of climate change, and turns to five famous leaders of nonviolent social movements for insight and inspiration in the struggle for climate justice. O'Brien develops a brief argument (in conversation with environmental theologian Whitney Bauman) for treating climate change as a global problem requiring a "'planetary' morality, which embraces the wide diversity of life on planet Earth in each of its diverse local expressions." Because climate change is rooted in "anthropocentric habits of thought and behavior," ethics responsive to the violence of climate change must expand their moral visions to include other creatures and earth as a whole.[76]

While O'Brien includes ecological degradation as part of his account of the violence of climate change, he also argues that concern for non-human species and natural processes should be valued "pragmatically" in movements for climate justice. "Small steps in the right direction that have been democratically agreed upon are far more powerful than boldly radical statements that are widely dismissed," he writes. Eco-centric accounts of climate violence are politically marginal, and make the claims of climate justice significantly more demanding. Extoling the example of Jane Addams, O'Brien urges pragmatism, which in this case means narrowing the scope of moral attention to the human dimensions of ecological violence in order to allow wide cooperation toward meaningful progress on climate justice.[77] O'Brien is willing to countenance what Goldtooth calls "violation of the sacred" in exchange for piecemeal, majoritarian improvements to climate politics. But the trade-off is made consciously, with a pragmatist's faith in the capacity of grassroots democracy to gradually cultivate the cultural and political shifts that may one day recognize the cries of the earth and the justice claims of indigenous communities.[78]

O'Brien's approach to the violence of climate change is also pragmatic in another sense. His book "begins not with an abstract claim but with a concrete challenge," i.e., the structural violence of climate change, understood at its many levels of moral, scientific and political complexity. By locating climate change in the realm of violence, O'Brien emphasizes that the problem's ethical demands are not entirely unprecedented; moral communities have successfully resisted violence before. His approach seeks to cultivate capacities to engage climate violence by learning from social movements, with attention to how their ways of seeking justice and peace present both practical tools for climate action and theo-ethical insight about life in a warming world.[79]

4. Doing Christian Ethics for Ecologies of Violence

When O'Brien describes his approach to climate ethics as "pragmatic," he refers to the work of Willis Jenkins, who distinguishes between two broad strategies, two ways of doing religious ethics in response to social-environmental problems. In Jenkins' taxonomy, a pragmatic strategy "starts from concrete problems and works with the ideas and practices generated from reform projects attempting to address them." It holds that "the meaning of moral beliefs and practices lies in the patterns of action they support," and therefore looks to how moral communities adapt their traditions "to see and solve problems." The ethicist's task is to help moral communities use their traditions better. The other strategy is "cosmological." It attempts to meet moral challenges by telling "a new story or retrieving a forgotten moral vision in order to reorient humanity's moral consciousness." Where a pragmatic strategy trusts practices to transform moral vision, a cosmological strategy wagers that renewed worldviews can reshape moral practices.[80] Where cosmology centers on core convictions and root

---

[76] (O'Brien 2017, pp. 106, 111).
[77] (O'Brien 2017, pp. 109–11).
[78] Cf. O'Brien (2017) discussions of the climate threats to Kivalina, pp. 100–1, 113–14.
[79] (O'Brien 2017).
[80] (Jenkins 2013, pp. 1–15).

metaphors, pragmatism looks to concrete cases of collective problem-solving. Taken together, the books discussed above indicate that efforts to help Christian ethics discern responsibilities for ecologies of violence will have to do both.

A major task for Christian ethics at the intersection of violence and the environment will be to re-envision social, political, and religious life within ecological systems—a challenge of moral cosmology. As Jennings and others point out, the segregation of corporate life from the wider communion of nature has circumscribed the Christian imagination in ways directly complicit with racialized violence, economic exploitation, and environmental desecration. It has also effectively obscured links between ecology, conflict, and structural violence, channeling Christian moral thought on politics and environment into separate pools, making it difficult to reckon with ecologies of violence whether in theory or in practice.

"After hundreds of years of thinking of war as primarily fought for political purposes," writes Douglas, "the return of resource wars, the weaponizing of environmental goods, the destabilizing effect of climate refugees, and the reshaping of mutually beneficial alliances (not to mention what will count as mutual benefit) ... will lead to a rethinking of the causes, types, exacerbating factors, and understandings of war in a warming world."[81] This is all true, and yet war will still be fought primarily for political purposes. The defining mark of the environmental age is not the supersession of ecological forces over political life, but their mutual entanglement. Ecology is political; politics involves ecological relations, is shaped by landscape and nature's processes, and always has environmental ramifications.

Northcott, Douglas, and Moe-Lobeda all, in their own ways, attempt to reform the Christian imagination toward the capacity to see and accept responsibilities for violent political ecologies. Northcott restores God's presence to creation in order to reverse the catastrophic rupture of nature from culture. Douglas locates God's presence in the movement of Christian tradition through time in order to help communities tell their formative stories in ways that orient them to the distinct moral demands of an environmental age. Moe-Lobeda develops the meaning of Christian love to encompass the non-human world and to confront violence hidden in the convergences of economic structures and ecological relations.

If environmental conditions affect, integrate, and convey relationships of violence and domination, the flip side is that peace and flourishing are bound up with ecology. Another important site of attention for Christian ethics could be to flesh out the theological significance of God's peace for the moral challenges of political ecology. A number of Christian leaders have already indicated the importance of expounding the ecological dimensions of Christian conceptions of *peace*. "In our day," stated Pope John Paul II in his message for the 1990 celebration of the World Day of Peace, "there is a growing awareness that world peace is threatened not only by the arms race, regional conflict and continued injustice among peoples and nations, but also by a lack of *due respect for nature*, by the plundering of natural resources and by a progressive decline in the quality of life."[82] "Protecting the natural environment in order to build a world of peace is ... a duty incumbent upon each and all" argued Pope Benedict XVI at the same celebration twenty years later.[83] Pope Francis built on such themes in *Laudato Si*.[84] While the Popes argue that environmental protections are crucial to peace, the World Council of Churches (WCC) insists that peace is generative of ecological integrity: "The earth calls for and is in desperate need of a vision of peace that will enable it to restore itself in accord with its own intrinsic dynamism."[85] For the popes, the WCC, and a number of other Christian environmental thinkers, environmental issues

---

[81] (Douglas 2019, p. 102).
[82] (John Paul 1990, §1). Emphasis in the original.
[83] (Benedict 2010, §14). For critical commentary, and a "creatiocentric" extension of Catholic Social Teaching's ways of linking environmental issues to peace and nonviolence, see (Thompson 2012).
[84] (Francis 2015). See also (Winright 2018).
[85] (World Council of Churches 2008).

are peace issues not primarily because ecological problems spark violence. Peace is a fundamental category of environmental ethics, they suggest, because biblical or theological conceptions of peace are holistic and expansive. The Hebrew word for peace, *shalom*, involves not only inter-human harmony within conditions of social justice, but further denotes God's ultimate intentions for the flourishing of all creation in loving fellowship with the Creator.[86] God's will for peace is coextensive with God's designs for creation, such that the earth's travail frustrates God's longing to draw the world into communion with Godself. According to this framework, ecological degradation sabotages *shalom*, and warped visions of peace devastate the environment.

Cosmological strategies become necessary, suggests Jenkins, when "a culture's moral inheritances can no longer be trusted."[87] Faced with a set of unexamined ethical challenges—ecologies of violence that are not only ignored but also entrenched and concealed within North Atlantic Christian traditions—it may be useful to let constructive theology mend the moral imagination. "Ethics may need the religious capacity to reconsider the basic story by which [the] culture lives."[88] On the other hand, Christian ethics has a tendency to overestimate the power of theological beliefs to transform cultures, and cosmological strategies direct attention to grand theories and big ideas, funneling energy away from "concrete problems, scientific learning, pluralist negotiations, and the dynamics of cultural change."[89] Pragmatic strategies attempt to correct these liabilities.

If the cosmological challenge is to re-envision human life within ecological systems, the pragmatic challenge is to equip ecological communities to practically engage problems linking violence and environment. A key step will be to attend carefully to the details of various types and instances of violent ecology. The four types outlined above are all quite different, and all take on distinct aspects when the scope of attention changes from general types to specific cases. Land conflict looks different in America's eastern coal country than it does in western ranchlands; both take on new valences where native peoples claim rights to ancestral lands; there are other kinds of differences between North American conflicts and those in the Middle East or in South Asia. Each form of ecological violence is embroiled in important debates in the natural and social sciences, and each has provoked morally significant political, legal, and philosophical discussions. Just as reckoning with the challenges of modern economy or contemporary politics requires scrutinizing over how each of these systems actually functions,[90] understanding what is at stake for Christian ethics in ecologies of violence will require getting acquainted with today's political ecologies.

Another step will be to consider how Christian communities and other movements around the world are already engaging ecologies of violence in practical ways. Collaboration with and critical reflection on real efforts to confront contextual problems is at the heart of Jenkins' pragmatic strategy, which runs on "the moral creativity in religious reform projects."[91] This may be particularly important when attempting to come to grips with problems like environmental conflict, the environmental impacts of war, land conflict, or the structural violence of climate change, because the tradition has virtually no history of scholarly reflection on these issues, and because its conceptual tools for addressing them are underdeveloped.

Allowing problems and the practical projects that engage them to tutor Christian ethics will require case-based analyses and place-based forms of moral reflection. Taking responsibility for ecologies of violence involves re-envisioning Christian ethics as a practice of orienting Christian life within the diverse relations constitutive of a place. Reflecting on cases of violence grounded in environmental

---

[86] Cf. (Wirzba 2003).
[87] (Jenkins 2013, p. 159).
[88] (Jenkins 2013, p. 166). This is roughly the argument and the approach taken by ecofeminist theologian Sallie McFague across a number of books responsive to climate change and other environmental challenges. Among others, see (McFague 1993, 2001, 2008).
[89] (Jenkins 2013, pp. 4–5).
[90] e.g., (Tanner 2019; Bretherton 2010).
[91] (Jenkins 2013, p. 5).

conditions or conveyed in ecological systems rivets attention to the geography of moral life, so the field of Christian ethics must find ways to geo-locate its work, perhaps by finding its source materials within embodied Christian communities living their body politics in confrontation with violent ecologies.

Both cosmological and pragmatic strategies for reckoning with ecologies of violence will need to employ a third approach: Christian ethics must develop a *dialogical* method. Where contemporary problems transgress traditional intellectual and agential boundaries, ethics needs ways to orient moral life in processes of integration, critique, collaboration and exchange. Doing Christian ethics for ecologies of violence involves several kinds of dialogue, including interdisciplinary investigations needed to grasp the issues, inter-religious and cross-cultural dialogues necessary to understand and address particular cases, theological exchanges between schools of environmental and political reflection, and participatory learning across movements of practical response. Christian engagements with ecologies of violence will inevitably take on the diverse and distinct theological and methodological habits of the Christian spectrum, but dialogue should characterize the full range.

Traci West argues that dialogue is central to doing Christian ethics because the field's central task is "to make responsible contributions to the shared values of our pluralistic world." Collaborating toward moral engagement with intersectional problems within conditions of pluralism entails putting the tradition's theo-ethical inheritances in conversation with the moral wisdom embedded in communities of practice. In *Disruptive Christian Ethics*, West develops a method of ethics driven by "conversations between text and social context," allowing "the theories and practices, texts and contexts that are examined [to] critique each other." Doing Christian ethics for ecologies of violence may press the field in the directions blazed by scholars like Traci West—toward ethics as dialogical negotiation over intersectional problems with the goal of "building more ethical communal relations."[92]

One key area for dialogue will be between environmental ethics and the ethics of war and peace, including conversations between each field's moral and theological frameworks and between the communities of practice that carry them. The reasons for such dialogues are clear. Having developed in mutual isolation, and now facing problems that outstrip their respective ethical competencies, in part by crossing into the other's domain, each stands to learn from the other what a Christian response to ecologies of violence might entail. Paradigms of war/peace ethics each have practical repertoires for criticizing violence, for limiting, preventing, and even healing it. They can stimulate debate about the acceptability, scope, ends and means of violence and warfare. Paradigms of environmental ethics have capacities for criticizing environmental degradation, and have shown themselves especially creative in working with inherited moral traditions to develop new forms of ethical responsibility. They also have experience articulating forms of responsibility that cross social, political, ecological, and bio-physical spheres of live.

The grounds for such dialogue are also transparent. Both subfields frame their moral inquiries under the general task of orienting Christian life in response to God. Although specialized ethical arenas, they share common, theologically articulated norms (e.g., love and justice), as well as key inheritances (e.g., scripture and other authoritative texts, theological motifs, and exemplars) that have always shaped Christian ethics, so that the sources and structures of human obligation and Christian responsibility within both subfields ultimately cluster around common themes or debates. Yet there are important differences between environmental ethics and the ethics of violence. While the two must now be interwoven, they cannot be collapsed into each other without problems. In practice, the two reason differently about what is at stake in ecologies of violence; they work with incommensurable criteria to evaluate adequate responses, and they supply divergent resources to get there. Still they must develop practices of critical collaboration if they are to contribute to practical reasoning about the connections between violence and natural environment.

---

[92] (West 2006, pp. xv–xxi).

The era of thinking ethically about justice and peace in abstraction from ecological systems and environmental conditions is passed. What this means for Christian ethics depends in part on how Christians come to interpret and perform the moral and theological significance of humanity's relations with non-human creation, and so on how ethics discerns the significance of *place* for moral reflection and Christian life. It also hinges on how Christians understand, evaluate, and inhabit their ecological connections with both neighbors and enemies, and so on how they adapt the tradition's theories and practices of violence, nonviolence, warfare and peacemaking. It will rely on developing dialogue as fundamental to the discipline, and allowing conversations across texts and contexts to stimulate moral imagination. In these exercises, Christians will find new ways to image God's peace amidst ecologies of violence.

Funding: This research received no external funding.

Conflicts of Interest: The authors declare no conflict of interest.

References

Agarwal, Anil, and Sunita Narain. 1991. *Global Warming in an Unequal World: A Case of Environmental Colonialism*. New Delhi: Centre for Science and Environment.

Alvarez, Alex. 2017. *Unstable Ground: Climate Change, Conflict, and Genocide*. Lanham: Rowman & Littlefield Publishers.

Austin, Jay E., and Carl E. Bruch, eds. 2000. *The Environmental Consequences of War: Legal, Economic, and Scientific Perspectives*. New York: Cambridge University Press.

Baker-Fletcher, Karen. 1998. *Sisters of Dust, Sisters of Spirit: Womanist Wordings on God and Creation*. Minneapolis: Fortress Press.

Barnett, Jon, and Stephen Dovers. 2001. Environmental Security, Sustainability, and Policy. *Pacifica Review* 13: 157–69. [CrossRef]

Benedict, Pope, XVI. 2010. If You Want to Cultivate Peace, Protect Creation. Message for the Celebration of the World Day of Peace. January 1. Available online: http://w2.vatican.va/content/benedict-xvi/en/messages/peace/documents/hf_ben-xvi_mes_20091208_xliii-world-day-peace.html (accessed on 20 July 2019).

Brauch, Hans Günter. 2009. Securitizing Global Environmental Change. In *Facing Environmental Change: Environmental, Human, Energy, Food, Health and Water Security Concepts*. Edited by John Grin, Brauch Hans Gunter, Heinz Krummenacher, Czeslaw Mesjasz and Patricia Kameri-Mbote. Berlin: Springer, pp. 65–102.

Bretherton, Luke. 2010. *Christianity and Contemporary Politics: The Conditions and Possibilities of Faithful Witness*. Malden: Wiley-Blackwell.

Broome, John. 2012. *Climate Matters: Ethics in a Warming World*. New York: W. W. Norton & Company.

Buhaug, Halvard, Jonas Nordkvelle, Thomas Bernauer, Tobias Böhmelt, Michael Brzoska, Joshua W. Busby, and Antonio Ciccone. 2014. One Effect to Rule Them All? A Comment on Climate and Conflict. *Climatic Change* 127: 391–97. [CrossRef]

Bullard, Robert. 1990. *Dumping in Dixie: Race, Class and Environmental Quality*. Boulder: Westview Press.

Bullard, Robert, Paul Mohai, Robin Saha, and Beverly Wright. 2007. *Toxic Wastes and Race at Twenty, 1987–2007*. Cleveland: United Church of Christ Justice and Witness Ministries, United Church of Christ.

Burke, Marshall, Solomon M. Hsiang, and Edward Miguel. 2015. Climate and Conflict. *Annual Review of Economics* 7: 577–617. [CrossRef]

Buzan, Barry, Ole Wæver, and Jaap de Wilde. 1998. *Security: A New Framework for Analysis*. Boulder: Lynne Rienner.

Conca, Ken, and Geoffrey D. Dabelko. 2002. *Environmental Peacemaking*. Washington, DC: Woodrow Wilson Center Presss.

Cone, James. 2001. Whose Earth Is It Anyway? In *Earth Habitat: Eco-Injustice and the Church's Response*. Edited by Dieter Hessel and Larry Rasmussen. Minneapolis: Fortress Press, pp. 23–32.

Detraz, Nicole. 2015. *Environmental Security and Gender*. New York: Routledge.

Deudney, Daniel. 1990. The Case against Linking Environmental Degradation and National Security. *Millenium: Journal of International Studies* 19: 461–76. [CrossRef]

Deudney, Daniel H. 1999. Environmental Security: A Critique. In *Contested Grounds: Security and Conflict in the New Environmental Politics*. Edited by Daniel Deudney and Richard A. Matthew. Albany: SUNY Press, pp. 187–219.

Diederich, Michael D. 1992. 'Law of War' and Ecology: A Proposal for a Workable Approach to Protecting the Environment Through the Law of War. *Military Law Review* 136: 137–60.

Diehl, Paul F., and Nils Petter Gleditsch, eds. 2001. *Environmental Conflict*. Boulder: Westview Press.

Douglas, Mark. 2019. *Christian Pacifism for an Environmental Age*. New York: Cambridge University Press.

Doyle, Timothy, and Sanjay Chaturvedi. 2012. Climate Refugees and Security: Conceptualizations, Categories, and Contestations. In *The Oxford Handbook of Climate Change and Society*. Edited by John S. Dryzek, Richard B. Norgaard and David Schlosberg. New York: Oxford University Press. [CrossRef]

Duffy, Rosaleen. 2014. Waging a War to Save Biodiversity: The Rise of Militarized Conservation. *International Affairs* 90: 819–34. [CrossRef]

Eckersley, Robyn. 2007. Ecological Intervention: Prospects and Limits. *Ethics and International Affairs* 21: 293–316. [CrossRef]

Elshtain, Jean Bethke. 1987. *Women and War*. Chicago: University of Chicago Press.

Farrell, Justin. 2015. *The Battle for Yellowstone: Morality and the Sacred Roots of Environmental Conflict*. Princeton: Princeton University Press.

Francis, Pope. 2015. Laudato Si: On Care for Our Common Home. In *The Holy See*. Vatican City: Libreria Editrice Vaticana.

Galtung, Johann. 1969. Violence, Peace, and Peace Research. *Journal of Peace Research* 6: 167–91. [CrossRef]

Glave, Dianne. 2006. Black Environmental Liberation Theology. In *To Love the Wind and the Rain: African Americans and Environmental History*. Edited by Dianne Glave and Mark Stoll. Pittsburgh: University of Pittsburgh Press, pp. 189–99.

Goldtooth, Tom B. K. 2017. Respect for Mother Earth: Original Instructions and Indigenous Traditional Knowledge. In *The Wiley Blackwell Companion to Religion and Ecology*. Edited by John Hart. Hoboken: Wiley.

Graeger, Nina. 1996. Environmental Security? *Journal of Peace Research* 33: 109–16. [CrossRef]

Grunawalt, Richard J., John E. King, and Ronald S. McClain, eds. 1996. Protection of the Environment During Armed Conflict. In *International Law Studies*. Newport: Naval War College.

Harris, Melanie L. 2017. *Ecowomanism: African American Women and Earth-Honoring Faiths*. Maryknoll: Orbis Books.

Homer-Dixon, Thomas. 1999. *Environment, Scarcity, and Violence*. Princeton: Princeton University Press.

Hsiang, Solomon, Kyle Meng, and Mark Cane. 2011. Civil Conflicts are Associated with the Global Climate. *Nature* 476: 438–41. [CrossRef] [PubMed]

Hupy, Joseph P. 2008. The Environmental Footprint of War. *Environment & History* 14: 405–21.

Jenkins, Willis. 2013. *The Future of Ethics*. Washington, DC: Georgetown University Press.

Jenkins, Willis. 2017. Is Climate Change Structural Violence. Paper presented at the Annual Meeting of the Society of Christian Ethics, New Orleans, LA, USA, January 5–8.

Jenkins, Willis. 2018. White Settler Christianity and the Silence of Earth in Political Theology. Political Theology Network, Symposium on Political Theology and Ecology. Available online: https://politicaltheology.com/naturalized-white-settler-christianity-and-the-silence-of-earth-in-political-theology/ (accessed on 2 August 2019).

Jenkins, Willis, Evan Berry, and Luke Beck Kreider. 2018. Religion and Climate Change. *Annual Review of Environment and Resources* 43: 85–108. [CrossRef]

Jennings, Willie J. 2010. *The Christian Imagination: Theology and the Origins of Race*. New Haven: Yale University Press.

Jensen, David, and Steve Lonergan, eds. 2012. *Assessing and Restoring Natural Resources in Post-Conflict Peacebuilding*. New York: Routledge.

John Paul, Pope, II. 1990. Peace with God the Creator, Peace with All of Creation. Message for the Celebration of the World Day of Peace. January 1. Available online: http://w2.vatican.va/content/john-paul-ii/en/messages/peace/documents/hf_jp-ii_mes_19891208_xxiii-world-day-for-peace.html (accessed on 20 July 2019).

Johnston, Laurie. 2015. Just War and Environmental Destruction. In *Can War Be Just in the 21st Century? Ethicists Engage the Tradition*. Edited by Tobias Winright and Laurie Johnston. Maryknoll: Orbis Books, pp. 96–111.

King, Martin Luther, Jr. 1991. A Time to Break Silence. In *A Testament of Hope*. Edited by James M. Washington. New York: HarperCollins, pp. 231–44.

Klare, Michael T. 2001. *Resource Wars: The New Landscape of Global Conflict*. New York: Henry Holt and Company.
Martinez-Alier, Joan. 2002. *The Environmentalism of the Poor: A Study of Ecological Conflicts and Valuation*. Northampton: Edward Elgar.
Martin-Schramm, James. 2010. *Climate Justice: Ethics, Energy, and Public Policy*. Minneapolis: Fortress Press.
McFague, Sallie. 1993. *The Body of God: An Ecological Theology*. Minneapolis: Fortress Press.
McFague, Sallie. 2001. *Life Abundant: Rethinking Theology and Economy for a Planet in Peril*. Minneapolis: Fortress Press.
McFague, Sallie. 2008. *A New Climate for Theology: God, the World, and Global Warming*. Minneapolis: Fortress Press.
Moe-Lobeda, Cynthia. 2013. *Resisting Structural Evil: Love as Ecological-Economic Vocation*. Minneapolis: Fortress.
Nixon, Rob. 2011. *Slow Violence and the Environmentalism of the Poor*. Cambridge: Harvard University Press.
Northcott, Michael S. 2007. *A Moral Climate: The Ethics of Global Warming*. Maryknoll: Orbis Books.
Northcott, Michael S. 2013. *A Political Theology of Climate Change*. Grand Rapids: Eerdmans.
Northcott, Michael S. 2017. Climate Change and Christian Ethics. In *The Wiley Blackwell Companion to Religion and Ecology*. Edited by John Hart. Hoboken: John Wiley & Sons, pp. 286–300.
O'Brien, Kevin J. 2017. *The Violence of Climate Change: Lessons of Resistance from Nonviolent Activists*. Washington, DC: Georgetown University Press.
Parenti, Christian. 2011. *Tropic of Chaos: Climate Change and the New Geography of Violence*. New York: Nation Books.
Parsons, Rymn J. 2010. Climate Change: The Hottest Issue in Security Studies? *Risk, Hazards & Crisis in Public Policy* 1: 87–116.
Purdy, Jedediah. 2015. *After Nature: A Politics for the Anthropocene*. Cambridge: Harvard University Press.
Rayfuse, Rosemary, ed. 2014. *War and the Environment: New Approaches to Protecting the Environment in Relation to Armed Conflict*. Leiden: Brill Nijhoff.
Reichberg, Gregory, and Henrik Syse. 2000. Protecting the Natural Environment in Wartime: Ethical Considerations from the Just War Tradition. *Journal of Peace Research* 37: 449–68. [CrossRef]
Roberts, J. Timmons, and Bradley Parks. 2006. *A Climate of Injustice: Global Inequality, North-South Politics, and Climate Policy*. Cambridge: The MIT Press.
Roberts, J. Timmons, and Bradley C. Parks. 2009. Ecologically Unequal Exchange, Ecological Debt, and Climate Justice: The History and Implications of Three Related Ideas for a New Social Movement. *International Journal of Comparative Sociology* 50: 385–409. [CrossRef]
Ruether, Rosemary Radford. 1975. *New Woman, New Earth: Sexist Ideologies and Human Liberation*. New York: Seabury Press.
Schmitt, Michael. 1997. Green War: An Assessment of the Environmental Law of International Conflict. *Yale Journal of International Law* 22: 1–109.
Shadle, Matthew. 2011. No Peace on Earth: War and the Environment. In *Green Discipleship: Catholic Theological Ethics and the Environment*. Edited by Tobias Winright. Winona: Anselm Academic, pp. 407–425.
Shue, Henry. 2016. *Climate Justice: Vulnerability and Protection*. New York: Oxford University Press.
Sideris, Lisa. 2003. *Environmental Ethic, Ecological Theology and Natural Selection*. New York: Columbia University Press.
Stockholm International Peace Research Institute. 1975. *Delayed Toxic Effects of Chemical Warfare Agents*. Stockholm: Amkqvist & Wiksell International.
Stockholm International Peace Research Institute. 1976. *Ecological Consequences of the Second Indochina War*. Edited by Arthur H. Westing. Stockholm: Almqvist & Wiksell.
Stone, Christopher D. 2000. The Environment in Wartime: An Overview. In *The Environmental Consequences of War: Legal, Economic, and Scientific Perspectives*. Edited by Jay Austin and Carl E. Bruch. New York: Cambridge University Press, pp. 16–35.
Tanner, Kathryn. 2019. *Christianity and the New Spirit of Capitalism*. New Haven: Yale University Press.
Thistlethwaite, Susan Brooks. 2015. *Women's Bodies as Battlefield: Christian Theology and the Global War on Women*. New York: Palgrave Macmillan.
Thompson, J. Milburn. 2012. Treating Nature Nonviolently: Developing Catholic Social Teaching on the Environment through Nonviolence. In *Violence, Transformation, and the Sacred*. Edited by Margaret R. Pfeil and Tobias L. Winright. Maryknoll: Orbis Books, pp. 225–38.
Tinker, George. E. 1997. An American Indian Theological Response to Ecojustice. *Ecotheology* 3: 85–109. [CrossRef]
Tinker, George E. 2008. *American Indian Liberation: A Theology of Sovereignty*. Maryknoll: Orbis Books.

United Nations Environment Programme. 2009. *From Conflict to Peacebuilding: The Role of Natural Resources and the Environment*. Nairobi: United Nations Environment Programme.

United Nations Environmental Program. 2009. *Protecting the Environment During Armed Conflict: An Inventory and Analysis of International Law*. Nairobi: United Nations Environmental Program.

United States Department of Defense. 2015. *National Security Implications of Climate-Related Risks and a Changing Climate*; Washington, DC: US Department of Defense.

Walzer, Michael. 2004. *Arguing About War*. New Haven: Yale University Press.

Warren, Karen, ed. 1997. *Eco-Feminism: Women, Culture, Nature*. Bloomington: Indiana University Press.

West, Traci. 2006. *Disruptive Christian Ethics: When Racism and Women's Lives Matter*. Lexington: Westminster John Knox.

Westing, Arthur H. 1990. *Environmental Hazards of War: Releasing Dangerous Forces in an Industrialized World*. London: Sage Publications.

Williams, Delores. 1993. Sin, Nature and Black Women's Bodies. In *Ecofeminism and the Sacred*. Edited by Carol J. Adams. New York: Continuum, pp. 24–29.

Winright, Tobias. 2018. Peace on Earth, Peace with Earth: Laudato Si' and Integral Peacebuilding. In *All Creation Is Connected: Voices in Response to Pope Francis's Encyclical on Ecology*. Edited by Daniel R. DiLeo. Winona: Anselm Academic.

Wirzba, Norman. 2003. *The Paradise of God: Renewing Religion in an Ecological Age*. New York: Oxford University Press.

Woods, Mark. 2007. The Nature of War and Peace: Just War Thinking, Environmental Ethics, and Environmental Justice. In *Rethinking the Just War Tradition*. Edited by Michael W. Brough, John W. Lango and Harry van der Linden. Ithaca: SUNY Press, pp. 17–34.

World Council of Churches. 2008. Peace on Earth and Peace with the Earth. Paper presented at the Memorandum from WCC Symposium Peace on Earth is Peace with the Earth: Peace of Creation, Geneva, Switzerland, September 14–18.

Zeitoun, Mark. 2013. Global Environmental Justice and International Transboundary Waters: An Initial Exploration. *The Geographical Journal* 179: 141–49. [CrossRef]

© 2019 by the author. Licensee MDPI, Basel, Switzerland. This article is an open access article distributed under the terms and conditions of the Creative Commons Attribution (CC BY) license (http://creativecommons.org/licenses/by/4.0/).

MDPI
St. Alban-Anlage 66
4052 Basel
Switzerland
Tel. +41 61 683 77 34
Fax +41 61 302 89 18
www.mdpi.com

Religions Editorial Office
E-mail: religions@mdpi.com
www.mdpi.com/journal/religions

www.ingramcontent.com/pod-product-compliance
Lightning Source LLC
LaVergne TN
LVHW070605100526
838202LV00012B/569